AF673932

Echoes of Ancient Indian Wisdom

The Universal Hindu Vision and Its Edifice

Dr (Mrs) Shantha N Nair

PUSTAK MAHAL®

PUSTAK MAHAL®
Administrative Office and Sale Centre
J-3/16 , Daryaganj, New Delhi-110002
☎ 011-23276539, 23272783, 23272784, 23260518
E-mail: info@pustakmahal.com
Website: www.pustakmahal.com

Branch Office
Bengaluru: ☎ 080-22234025, 40912845
E-mail: pustakmahalblr@gmail.com

© Pustak Mahal, Delhi
ISBN 978-81-223-1020-7
Edition : 2026

The Copyright of this book, as well as all matter contained herein (including illustrations) rests with the Publishers. No person shall copy the name of the book, its title design, matter and illustrations in any form and in any language, totally or partially or in any distorted form. Anybody doing so shall face legal action and will be responsible for damages.

Printed at : Sharma Printers, Delhi

Dedicated to

all my teachers

with great respect

and humble pranams

Acknowledgements

I am deeply indebted to all the authors, scholars, learned professors, philosophers, spiritual leaders and saints, and others, whose works and websites I had referred to for writing this book. Some offered the translations of the original scriptures, some elaborated on their contents, some offered critical appreciation, while others had criticisms and condemnations. All these helped me in forming this book in greater or lesser measure. The number of books and articles that I went through and the websites that I surfed, are so numerous that it is not possible for me to extend my thanks to each and every author of those books, articles and websites individually.

I am grateful to my husband Sri K C N Nair for all his support, encouragement, critical views and advice. I appreciate the assistance and cooperation extended to me by my son Uday Gowri Shankar and my daughter-in-law Roopa Uday. My son, who has more knowledge of the great scriptures than myself, helped me through our discussions, at every step, to get the necessary clarity of thought. I will be failing if I do not mention the contribution made by my little grandson Pranav Shankar whose innocent remarks and comments I could make use of in this book. I extend my very special thanks to him. After all, the only difference between a saint and a child is that while the child's innocence is due to ignorance, that of the saint is with full awareness.

Contents

Preface

When I started writing this book, I never expected that it would be such a Herculean task. As and when I went deeper and deeper into the subject, I realised the extent of depth and vastness of the ancient Indian wisdom. Even after putting in great effort, I could only touch upon its periphery. It was like trying to reach the farthest limit of the sky or touching the deepest layer of the earth. At every step, it was very difficult for me to proceed further. Nonetheless, with my limited strength, I decided to dive deep into the ocean of the great, inexhaustible and vast ancient knowledge to get at least a handful of pearls of wisdom. I thought I would be able to go deeper and deeper into the ocean. But after some time, I realised that I was still on the surface. This, however, did not dishearten me in any way. I did not stop. With greater determination than before, I dived again as deep as I could, until I got exhausted and came up to the shore after gathering whatever little treasure of knowledge I could gather.

My desire overtook my limitations and finally I ventured to complete this work at any cost. The two saving graces were my deep interest in the subject and also my association with the Hindu Scriptures.

Ever since my childhood, I had had great respect, intense admiration and deep appreciation for the ancient Hindu religion and also great curiosity to know about *Sanatan Dharma* or Universal Religion. But this eagerness did not make me in any way, a fanatic.

I respect all religions of the world and it is my deep conviction that the end of all religions is the same, though their paths vary depending upon the times they were founded. The misrepresentation of the principles of the religions and the inadequate interpretations of those principles are, in my opinion, the most important reasons for cropping up of many religions and many sects in the same religion. However, all are founded with the best of intentions, that is, for peace and happiness for man in the world and beyond. But as time passed on, many of the followers of the various religions and sects forgot all about the fundamental unity of ideas in them, and began to quarrel among themselves about the superiority of one or the other religion or sect. In the name of religion and sect, conflicts arose and the world that is one single home of mankind got disintegrated.

If there has to be any change for better, then people should realise the fundamental oneness of all religions and sects and show respect and regard for all the religions and sects. This knowledge will make man more broadminded. Then only there will be peace and happiness in the whole world.

My eagerness to know more and more about the Hindu religion, in which I was born and brought up made me read the fathomless scriptures of *Shrutis*, and the *Smritis*, but only in their translated versions in English language as I had little knowledge of Vedic or even classical Sanskrit. Then, the idea of writing a book on this wisdom arose in my mind and I started this venture. But my effort and work is in no way exhaustive or scholarly. If I compare the treasure of ancient Indian Scriptures to all the oceans of the world, or even much more than that, what little I have presented here, undoubtedly forms only an infinitesimally small part of a single wave or even less. In spite of my limitations regarding knowledge and language if I have written something about the great, sacred, and eternal universal wisdom of India, it is only because of my interest to write something if not everything about the great ancient works, that overtook my inability and incapacity. The learned ones who happen to go through this work may find loopholes in it but my intention here is only to share whatever little knowledge I obtained with as many people as possible through this writing.

One solace that I have is the fact that even the great thinkers, learned scholars and spiritual leaders have accepted the vastness and complexity of this subject. It is not easy to understand and interpret correctly the great spiritual literature of India as it is very ancient and is written in Vedic Sanskrit. It offers multiple interpretations and has hidden meanings. How one understands it depends upon his knowledge of the ancient Vedic mythology, ancient Vedic History, spirituality, Vedic Sanskrit, and his mental makeup.

I, with all my limitations, have sincerely tried my level best to give a general and brief outline, or rather a macro view, of the ancient treasure of India, to a certain extent. How far I could succeed in my endeavour and how far I have been able to do justice in my attempt, I do not know. It is up to the readers to decide.

1

Shruti and Smriti

Shruti

The ancient Indian scriptures are divided into two categories — the *Shruti* and the *Smriti*.

The Vedas belong to the category of *Shruti*. All the other scriptures that have Vedas as the basis are called *Smriti*. While Vedas were written in Vedic Sanskrit that is known as *Vaidhika* or eternal, the *Smritis* were written in classical Sanskrit known as *Laukika* or worldly, that was spoken by the people.

Shruti means what is heard or revealed. The *rishis* did not create Vedas. They heard the eternal truths, which the God revealed to them. This makes the Vedas truths without beginning or end. They are superhuman and without authors. They contain the earliest knowledge of mankind and are the oldest scriptures on earth, almost as old as the human civilisation. They constitute one of the most valuable treasures of the earth and a glorious gift to mankind as a whole. The *Shrutis* are considered as the primary authority. They are known as the *Prabhu Samhitas* that means, commanding treatises with great authority. It is said that the Vedas are the source of all the other scriptures in the world. They are also considered the roots of Indian culture and wisdom. They are the crowning glory of India.

Sanatan Dharma

Vedas form the basis of one of the most ancient and the most tolerant religions of the world, namely *Sanatan Dharma* or the Hindu religion that is followed by nearly 13% of the world's population forming approximately one billion people. This is, in spite of the fact that the *Shrutis,* on which the Hindu religion is based, were passed on from generation to generation orally for a very long time. It was only after several thousands of years that they were penned down. They were mainly written either on copper plates or on palm leaves. Some of these, if not all, exist even today in spite of the ravages of time and also the fact that they were preserved in a tropical climate where everything perishes quickly. The absolute number and the percentage of the world population following Hinduism did not enhance rapidly or even significantly because Hindu religion did not believe in the religious conversions of people from other religions either by force or by persuasion or by any other means. In fact, the *Upanishads* categorically state that the sacred and the secret great principles should be taught only to those who crave for that knowledge and not to the others. This secrecy, in course of time, also became a bane for this religion. It was only after a very long time when the sacred deep-rooted principles of this religion began to be misused and misrepresented; and on account of that, when it started showing the marks of decline, Adi Shankara emerged on the scene. He eliminated the misconceptions about Hinduism from the land by means of debates, discussions, discourses, writings and establishing *Mutts* in all the four corners of India by travelling throughout the country. Thus, he brought back the past glory of the Hindu religion. Hinduism is the third largest religion in the world today.

Vedas that have stood the test of time are considered the highest and fundamental religious authority of the Hindu religion. Even today, the Vedic laws govern the individual, social, legal and most importantly, the religious customs of the Hindus all over the world. The Hindu religion or Hinduism, as it is popularly called, differs from most of the other religions of the world as it has no single founder, system or God, neither does it have a single belief or mode of worship. It is a religion that is highly liberal and highly democratic in its purest form. One can follow any path prescribed by the scriptures, any God of one's choice suiting to his temperament and one can view God in any kind of relationship as one desires. The innumerable Gods or deities are taken as manifestations of the one Supreme God — the Almighty, the Universal, eternal, non-perishable power — the *Brahman*, that has no form or qualities. The average humans cannot grasp, understand, assimilate and realise this eternal truth of the Ultimate *Brahman*. So it becomes essential to elevate their understanding by gradual stages. Therefore, there is the need for various deities, rituals and so on.

The Hindu religion is called *Sanatan Dharma* — *Sanatan* means 'Eternal' and *Dharma* means 'Laws'. *Sanatan Dharma* refers to the eternal and imperishable cosmic laws or the Laws of Nature. In that sense, it is a Universal religion. Further Vedas, on which the Hindu religion is based upon, are the most ancient of all scriptures in the world. Hence the Hindu religion can be considered as the mother of all religions. It is the most ancient, which existed even prior to the founding of all other religions, and it also contains the basic principles of every religion. The mother gives birth to children, but neither she compares herself with her children nor is she jealous of their growth. Because, the glory of the children belongs to her and she knows that well. This is the relationship of *Sanatan Dharma* with the other religions of the world.

Religion

The word religion comes from the Latin word *re-ligare* meaning 'to rebind'. So religion is that which rebinds man to the eternal source or to the eternal law of the very existence of man. Hindu religion, therefore, refers to that religion, the basis of which is the eternal cosmic laws. Hinduism is nothing but a way of life. It teaches how one should live in accordance with the Cosmic Laws and lead a contented, happy, peaceful life on earth by gaining both material as well as spiritual wealth and attain *nirvana*. All the innumerable scriptures, with Vedas as their basis, convey the same message. The aim of the Vedas is to guide the soul towards God realisation. In its broad sense, all religions have the same root, namely spirituality and the end goal of all religions is also the same that is to bring out the divinity and purity in man and to make man attain liberation (*mukti*) or salvation (*nirvana*) or any other term as mentioned in the other religions. All aim at making the man pure and divine. All religions stress the need for good qualities like charity, love, kindness, compassion, and honesty for man to become divine and to maintain peace, harmony and happiness. Their paths may differ but they start and end with the same. These paths are like instruments that are to be used for reaching the goal which remains the same for all the religions in the world. It is up to the man how he makes use of religions in a proper manner. A knife in the hands of a gardener gives good results whereas the same knife results in grave consequences if it is in the hands of a small child who is utterly ignorant of its use. All the religions teach the same truth in different ways. No path is superior or inferior to the other. Just as a particular destination can be reached through several routes – some easy to walk but slightly roundabout, the other not very smooth but quick to reach – the paths shown by different religions, sects and even methods employed may vary, but whichever path one follows he is sure to reach the destination. The hatred among different religions and sects of the same religion and the resulting violence only reveal the narrow-mindedness and lack of proper understanding of the real purpose behind all the religions of the world. The great religious founders would never have expected about such a sorry state of affairs in the name of religion. The real aim of all the religions is to make the man enlightened by bringing out the divinity in him. Religion is not meant for hatred, violence and all those things that end in unhappiness and lack of peace for mankind. When all humans, irrespective of caste, creed, sect, nationality and religion will realise this truth, then there will be everlasting peace and happiness on earth. In this sense, Vedas are the most ancient scripture considered as the source and end of all religions of the world.

The Four Vedas

The two basic ideas of all the four Vedas, namely, the *Rig Veda,* the *Yajur Veda,* the *Sama Veda* and the *Atharva Veda* are truth (*satya*) and eternal order (*rita*). The ultimate goal of the Vedas is the well-being or welfare of all living beings on earth, their spiritual upliftment and finally liberation (*mukti*) of all human beings by achieving the unison of the individual soul along with the cosmic soul, with the realisation of the ultimate truth — the imperishable and everlasting *Brahman.*

Rig Veda is the earliest of all the Vedas. Its last hymn is a universal prayer for welfare of the entire mankind. The hymn reveals the great truth that all living beings are one and the same. This way it exemplifies the universal outlook of the ancient sages of India.

It says —

समानी व आकूतिः समाना हृदयानि व।
समानमस्तु वो मनो यथा वः सुसहासति।।
Samānī va ākūtiḥ samānā hṛdyāni va
Samānamastu vo mano yathā vaḥ susahāsati

(May the whole of the mankind be of one mind, have a common goal, and the hearts with united love and may the mind and soul be one and the same for all to live a life of happiness.)

The famous *Gayatri Mantra* that is regarded as the mantra of spiritual light, given by Sage Vishvamitra in the *Rig Veda* 3.62.10 is a prayer for peace, amity and prosperity on earth.

It says —

ॐ भूर्भुवः स्वः तत्सवितुर्वरेण्यं भर्गो देवस्य धीमहि।
धियो यो न प्रचोदयात्।।
Auṁ bhūr bhuvaḥ svaḥ tat savitur vareṇyam′
Bhargo devasya dhī mahi dhiyo yo na pracodayāt

(I invoke the earth plane, the astral plane, the celestial plane, the plane of spiritual balance, the plane of human spiritual knowledge, the plane of spiritual austerities, and the plane of ultimate Truth. Oh, the Creator of the Universe, we meditate upon thy supreme splendor, the great Spiritual Light that is the brilliance of all Divinity. May thy radiant power illumine our intellects, destroy our sins, and guide us in the right direction.)

The universal outlook of the Vedic seers can be found in many of the other mantras as well. The wide vision found in the *Shanti Mantra* provides ample proof for this.

ॐ सहनावावतु सहानव भुनक्तु,
सहवीर्यं करावावहे।
तेजस्वी नव अधीतमस्तु,
मा विदिविशा वा हवे।।
Auṁ sahanāvāvatu sahānav bhunaktu
Sahavīryam′ karavāvahe

Tejasvī nav adhītmastu
Mā vidiviśā vā have

(May we be protected together, may we be nourished together, may we work together with great vigour, may our study be enlightening, and may no obstacle arise between us. Let us move together in unison. Let us live in harmony.)

Another prayer says —

असतो मा सद् गमय तमसो मा ज्योतिर्गमय।
मृत्योर्मामृतं गमय।।

शतपथ ब्राह्मण–(14/1/1/30)

Asto mā sadgamaya tamaso mā jyotirgamaya
Mrityormāmṛtaṁ gamaya

(Oh God, lead us from unreal to the real, from untruth to truth, from darkness to light, from death to immortality.

Another prayer says —

सर्वेषां स्वतुः भवतु सर्वेषां शान्ति भवतु।
सर्वेषां पुमां भवतु सर्वेषां मंगलं भवतु।।
Sarveṣaṁ svatuḥ bhavatu sarveṣaṁ śanti bhavatu
Sarveṣaṁ pumām′ bhavatu sarveṣaṁ mañgalam′ bhavatu

(May there be good for all, peace for all, may all be fit for perfection, and may all experience that which is auspicious.)

सर्वे भवन्तु सुखिनः सर्वे सन्तु निरामया।
सर्वे भद्राणि पश्यन्तु मा कश्चिद् दुःखभाग्भवेत।।
Sarve bhavantu sukhinaḥ sarve santu nirāmayā
Sarve bhadrāṇi paśyantu mā kaścid dukhbhāgbhavet

(May all be happy, all be healthy, may all experience what is good, and let no one suffer.)

Such a strong, solid and advanced spiritual foundation, including all that is noble and sacred, has made the people of India broad-minded and peace-loving, highly knowledgeable and full of wisdom. The first University in the world was established in India around 700 BC in Takshashila with more than 10,500 students. Evidence suggests that students from all over the world studied more than 60 subjects here. History proves the fact that India never invaded any country at least in the last 10,000 years but was attacked by others. Every time she was attacked, she lost much of her literary, spiritual, religious and cultural treasures, but in spite of that she still retained her past temperament and culture in great honour. The firm and solid foundation provided by the ancient Indian seers in the form of the great *Shruti* and *Smriti* enabled the Indian culture and civilisation to withstand the harsh ravages of time.

Smriti

Except Vedas, all the other scriptures which are born out of the Vedas are considered as *Smriti.*

These are the secondary scriptures based on the teachings of Vedas. They are placed next to Vedas in authority. These are called *Smriti Samhitas* or friendly treatises and comprise *Puranas, Itihasas, Vedangs, Upa Vedas, Darshanas, Vedanta Sutras, Agamas, Kalas,* and other texts based on the four Vedas and also later writings based on the Vedas. *Smritis* are the recollections of the experiences of the ancient seers.

Smritis are also known as the *Dharma Shastras*. The *Smritis* lay down *Dharmic* laws for regulating the individual, family, social and national obligations of people. They explain the codes of conduct for mankind in day-to-day life. Whatever may be the classification, the objective of both *Shruti* and *Smriti* is the same that is the liberation, and freedom from sorrow. Actually there is no single opinion about what *Smritis* are. According to some, there are 20 *Smritis.* Others say there are 57 *Smritis.*

The ***Itihasas*** and ***Puranas*** mainly explain the *Karma Kand* of the Vedas. In these, the divine wisdom of the Vedas is made more relevant to ordinary men and women. These are meant for ordinary people who cannot understand the knowledge of the Vedas in its pure form. So the Vedic truths are taught through events and stories in *Itihasas* and *Puranas*. The description of God here is more personal. God, the Creator, loves, inspires and protects them. The divine wisdom of the Vedas is made easy here for the common man to understand. These appeal mostly to the heart. These are the books of mythology and legend.

Vedangs that are explanatory part or *anga* of the Vedas help us in understanding the various aspects of Vedic knowledge.

The *Upa Vedas* are secondary Vedas, which apply the Vedic knowledge in practical life. The *Darshanas* that are mainly six in number are the systems, which explain the Vedic philosophy in a scholarly and rationalistic manner.

The *Vedanta Sutra* written by Vyasa himself, contain the essence of all the four Vedas. Here the wisdom of *Upanishad*, that Absolute truth is the Supreme Godhead and is the cause of all, is explained through logical argument.

The *Agamas* are both theological as well as practical and relate to the worship of Gods.

The *Kalas* deal with various sciences including mathematics, the science of sounds, sculpture, cookery, and so on.

The special texts based on the Vedas explain the aphorisms. These are the critical studies of the commentaries and guides for the easy understanding of the original texts. The later writings include the wise sayings, the scholarly compositions or dramas, the rhetorical texts or *slokas*, *strotas* and *bhajans* for worshipping the divine.

2

The Vedas – Origin, Content, Shakhas and Structure

Origin of the Vedas

The most sacred books of ancient India, namely the Vedas are the earliest, eternal, divine, holy and impersonal spiritual truths that existed from time immemorial as vibrations in Space with no beginning and end.

They are *Anadi* or eternal and *Aparushaya* or super human without a beginning or an end and therefore, not created by human beings and without any author.

They are *Amnaya*, the root texts of tradition and *Nigama*, the traditional wisdom transmitted from generation to generation.

They are also *Trayi*, the texts consisting of mantras, prose and melodies. The ancient seers detected these revered truths by the divine grace of God. They are the revelations of the ancient seers. The *rishis* through their intuition heard the truths directly from God. The sublime knowledge was revealed to the ancient seers of India during their meditation in the state of their supra-normal consciousness. Hence Vedas are also called *Shrutis*.

Shrutis are the oldest of all scriptures and can be treated as the source of all religions of the world. In a broad sense, Vedas belong to the whole of humanity because it encompasses the human life in general.

As Dr Radhakrishnan has stated —

'The Vedas are the earliest documents of human mind.'

The *rishis* did not invent the knowledge. They discovered it as a result of their prolonged and intense meditation and penance. Hence the Vedas are considered as the spiritual experiences of the ancient seers.

It is said that fixing a date of origin the Vedas is unnecessary and meaningless, as the period of the Vedas can never be ascertained with precision. Further, understanding the Vedic truths which are the fruits of Vedas are more important than knowing the date of their origin which can at best be only approximations or even guesswork at times. However, the versions and the opinions of scholars differ regarding the antiquity of Vedas.

Views on the Origin of Vedas

The *Brihad Aranyaka Upanishad* (4.5.11) says that the four Vedas emanated from the breathing of God himself.

In *Srimad Bhagavata Purana,* it is stated that the Vedas are the supreme personality of Lord Narayana and are self-born.

According to one view, the sound of the *Pranava mantra 'AUM'* and the Vedas were taught by the supreme *Nirguna* Brahman, which is that Universal supreme power without attributes that was responsible for the creation, maintenance and dissolution of the Universe. In course of time, the *rishis* heard these truths as a result of their intense and prolonged meditation.

Another interpretation describes origin of Vedas in the present *Kalpa*. A *Kalpa* is the period of existence of the world at the end of which the world will be destroyed for a new beginning in another new *Kalpa*. One *Kalpa* is equivalent to 4320 million years, which is one day for Brahma, the Creator. A month for Brahma is supposed to be equivalent to 30 *Kalpas* or 129.6 billion years. The present *Kalpa* is believed to have started about 1972 million years ago, and 50 years of Brahma is over now. After the great deluge at the end of the last *Kalpa*, Rudra, the deity at that time created Brahma for creating the present *Kalpa* called *Shvetavaraha Kalpa*. He taught Brahma the technique of creation. Brahma, the *Prajapati* meditated upon Rudra, who appeared before him as *Pranava Mantra (AUM)*.

Brahma prayed to the Almighty for knowledge and the God blessed him with the Vedas. It is said that the Vedas came from *Pranava Mantra*, the *Rig Veda* from the letter '**A**', *Yajur Veda* from the letter '**U**', the *Sama Veda* from the letter '**M**', and the *Atharva Veda* from the *ardh mantra* '**M**'.

According to another belief, all the Vedas originated from Lord Vishnu. From the Lord, the knowledge came down to Brahma, the Creator, at the very beginning of creation of the world which again is believed to be about 155.52197 trillion years ago and Brahma in turn revealed them to the ancient sages.

Yet another view says that God gives the Vedas to this world at the beginning of each cycle of creation and withdraws them again at the end of it. It means that God Himself revealed them to the ancient seers.

All these beliefs bring forth the conclusion that the Vedas existed even from the beginning of the Universe, that is, about 311 trillion years ago.

Theories on the Origin of Vedas

Apart from the views, there are some theories put forward by those who advocate the Aryan invasion and Aryan migration.

According to the Aryan invasion theory, the Aryans who were associated with the Iranians and with the Indo-European group having their origin in Russian steppes or in Central Asia, invaded India and pushed *Dasyus*, the original inhabitants to Peninsular India. They composed the Vedas. They were a warring group and they conquered the native people who worshipped the Nature Gods. The proponents of this theory state that many Persian writings and the Vedas seem to be similar as far as the Gods and the beliefs are concerned. But this theory of Aryan invasion has been refuted now, as there are not enough evidences to support this theory. There are no archaeological evidences of any Aryan invasion. On the other hand, it is found that there is continuity in the culture and civilisation here. It is understood that the Vedic culture was already very old, by the time that is ascribed to the Aryan invasion. Further, Jeffrey Armstrong opines that Sanskrit is the mother language even for the ancient languages of Greek like Latin and for all other languages of the world.

There are also a few who subscribe to the theory of Aryan migration. They opine that a small number of people who had migrated to the Indus Valley area in India, wrote the Vedas. But this migration theory too has been opposed now. This is because the term *Aryavarta* refers to the abode of noble and excellent ones and the word *Arya* in Sanskrit is a word of honourable address and it does not refer to any particular race or group. So the term *Arya* cannot refer to those who invaded our land. It is believed that some of the Vedic mantras were written nearly five to six thousand years ago. It goes beyond the period mentioned in the theory of Aryan invasion and Aryan migration.

Further the gap between the end of Harappan Civilisation and Vedic history is traditionally estimated around 1000 years and the place Harappa is never mentioned anywhere in the *Rig Veda* the oldest of all Vedas.

Jeffrey Armstrong in his book *Greatness of the Vedas* explains that the proponents of the Aryan invasion theory speak about the Aryans who rode on horse back, invaded and subjugated India, and wrote the Vedas. But, he says, one must understand that Vedas contain astronomical calculations that go back to the period when the horseriding culture was not known to people. People were proficient in other disciplines, such as astronomy, astrology, and so on. It is also found that during the Vedic period there was an advanced and sophisticated maritime culture. Trade was carried on along the sea route. There were towns and small kingdoms that showed an advanced urban culture. Arts and crafts, agriculture, and science were all highly developed.

Kurt Schildmann, a German linguist, says that his study of the ancient inscriptions in the caves of Peru and the United States shows that they are similar to the Indus Valley Sanskrit. It suggests that the sea fares from India might have reached America thousands of years before. Finally the Vedas, if at all, were written by the invaders, (as per the Aryan invasion and migration theories which are refuted now) why did they not write the great scriptures in their own land before they invaded or migrated to India? What was the need for them to come all the way to another country for revealing the great truths? Why did they not write them in their own language? Or did they confiscate the sacred scriptures along with the other material wealth of India? The sages might not have been concerned about such an act because to them all living beings were one and the same. Their concern was only to impart the ancient and sacred knowledge to mankind as a whole, and not just possessing them and keeping them in their own hands. For them, only the conquest of the inner-self mattered.

All these views and counter views clearly show that it is impossible to know the origin of the Vedas accurately. At the most, one can only come to the conclusion that Vedas are as old as human evolution.

Further, the political and geographical boundaries of the nations keep on changing from time to time. Some of the places have also disappeared from the maps. What happened to Dwarka, after Lord Krishna left this earth? What happened to Dhanushkodi in the recent history? What was the map of India prior to the year 1947? Several places of the past have got submerged in the sea. History has records of unification of countries (for example, unification of East and West Germany) and also their bifurcation resulting in the creation of nations with new political boundaries. So it is very difficult to know the exact jurisdiction and who the original natives of any country were for that matter. Who were the sages? The exact location they belonged to should not bother us much, because, one thing that is certain is that the most ancient scripture of the humans, namely, the Vedas were composed in the sacred land of India. This itself is a matter of great pride for the people of this land. But more than that, the entire mankind, irrespective of the nations they belong to, should feel proud of our ancestors for this priceless and everlasting gift to the mankind as a whole.

Whatever may be the views pertaining to the origin of the Vedas, there are no two thoughts about the fact that the Indian sages were the media through which the knowledge of Vedas was passed on. They were blessed with the divine grace, the outcome of which was the Vedas. Nonetheless, the political and geographical divisions have significance in the material world only not in the spiritual realm. What is important is to understand the fathomless, everlasting and ultimate knowledge contained in the Vedas and be thankful to those, who have composed them and gave us greatest treasure rather than debating upon the questions as to when and by whom the Vedas were composed.

All the above arguments prove that there is no consensus of opinion regarding the date of origin and the authorship of the Vedas. Everyone tries to conjecture depending upon the information available. It is like five blind people trying to describe an elephant. While there may be or may not be some truth in their arguments, none can be totally correct. Hence it is better to set aside the arguments relating to the origin and authorship of the Vedas, as this will not serve the purpose for which they were passed on from generation to generation.

Vedic Period

For a long time, the knowledge of Vedas was imparted orally to the successive generations. This process continued for many centuries before they were written down. It is believed that the sage Veda Vyasa classified them about 5000 to 6000 years ago and that they were written down on the banks of the legendary Saraswati River, which got dried up in the course of time. Veda Vyasa compiled the scattered knowledge of the ancient seers, into four parts which came to be known as the four Vedas.

All the mantras that are in praise of deities were grouped together to constitute the ***Rig Veda***.

The mantras sung to the prescribed tunes melodiously formed the ***Sama Veda***.

All those mantras that were both in verse and prose and dealt with the sacrifices were classified as ***Yajur Veda***.

Finally, all the mantras that were essential and highly helpful in the everyday life of humans became the ***Atharva Veda***.

In Indian History, the period from 1500 BC to 1000 BC is called the Vedic period. Vedas were supposed to have been written in *Brahmi* or Vedic Sanskrit during that period. According to some, the origin must have been prior to 1500 BC.

It is said that Veda Vyasa, also known as *Krishna Dwaipayana*, who collected and classified the Vedas and also wrote the *Puranas* and *Itihasas*, lived during the time of Shantanu, the great grandfather of the Pandavas and Kauravas. His real name was Krishna. He was the son of sage Parashara and Satyavati, a fisher woman. Since he was born on an island, he was called *Dwaipayana* (islander), and since he lived near Badrikashram, he was also referred to as *Badarayana*.

It is also believed that *Vyasa* refers to a title rather than a person and that in all *yugas, Vyasas* are born. *Krishna Dwaipayana* was the *Vyasa* of *Dwapara Yuga.* There were 28 *Vyasas* altogether and *Veda Vyasa* was the last among them.

According to another view, *Vyasa* means composition or classification. Since he classified Vedic Knowledge into four Vedas, and then sub-divided them into 1180 recessions, he was called *Vyasa Maharshi*. After compiling the Vedas and arranging them in their present form, he gave each of these Vedas to each of his four disciples. He gave *Rig Veda* to **Paila**, *Yajur Veda* to **Vaishampayana**, *Sama Veda* to **Jaimini**, and the *Atharva Veda* to **Sumantu**. These four sages taught them to their disciples and they in turn passed them on to the later generations.

But some are of the view that *Vyasa Krishna Dwaipayana* may not be a single individual but symbolic of all Vedic schools which were present in India at that time. Also, there are others who believe that the Vedas were composed around 6000 BC or even earlier.

Regarding creation, one of the hymns in *Rig Veda* (10.129) states —

> इयं विसृष्टिर्यत आबभूव यदि वा दधे यदि वा न।
> यो अस्याध्यक्षः परमे व्योमन्तसो अंग वेद यदि वा न वेद।।
> Iyaṁ visṛṣtiryat ābabhūv yadi vā dadhe yadi vā na
> yo asyādhyakṣhaḥ parame vyomaṇtso aṇga
> veda yadi vā na veda
>
> *'Who knows for certain about origin of the creation of the world and when creation took place; since no one knows about it. Only He who surveys from the lofty skies knows or perhaps even He may not know.'*

The same statement can be applied to the origin of the Vedas as well.

Content of the Vedas

In Sanskrit language, *Vid* means to know, that is, knowledge or truth. It also refers to wisdom or even vision. The word Veda is derived from the word *Vid* and they form the repository of all knowledge.

The vast body of spiritual knowledge found in the Vedas is infinite and indestructible.

Symbolism

The human knowledge is available in the Vedas in symbolic form. It contains knowledge about discoveries and inventions of all times including the modern knowledge on almost all the aspects. They cover various areas from nature to everyday life. They are full of knowledge and wisdom. They act as a guide for man in his quest for the four goals in life namely, *Dharma* relating to spiritual wisdom, *Artha* relating to his material welfare, *Kama* relating to sensual pleasure and happiness and *Moksha* the salvation. That is why Vedas are considered the ultimate source of all material as well as spiritual wisdom. All branches of knowledge, both mundane and transcendental, are found in them. They proclaim the lofty truths through the mantras, the sounds of which have energising character. They teach about the spiritual well-being of one and all. They also deal with the ideals of social life, the duties of society and the spiritual life of man. In essence, they deal with Nature, Creation and God.

The Brahman

The Vedas proclaim that the one *Brahman*, which is nothing but the truth is manifested in different deities. Every God represents the ideas of truth (*satya*) and eternal order (*rita*). One can adhere to any path but should have faith and devotion and then he will be led towards the ultimate truth or knowledge. Vedas give many paths to liberation. Different paths can be followed to discover the truth. Sacrifices, *yajna* or rituals are also discussed in them. They tell us about the conduct of sacrifices, ways of worship, methods of meditation, and so on. Whosoever may be the deity, the ritual is the same. They also give instructions for keeping the body and mind healthy.

In Vedas, we find the worship of different cosmic principles such as *Agni* (fire), *Vayu* (wind), *Jal* (water), *Prithvi* (earth) and *Aakash* (space). They also speak about atomic energy and nuclear growth. Almost every thing under the sun is included in the Vedas. The Vedas proclaim 'Unity with the Divine' as the highest goal of mankind.

Thus the Vedas are the ultimate source of all wisdom. They are the oldest, the most comprehensive and the universal scripture of mankind representing the ancient Hindu thought and forms the basis of *Sanatan Dharma* or universal religion that all Hindus follow. Even today, the laws of Vedas regulate the social, legal, domestic and religious customs and traditions of Hindus. It is said that the Vedas are the storehouse of ancient Indian wisdom that form the foundation of all the religions of the world. This is the reason why they are described as *Sat-Chit-Ananda* that means unending, full of knowledge, and providing unlimited happiness.

The subject matter of the Vedas can be classified into three sections —

- The *Karma Kand* or the ritualistic section dealing with various sacrifices and rituals and worship of various deities
- The *Upasana Kand* or the worship section that explains the different kinds of worship and meditation
- The *Jnana Kand* or the knowledge section that tells about the highest knowledge of *Nirguna Brahman*

The rituals mentioned in the *Karma Kand* are relegated to the background in the *Jnana Kand.* It clearly reveals that as long as one takes the world to be real, and seeks material pleasures of the world, one has to perform the required Karma to realise the goal of material happiness. When one advances further in wisdom, the world no longer appears to be real and material comforts and happiness become useless. At that time, the rites and sacrifices become unnecessary as the man acquires the eternal knowledge. The *Karma Kand*, in this manner, prepares one for the *Jnana Kand.* The *Karma Kand* is the first step to make one realise the truth. An ordinary man has to go through a life of rituals and sacrifices to get the necessary maturity of thought. Sacrifices involving material things help one reduce his ego and attachment to worldly things. Once that objective is realised, performing sacrifices will become totally unnecessary as one sacrifices his ego and becomes fit to seek the ultimate knowledge.

Jeevatma and Paramatma

When one goes beyond the material pleasures of the world and considers them unreal and temporary, then only one is able to go beyond the three *gunas*, namely, *satwa*, *rajas* and *tamas*. The example of flower and fruit clearly explains this. Fruit cannot originate without flower. The flower, no doubt, is beautiful. But the fruit that is required emerges only when the flower withers and droops and ultimately falls down. Similar is the case with *Karma Kand* and *Jnana Kand.* The various disciplines found in the Vedas like, performing rituals and sacrifices, performance of duties according to one's own *dharma*, engaging oneself in social obligations, and social functions, practising austerities, all these are meant to purify one's body and mind. The *Karma Kand* is meant for this. Once the cleansing is over, one becomes physically and mentally fit and gets the wisdom to gain the inner vision. In a flash, one experiences the unity of *Paramatma*, the cosmic energy or *chaitanya* with one's self or *Jeevatma.* The cosmic energy is not visible to us, but that is not a ground to negate its existence. Just as in electricity, the energy can be known only through its flow in the electrical appliances, the cosmic energy or the *Paramatma* can be seen through its innumerable creations.

According to science, the world is embraced by the concepts of time and space. The Vedas advocate that truth can be realised only by freeing oneself from the concepts of time and space and by forgetting time and space. This is possible when we turn our gaze inward, in which we forget ourselves as in a deep sleep. The common goal of all the Vedas is the well-being of living creatures, the upliftment of *Jeevatma* or the individual self, and finally the eternal unity of the *Jeevatma* with the *Paramatma.* In essence, the Vedas aim at liberation of the self while living in the world. However, we cannot find systematic logical sequence or doctrines in the Vedas. Every verse or mantra has multiple meanings. This makes the Vedas ambiguous, difficult to understand and at the same time symbolic.

According to Vedic knowledge, the Vedic sound is divided into four phases. These can be grasped fully only by the sages. While the first three of these are located internally, within the living entity, the fourth phase of the Vedic sound is manifested externally as speech. Even this fourth phase, which is located externally, is very difficult to understand. The four phases are as follows —

- The Spiritual phase, known as *Para* is located down within. It is located in the *Adhara Chakra.*
- The Mental phase, known as *Pashyanti* is located in the *Manipura Chakra,* located in the area of navel.

- The Intellectual phase, known as *Madhyama* is located in the heart area, in the *Anahata Chakra.*
- The Sensory phase, known as *Vaikhari* is manifested externally and includes all the vital energies that are found within the Universe and beyond.

In the *Skand Purana,* Vedas are personified as living beings —

- The *Rig Veda* is personified as a short man, with fair complexion, and holding a rosary.
- The *Yajur Veda* is personified as a thin man of medium height with yellow complexion, holding a rosary and a thunderbolt.
- The *Sama Veda* is referred to as a tall man with a glowing complexion, holding a rosary with a conch shell.
- The *Atharva Veda* is personified as a pale, red-eyed person holding a rosary and a short sword.

It is also believed that four planets preside over the Vedas, *Guru* or Jupiter over *Rig Veda, Shukra* or Venus over *Yajur Veda, Mangal* or Mars over *Sama Veda* and *Budha* or Mercury over *Atharva Veda.*

Shakhas of the Vedas

According to the *Muktikopanishad,* there were approximately a total of 100,000 verses in the 1180 branches of the Vedas. But now only 20,379 verses are available —

- 10,552 of the *Rig Veda* verses in 10 mandals
- 1975 verses of the *Yajur Veda* in 40 chapters
- 1875 verses of the *Sama Veda* in 21 chapters
- 5977 verses of *Atharva Veda* in 20 chapters

Out of the 1180 branches of the Vedas, only very few *shakhas* or branches are available now.

According to **Patanjali**, originally there were 21 branches of the *Rig Veda,* 1000 branches of the *Sama Veda,* 101 branches of the *Yajur Veda* consisting of 86 branches of the *Krishna Yajur Veda* and 15 that of *Shukla Yajur Veda* and 9 branches of the *Atharva Veda.* But only 20 branches of all the Vedas put together are available to mankind now. They are in the form of manuscripts, and a few in fragmentary conditions.

According to **Shaunaka,** there are 5 *shakhas* in the *Rig Veda,* 42 to 44 *shakhas* in the *Yajur Veda,* 12 in the *Sama Veda* and 9 in the *Atharva Veda.*

However the *shakhas* available now include the following —

- *Shakla Shakha* and fragments of *Bhashkala Shakha* of the *Rig Veda*
- *Vajasaneyi, Madhyandina, Kanva, Taittiriya, Maitrayani, Charaka Katha* and *Kapisisthala* of the *Yajur Veda*
- *Jaiminiya* and *Kauthuma* of the *Sama Veda*
- *Shaunakiya* and *Paippalada* of the *Atharva Veda*

It is also believed by some that each branch of the Vedas had 1130 each of the *Samhitas, Brahmanas, Aranyakas* and *Upanishads.* But now many are lost. Only less than 6% of the original Vedas are available now.

Structure of the Vedas

Vyasa classified all Vedic knowledge into four Vedas, the *Rig Veda,* the *Yajur Veda,* the *Sama Veda* and the *Atharva Veda.* Each Veda has four divisions or sections. These are *Samhitas, Brahmanas, Aranyakas* and *Upanishads.*

- The first section is *Samhita* which is the oldest. It is the hymn section.
- The second is the section of *Brahmanas* that deals with the ritualistic teachings.
- The third section is the *Aranyaka.* It is called the theological section.
- The fourth and the final section is the section of *Upanishads* that is called the philosophical section.

The *Samhitas* and *Brahmanas* correspond to the *Karma Kand,* the ritualistic section of the Vedas for the attainment of material prosperity on earth and celestial luxuries or heaven after death. These relate to the *yajnas* and Vedic rituals along with the performance of good *karmas.*

The *Aranyakas* and *Upanishads* correspond to the *Upasana* and *Jnana Kand* respectively. The *Upasana Kand* is concerned with different kinds of worships and meditation and the *Jnana Kand,* called the knowledge section, tells about the highest knowledge of *Nirguna Brahman* and shows the path of God realisation. The *Aranyakas* and *Upanishads* give spiritual knowledge leading to liberation or *Mukti*, that is freedom from ignorance and sorrows of life and the realisation of the ultimate truth.

It is said that if *Samhita* is compared to a **tree**, the *Brahmanas* are its **flowers** and the *Aranyakas* are the **unripe fruits** and the *Upanishads* are the **fully ripe fruits**. It is also said that just as in the case of a tree, the leaves and flowers outnumber the fruits, in the case of Vedas, the *Karma* and the *Upasana Kands* outnumber the *Jnana Kand.*

Samhitas and *Brahmanas* relate to *yajnas* and rituals and they form 75% of the Vedas, 19% relate to the meditational and theological aspects found in the *Aranyakas* and only 6% relate to *Jnana Kand,* the philosophical and knowledge section of the *Upanishads.*

These four sections are found in all the four Vedas. But in the case of the *Rig Veda, Shukla Yajur Veda* and the *Atharva Veda,* there is a clear separation between the *Samhita* and the *Brahmana* sections.

In the other Vedas, there is no clear distinction between the *Aranyaka* and *Upanishad* sections as one shades into the other.

It is said that the four parts of the Vedas namely the *Samhita, Brahmana, Aranyaka* and *Upanishads* correspond to the four stages or *ashramas* in a man's life namely, *Brahmacharya*, *Grihasthashrama*, *Vanaprastha* and *Sanyasa*.

As a student or *Brahmachari,* one is supposed to chant the mantras and lead a controlled and virtuous life. Then as a householder or *Grihastha*, which is the second stage in a man's life, one is expected to observe the injunctions put forth in the *Brahmanas.* In his third stage of life, namely *Vanaprastha*, which is the forest dweller's stage, one is supposed to meditate upon the underlying spiritual truths behind the rituals as found in the *Aranyakas* and practise renunciation. Finally as stated in the *Upanishads,* as a *Sanyasi,* one has to seek the ultimate truth and know *Brahman* for liberating oneself.

1. Samhitas

Samhita means collection. It contains sacred devotional hymns. It is the mantra or the first portion of the Vedas. The mantras are mostly addressed to Nature Gods and Goddesses. These form the basis for the *Brahmanas, Aranyakas* and *Upanishads*.

The mantras contained here are mostly in verse. The *Samhitas* or mantras or hymns or chants are the original, the oldest, and main texts of the Vedas. These contain poems containing prayers, hymns and incantations praising the Supreme God who created the Universe, the various deities who personify the Supreme Power, and also certain sages. These have divine power and are meant as general prayer. The mantras or hymns are sung to propitiate the celestial Gods during *yajnas* or ceremonies, to protect oneself from evil forces, and for seeking assistance in performing one's duties in life. They address subjects such as mystery of creation, divinity, aspects of Nature, everyday life and behaviour. There are hymns pertaining to the evils in gambling and so on. This portion also contains answers to the questions as to who created life, the Nature of the Universe and so on. The sacred mantras are written in verses and they are to be chanted in proper tune as prescribed in the Vedas.

The early Gods namely, Indra, Varuna, Yama, Surya and the *Trimurtis* who are responsible for creation, maintenance, and destruction of the Universe, namely Brahma, Vishnu and Shiva are mentioned in the *Mantra Samhitas.*

The *Samhitas* are five in number. They are, the *Rig Veda Samhita,* the *Shukla Yajur Veda Samhita,* the *Krishna Yajur Veda Samhita,* the *Sama Veda Samhita,* and the *Atharva Veda Samhita.*

It is said that there were 1180 branches of *Samhitas* in all the four Vedas. There are 20,389 or even 20,500 mantras in the *Samhita* portion of the Vedas. Of these approximately, 10,552 slokas are found in the *Rig Veda,* 1975 are in the *Yajur Veda,* 1875 slokas are in the *Sama Veda,* and there are 5987 slokas in the *Atharva Veda.* The Vedic mantras number more than 70 million. The effectiveness of mantras depends upon the mental discipline, correct recitation and breathing. It is mentioned in *Agni Purana* that mantras become very effective if they are recited quietly in the mind.

2. Brahmanas

The *Brahmanas* date back to 900 BC-500 BC. They are the oldest prose writings in any Indo-European language and form the second portion of the Vedas. They explain the hymns of the *Samhitas* and Vedic sacrifices and the way they are to be performed. They deal with *Karma* and are guides for the proper performance of rituals and sacrifices. The rituals can be interpreted in different ways. They can be considered as theological treatises of the Vedas. These explain the formulae for the rituals, their rules and regulations in minutest details. They further outline the performance of the various religious duties. They discuss the rituals that are performed for specific purpose with the objective of getting a specific effect.

The minute details of how a mantra is to be used by the householder while performing the sacrifices and rituals, which *yajna* is to be performed in what manner, the details of the actual performance of the *yajna*, the description of the worship of various forms of God, the significance of the mantras, description of the offerings, different kinds of ceremonies and rituals, their methods, methodologies, the rules, formulae and regulations and directions for performing the complicated rituals, the origin and meaning of the sacrifices; the importance of prayers and sacrifices, are all elaborately explained here.

They also outline the religious duties of people. They give guidance to the priests who perform the sacrifices. The duties of men following different occupations, the eternity of the Vedas, the popular customs and traditions, historical details, praising the ancient heroes, the description of the origin, creation and evolution of the Universe are some of the other subjects dealt with in *Brahmanas.*

Mystical Explanations

In short, *Brahmanas* can be considered as manuals for ritual worship and prayer. They give mystical explanations of the ceremonial aspects of religious life and also give directions and procedures to be followed in the performance of sacrifices and their correct observance. It is believed that all that one wishes to have can be obtained by performing the Vedic rituals in proper manner, with the knowledge of their real meaning but not with their mechanical performance.

They are so powerful that they can even make the performer control the process of Nature and Gods.

Brahmanas explain the hymns of the *Samhitas* and are in both prose and verse form. The fire God, *Agni* to whom all the offerings are made during the rituals, is given an important place here.

The *Brahmanas* are divided into *Vidhi* and *Arthavada. Vidhi* are commands in the performance of Vedic sacrifices, and *Arthavada* praises the rituals, the glory of the *Devas* and so on. The belief in reincarnation is seen in *Brahmanas.*

The *Samhitas* in each Veda had *Brahmanas* associated with them numbering around 1180. But only a few are available now. The *Brahmanas* that are available now are —

1. *Aitareya Brahmana*
2. *Chandogya Mantra Brahmana*
3. *Devatadhyaya Brahmana*
4. *Gopatha Brahmana*
5. *Jaiminiya Arsheya Brahmana*
6. *Jaiminiya Brahmana*
7. *Jaiminiya Upanishad Brahmana*
8. *Kanviyam Shatapatha Brahmana*
9. *Kathaka Brahmana*
10. *Kaushitaki Brahmana*
11. *Kauthuma Arsheya Brahmana*
12. *Samavidhana Brahmana*
13. *Samhitopanishad Brahmana*
14. *Shatapatha Brahmana*
15. *Shadvimsa Brahmana*
16. *Shankhayana Brahmana*
17. *Taittiriya Brahmana*
18. *Taittiriya Chardi Brahmana*
19. *Tandya Brahmana*
20. *Vadhula Anvaakhyaana Brahmana*
21. *Vamsa Brahmana*
22. *Fragments of lost Brahmanas*

3. Aranyakas

Aranyakas relate to the meditation section of the Vedas. They were believed to have been composed around 700 BC. These are considered part of *Brahmanas. Aranyakas* are forest books. They give mystical, symbolic and philosophical interpretations in metaphysical and cosmic terms and the inner meanings of the mantras of *Samhitas* and the rituals and sacrifices explained in the *Brahmanas* give the logical reasoning for following them and deal with *Upasana.*

These are treatises for the hermits who had retired to the forests in search of knowledge and ultimate truth. *Aranya* in Sanskrit means forest. *Aranyakas* are intended for those who are in the third stage of life namely, *Vanaprastha* and they prepare the *Vanaprasthis* or hermits for *Sanyasa.* Just as the *Samhitas* in each Veda have *Brahmanas,* each of the *Brahmanas* has got an *Aranyaka.* They deal more with God. The forms and aspects of God that is worshipped, the manner and mode of worship, are all explained here in detail. It is called *Videhi Bhakti* or worshipping God in a strictly formulative manner. How to sit for prayer, which side to face, during what part of the day to offer the prayer, what mantra to be chanted, which ritual to be performed before and after prayer and so on, are clearly explained here.

They also prescribe the alternatives in the form of different types of meditation to be practised when the elaborate ceremonies would not be possible for the *vanaprasthis* who live the life of hermits in the forests. The *Aranyakas* help them in knowing the hidden meaning and significance of the rituals and sacrifice. The mystical and philosophical interpretations of the mantras and rituals as found in the *Samhitas* and the *Brahmanas* become clear to them at this stage. The emphasis here is more on knowledge and meditation rather than chanting the mantras and performing the rituals. However, the hermits in the forests perform a few *yajnas* too. Hence the *Aranyakas* can never be clearly and absolutely distinguished from the *Brahmanas.* They form the basis of *Vedanta* or *Upanishads.*

Out of the 1180 *Aranyakas,* only a few are available now. It is believed that the *Aranyakas* were composed much later than the *Brahmanas.* The *Aranyakas* together with the *Upanishads* form the *Jnana Kand* or the section of knowledge. The *Aranyakas* now available are —

1. *Aitareya Aranyaka*
2. *Kathaka Aranyaka*
3. *Maitrayaniya Aranyaka*
4. *Shankhayana Aranyaka*
5. *Taittiriya Aranyaka*
6. *Talavakara Aranyaka*

4. Upanishads

The term *Upanishad* comes from the Sanskrit words *Upa Ni* (under and near) and *Shad* (to sit). It is the teaching, which the *guru* imparts when the disciples sit very near or very close to him so that no one overhears his teachings.

According to Adi Shankara, the term is derived from the word *Shad* that means 'to destroy'. *Upanishad* refers to that knowledge of *Brahman* by which ignorance is destroyed. The word also implies inner and mystic teachings of the sages to their disciples who belong to different groups. Sometimes the disciple is the wife of the saint himself, sometimes it is a young boy who could be his son or his student, still at another time, it could be a king as well.

Upanishads are also referred to as *Shruti Prasthana* or revealed scriptures from which knowledge of *Brahman* is obtained. *Upanishads* are also referred to as *Shruti-Siras*, meaning the head or crown of the Vedas that form the *Shruti.*

The *Upanishads* are also known as *Vedanta,* because they are the concluding portion or the culmination of Vedas or knowledge itself and also because, chronologically *Upanishads* came at the end of the Vedic period. They are continuation and development of the fundamental ideas and temperament of the Vedas. They are the philosophical treatises and explain the mystical aspects of the Vedas. In *Upanishads,* the importance of the mantras, rituals and Vedic sacrifices found in the *Samhita* and *Brahmana* portions of the Vedas are relegated to the background while the concept of Brahma that is all-pervading is brought to the limelight. The *Karma Kand* of the Vedas that include the *Samhita* and *Brahmana* portions of the Vedas, explain a way of life with the performance of actions and duties to discipline and purify oneself.

Jnana Kand

The *Jnana Kand* consisting of the *Aranyaka* and *Upanishad* portions speak about forsaking all Vedic *Karmas* and meditating on the truth expounded by the *Upanishads.* Some *Upanishads* even go to the extent of declaring the Vedic rites and the sacrifices as inferior knowledge. The seers of ancient India knew very well that conquest of the inner rather than the outer world alone can provide lasting happiness to man. Hence, they focused their attention from the outer objective world to the subjective, inner world of man. They advised us not to waste time in mere rituals but seek refuge in *Brahman* through meditation and introspection.

As Sri Aurobindo had remarked —

'*Upanishads are the records of the deepest spiritual experiences of the ancient seers. Upanishads are truth, seen, felt, lived and held by the innermost mind and soul.*'

However, many of the ideas contained in the spiritual vision and philosophical arguments of the *Upanishads* are very difficult to understand and are still obscure to us.

As David Frawley has said —

'The modern mind has yet to penetrate the veil protecting the ancient mysteries.'

The *Upanishads* teach *Atma Vidya* and the practical means of realisation of *Brahman*, the ultimate and eternal truth. They point out that through meditation that single Truth which is the ultimate reality can become a living reality, and the difference between the individual-self and the Universal-self can melt away. In that state, when the individual dissolves or merges with *Brahman,* one becomes a *sanyasi* and he fully understands the four *Mahavakyas* or the Great Mantras found in the great *Upanishads* that form the basic principles of Hinduism.

The first of these is *Prajnanam Brahma* stated in the *Aitareya Upanishad* of the *Rig Veda.* It means realisation of the *jnana,* which is the highest *Brahman* or the supreme intelligence. Through our innermost, supreme and divine intelligence, we can merge with the supreme *Brahman.*

The second is *Aham Brahmasmi* found in the *Brihad Aranyaka Upanishad* of the *Yajur Veda.* It means, 'I am *Brahman*' or 'I am consciousness.' It shows that the *jeevatma,* the individual self and the *Paramatma*, the universal soul are one and the same. In short, it states that God is in us and not outside of ourselves.

The third is *Tat Tvam Asi* given in the *Chandogya Upanishad* of the *Sama Veda*. It means, the *Paramatma* and you are one and the same. We are what we think.

The fourth and the last of the *Mahavakya* is *Ayam Atma Brahma* from the *Mandukya Upanishad* of the *Atharva Veda* that means, 'I am the Soul or *jeevatma*, which is a spark of *Paramatma*'. It means that the self, that is in me and in all the other beings is *Brahman*.

Upanishads form the fourth and the most important and final section of the Vedas. They are believed to have been composed over a long period of time covering several centuries, the most important period was between the 7th and 5th centuries.

The *Brihad Aranyaka* and the *Chandogya Upanishads* that are considered as the earliest, are dated between 800 BC and 400 BC.

The later ones are said to belong to the period around the 5th century BC. It is believed that the *Upanishads* were prevalent even some centuries before the time of Sri Krishna and Gautama Buddha.

Upanishads deal with the nature of reality, individual soul, and the Universal soul. A few *Upanishads* are the extended portion of *Aranyakas.* Some are in prose, some are in verse, and some are partly in prose and partly in verse. *Upanishads* are in the form of stories, dialogues, discourses, arguments, discussions, chants or hymns. These are highly metaphysical and philosophical. Some *Upanishads* are very long and certain others are very short. For example, the *Mandukya Upanishad* has only 12 very short paragraphs written in prose, whereas, the *Brihad Aranyaka Upanishad* is very long.

Upanishads are considered the most important part of the Vedas. They are the mystical or philosophical sections of the Vedas. These deal with *Tattva Jnana*. They contain the essence of the knowledge contained in the Vedas. These can be considered as the gist and goals of Vedas. They reveal truths about the individual soul, world and the Universal soul. The purpose is to achieve complete knowledge for a full and complete life and to know the real self. This portion of the Vedas is meant for people who are in the *sanyasa* stage, which is the fourth and the final stage in the life of a man.

Spiritual Vision

Upanishads give the necessary spiritual vision through philosophical arguments, episodes, commentaries, stories and metaphysical dialogues. They help uncover the process of creation, life, the essence of life, and the life beyond, that form the path of *Jnana Yoga. Upanishads* teach to renounce the worldly attachments and surrender to God and thereby show the path of God-realisation. They emphasise the role of *Jnana* or knowledge for achieving God-realisation, that is same as self-realisation. The knowledge of soul or *Atman* or self is the same as the knowledge of *Brahman* or Universal soul, which is the source of all existence. Hence, they are called as *Jnana Kand* or knowledge section of the Vedas. In the quietness of the forest, the sages revealed and communicated their knowledge only to those deserving pupils who were sitting close to their *guru's* feet in great devotion with all eagerness to learn the highest truth, listening to their teachings in the most attentive manner. The disciples approached the teacher with metaphysical questions and got the answers from him. The truth was taught only to such devoted disciples. Such teachings were not meant for those who were not mature or capable enough to understand and cherish the value of such teachings. In short, *Upanishads* are said to be the summit of thought on man and Universe and are supposed to uncover the secret wisdom. This wisdom they point out can be obtained only through strong personal effort because truth can be known only through direct experience. It is known only when one goes beyond mind.

In Hinduism, Lord Shiva as Dakshinamurty is regarded as the supreme Guru. It is said that the four sages, Sanaka, Sanananda, Sanatan, and Sanat Kumar once approached Lord Dakshinamurty for getting enlightenment about the supreme truth. Lord Shiva after hearing their request went and sat under a banyan tree. There he sat silently in the *Chinmudra* yoga posture facing southwards. The sages also sat near him with the utmost devotion. Lord Shiva did not speak a single word. But the four sages got their doubts cleared. It only shows that the final stage of teaching is through silence. At that stage, the Divine Grace flows from the teacher to the disciples and one automatically gains the knowledge. That state cannot be explained. It has to be experienced and such an experience is achieved only through the Divine Grace.

Vedic Doctrines

The *Upanishads* push human thought to its peak and even beyond. They form the core of Hindu philosophy. One can find all the fundamental teachings of Hinduism, namely, the concepts of *Karma* or action, *Punarjanma* or rebirth, *Moksha* or salvation, *Atman* or soul, and *Brahman* or Supreme Lord in them. The prime Vedic doctrines like self-realisation, yoga and meditation are also explained here. *Upanishads* speak of the identity of the *jeevatma* or the individual soul and the *Paramatma* or the Universal soul which has no form, gender or quality.

Vedanta asserts that the Absoute truth of the Universe is *Brahman*. The individual soul or *jeevatma* originates and merges with the *Paramatma* or the Universal soul.

'*Soul is God's spirit that dwells in every living being*' says *Bhagavad Gita* which is considered to contain the essence of all *Upanishad* teachings.

The *Upanishads* discuss the higher level of knowledge that relates to all imperishable knowledge that is different from that lower level of knowledge relating to all empirical sciences, and the knowledge of material things. They advocate the attainment of the knowledge of of the Self or the realisation of *Brahman* who is *Sat* (existence), *Chit* (consciousness) and *Ananda* (bliss).

The *Upanishads* teach us that by going beyond Space and Time, one can realise *Brahman* through self-analysis. *Upanishads* themselves were the result of continued introspection, contemplation and concentration of the sages that led to the clarity of their vision resulting in all spiritual understanding culminating in the achievement of direct and intuitive glimpses of the philosophical and spiritual truths. The three stages in the process of self-realisation are —

- The study of *Upanishad* under proper guidance
- A firm conviction of what is studied through introspection and logical thinking
- Constant and continuous meditation

However, one is supposed to practise self-control, generosity, and compassion before entering this stage.

Along with the subjects like yoga, meditation, reincarnation, self-realisation and so on, the *Upanishads* also deal with subjects like ancient history, cosmology, the art of living properly according to the moral code of conduct while performing one's duties and responsibilities as per one's own circumstances in life and so on. The purpose is to elevate man gradually from the material well-being to the higher level of spiritual well-being. Finally, through negation of all and everything, up to the Supreme, the *Upanishads* establish the Absolute truth that is beyond all names, forms and qualities.

Self and Cosmos

Upanishads mostly deal with the questions about Self and its relationship with the Cosmos, the nature of ultimate reality and so on. They arrive at the conclusion that *Paramatma* or *Brahman* is pure consciousness. Each individual soul lives countless lives according to its own *Karma*. In each birth, the individual soul enjoys and suffers the results of its good and bad actions. It takes birth again and again until it unites with the *Brahman* and once the merger or unification takes place, the soul gets freed from the cycle of births and deaths. At this stage, one becomes mature enough to severe oneself from all *Karmas*. For such a person, there are no more births and deaths.

In *Upanishads,* intuition rather than reason is given a prominent place. Again here we find projection of hypothesis and their rejection later, on the basis of new knowledge. The core of the teaching of the *Upanishads* is that the individual realises the ultimate Truth by means of an inward journey by entering into oneself and merging with the *Brahman.* One who cultivates all qualities like calmness of mind, controlled and quiet temperament, endurance, patience, sympathy, empathy, broadmindedness, humility and one who is eager to realise the ultimate Truth alone can reach the goal.

Again, the fundamental idea underlying all the *Upanishad* teachings is the concept of one God, all the other Gods being only the manifestations of this single supreme power and the identification of the Self (*Jeevatma)* with the Universal soul (*Paramatma* or *Brahman*).

Most of the earlier *Upanishads* are attached to a Veda through *Brahmana* or *Aranyaka.* But there are also *Upanishads,* which are separate texts. The later *Upanishads* represent Shiva, Vishnu and Shakti as manifestations of the supreme reality. Many divergent are views woven together in *Upanishads.* However, we can notice one common uniform principle running through all thoughts.

Sages in Upanishads

One main figure found in many of the *Upanishads* is the name of the sage Yajnavalkya. He taught the great doctrine of *Neti-Neti.* It means that truth can be found only through negation of all thoughts about it. Other important sages who are associated with *Upanishads* are Uddalaka Aruni, Shwetaketu, Shandilya, Aitareya, Pippalada, Sanat Kumara, and earlier Vedic teachers like Manu, Brihaspathi, Anasuya and Narada. As a result of continuous and constant inward concentration and contemplation that was effortless on their part, the sages could ascend to the transcendental state of consciousness that culminated in obtaining direct intuitive glimpses of the greatest philosophical and spiritual wisdom. However, these great teachers did not claim any credit for themselves for revealing the great wisdom of the *Upanishads.* On the other hand, in all humility, they maintained that they only transmitted the age-old wisdom. In short, as Sri Aurobindo had said, "*Upanishads* are the supreme work of the Indian mind that is the summit of ancient human thought."

According to one belief, there were around 1081 *Upanishads* that means as many *Upanishads* as there were branches in each Veda.

- 21 in *Rig Veda*
- 109 in *Yajur Veda*
- 1000 in *Sama Veda*
- 50 in *Atharva Veda*

Some state that there were 200 *Upanishads.* Others give the number as nearly 120. According to *Muktikopanishad,* there are 108 *Upanishads.* These 108 *Upanishads* are classified under different groups. There are some differences in the number of *Upanishads* belonging to different groups as per different estimates. A few *Upanishads* are considered as *Principal Upanishads.* The number of *Principal Upanishads* varies according to different estimates. According to *Muktikopanishad,* there are 12 *Principal Upanishads.* They are, namely, *Isha, Kena, Katha, Taittiriya, Aitareya, Prashna, Mundaka, Mandukya, Chandogya, Svetasvatara, Brihad Aranyaka* and *Maha Narayana. Adi Shankara* considered 10 of the earliest *Upanishads* as *Principal Upanishads* and commented upon them. They are *Aitareya, Brihad Aranyaka, Isha, Taittiriya, Katha, Chandogya, Kena, Mundaka, Mandukya* and *Prashna.* Some include *Kaushitaki* and *Maitreyi Upanishads* also in the category of early *Upanishads.* Of these, *Brihad Aranyaka* and *Chandogya* are considered very old. The earlier *Upanishads* are believed to have been written between 700 BC and 600 BC.

Among the later *Upanishads*, some are believed to have been written even as late as 14th or 15th centuries. The *Taittiriya, Aitareya, Kaushitaki, Kena, Katha, Isha,* and *Mundaka* belong to roughly about the 6th century BC, approximately, the period of Buddha. The *Upanishads Prashna, Svetasvatara, Mandukya, Maha Narayana* and *Maitreyi* are said to belong to the period after Buddha.

The number of Upanishads as per their Grouping and the Vedas associated with them

(RV – Rig Veda, KYV – Krishna Yajur Veda, SYV – Shukla Yajur Veda, AV – Atharva Veda)

Group	RV	KYV	S YV	SV	AV	Total
Principal Upanishads	1	2	2	2	3	10
Saktha Upanishads	3	1	0	0	5	09
Sanyasa Upanishads	1	6	7	4	4	22
Samanya Upanishads	3	8	6	4	1	22
Shaiva Upanishads	1	4	0	2	6	13
Vaishnava Upanishads	0	2	1	2	9	14
Yoga Upanishads	1	9	3	2	3	18
Total	**10**	**32**	**19**	**16**	**31**	**108**

The 108 *Upanishads* as per their groupings are —

Principal Upanishads–10

- *Aitareya (Rig Veda)*
- *Katha (Krishna Yajur Veda)*
- *Taittiriya (Krishna Yajur Veda)*
- *Brihad (Shukla Yajur Veda)*
- *Isavaya (Shukla Yajur Veda)*
- *Chandogya (Sama Veda)*
- *Kena (Sama Veda)*
- *Mandukya (Atharva Veda)*
- *Mundaka (Atharva Veda)*
- *Prashna (Atharva Veda)*

Saktha Upanishads–9

- *Bhahvricha (Rig Veda)*
- *Sowbhagya Lakshmi (Rig Veda)*
- *Tripura (Rig Veda)*
- *Saraswati Rahasya (Krishna Yajur Veda)*
- *Annapurna (Atharva Veda)*
- *Bhavana (Atharva Veda)*
- *Devi (Atharva Veda)*
- *Sita (Atharva Veda)*
- *Tripura Tapani (Atharva Veda)*

Sanyasa Upanishads–22

- *Nirvana (Rig Veda)*
- *Avadhuta (Krishna Yajur Veda)*
- *Brahma (Krishna Yajur Veda)*
- *Katha Rudra (Krishna Yajur Veda)*
- *Svetasvatara (Krishna Yajur Veda)*
- *Tejo Bindu (Krishna Yajur Veda)*
- *Varaha (Krishna Yajur Veda)*

- *Advarya Taraka (Shukla Yajur Veda)*
- *Bhikshuka (Shukla Yajur Veda)*
- *Jabala (Shukla Yajur Veda)*
- *Parama Hamsa (Shukla Yajur Veda)*
- *Satyayaniya (Shukla Yajur Veda)*
- *Turiyatita Avadhutha (Shukla Yajur Veda)*
- *Yajnavalkya (Shukla Yajur Veda)*
- *Aruneya (Sama Veda)*
- *Kundika (Sama Veda)*
- *Maitreyi (Sama Veda)*
- *Sanyasa (Sama Veda)*
- *Narada Parivarjaka (Atharva Veda)*
- *Para Brahma (Atharva Veda)*
- *Parama Hamsa (Atharva Veda)*
- *Pashupata Brahmana (Atharva Veda)*

Samanya Upanishads–22

- *Atma Boda (Rig Veda)*
- *Kaushitaki (Rig Veda)*
- *Mudgala (Rig Veda)*
- *Akshi (Krishna Yajur Veda)*
- *Ekakshara (Krishna Yajur Veda)*
- *Garbha (Krishna Yajur Veda)*
- *Pranagnihotra (Krishna Yajur Veda)*
- *Sareerika (Krishna Yajur Veda)*
- *Sarvasara (Krishna Yajur Veda)*
- *Skand (Krishna Yajur Veda)*
- *Sukha Rahasya (Krishna Yajur Veda)*
- *Adhyatma (Shukla Yajur Veda)*
- *Mantrika (Shukla Yajur Veda)*
- *Muktika (Shukla Yajur Veda)*
- *Niralamba (Shukla Yajur Veda)*

- *Paingali (Shukla Yajur Veda)*
- *Subala (Shukla Yajur Veda)*
- *Maha (Sama Veda)*
- *Maitrayani (Sama Veda)*
- *Savitri (Sama Veda)*
- *Vajra Suchika (Sama Veda)*
- *Surya (Atharva Veda)*

Shaiva Upanishads–13

- *Aksha Malika (Rig Veda)*
- *Dakshinamurthy (Krishna Yajur Veda)*
- *Kaivalya (Krishna Yajur Veda)*
- *Kalagni Rudra (Krishna Yajur Veda)*
- *Pancha Brahma (Krishna Yajur Veda)*
- *Jabali (Sama Veda)*
- *Rudraksha Jabala (Sama Veda)*
- *Atharva Sihkha (Atharva Veda)*
- *Atharva Shira (Atharva Veda)*
- *Bhasma Jabala (Atharva Veda)*
- *Brihad Jabala (Atharva Veda)*
- *Ganapati (Atharva Veda)*
- *Sarabha (Atharva Veda)*

Vaishnava Upanishads–14

- *Kali Santarana (Krishna Yajur Veda)*
- *Maha Narayana (Krishna Yajur Veda)*
- *Avyakta (Sama Veda)*
- *Vasudeva (Sama Veda)*
- *Dattatreya (Atharva Veda)*
- *Garuda (Atharva Veda)*
- *Gopala Tapaniya (Atharva Veda)*
- *Haya Greeva (Atharva Veda)*
- *Krishna (Atharva Veda)*

- *Narasimha Tapaniya (Atharva Veda)*
- *Rama Rahasya (Atharva Veda)*
- *Rama Tapani (Atharva Veda)*
- *Tripad Vibhuthi Maha Narayana (Atharva Veda)*

Yoga Upanishads–18

- *Nada Bindu (Rig Veda)*
- *Amrita Bindu (Krishna Yajur Veda)*
- *Amritananda (Krishna Yajur Veda)*
- *Brahma Vidya (Krishna Yajur Veda)*
- *Dyana Bindu (Krishna Yajur Veda)*
- *Kshurika (Krishna Yajur Veda)*
- *Rudra Hrudaya (Krishna Yajur Veda)*
- *Yoga Kundalani (Krishna Yajur Veda)*
- *Yoga Shikha (Krishna Yajur Veda)*
- *Yoga Tattva (Krishna Yajur Veda)*
- *Hamsa (Shukla Yajur Veda)*
- *Mandala Brahmana (Shukla Yajur Veda)*
- *Trisikhi Brahmana (Shukla Yajur Veda)*
- *Darshana (Sama Veda)*
- *Yoga Choodamani (Sama Veda)*
- *Atma (Atharva Veda)*
- *Mahavakya (Atharva Veda)*
- *Shandilya (Atharva Veda)*

3

The Vedas — Interpretations, Criticism and Symbolism

Interpretations of the Vedas

The ancient scriptures, particularly the Vedas, that formed the basis for all the other scriptures of India, are interpreted differently by different people according to their mental disposition, understanding and knowledge. A large number of people consider Vedas as the pinnacle of wisdom. But there are some others who view the Vedas as expressions of barbaric nomads of the Vedic times. They consider the hymns of the Vedas as childish and primitive. This latter view only shows the lack of proper knowledge and understanding of the Vedas and the myopic vision and ignorance on their part. How one understands the Vedic verses depends upon one's level of knowledge. A child who has just started learning the alphabet says that any word that is written down with letter 'A' but not followed by the letter 'B' is wrong. For him, the word 'CAT' is not correct, since in this word the letter 'C' is followed by the letter 'A'. According to him, it should be followed by the letter 'D' because in the understanding of the child the letter 'A' is to be followed by the letter 'B' and then 'C' and so on. One cannot blame the child because that is his level of understanding.

How much knowledge one can gather depends upon his capacity to contain. As a proverb in Malayalam quotes: ***Nazhi kollindodethe nanazhi kollumo*** *(A vessel of a particular measure cannot be expected to hold more than its capacity.)*

Similarly a person whose understanding is very limited cannot be expected to know the real content of anything. His understanding is limited to the extent of his knowledge. The ancient Indian scriptures are like an ocean. They are also highly complex and are very difficult to understand. This complex nature and depth of their knowledge has led to several interpretations depending upon the knowledge of the person who interprets them. However, condemning those scriptures totally and passing judgments over them only reveals total ignorance. For a person who is not having the required knowledge, the hymns of the Vedas may sound childish, primitive and barbaric but for a knowledgeable person it would not be so. Only the person who can dive deep into the ocean of Vedas will be able to obtain its pearls of wisdom.

The earliest commentators of the Vedas including Yaska, found three meanings in the Vedic verses. The first one is related to the knowledge of the **external worship and rituals,** the second is interpretation related to the **knowledge of the Supreme power** of the Universe called God, and the third and the most important of all the meanings is the **spiritual knowledge** relating to the Self.

The Vedic hymns can be interpreted in two ways.

Firstly, they can be taken to mean a poetical and legendary account of Vedic spiritual understanding, a description of the happenings in the Vedic times and everything connected with the Vedic civilisation, culture, life pattern and the desires and wishes of the people of those times.

Secondly, they can be interpreted in their mystical sense. Vedas composed poetically in Vedic Sanskrit in the background of Vedic history are very beautiful, yet at the same time highly mysterious and very difficult to understand as they have vast hidden content. They are interpreted in different ways by different people according to their level of understanding, knowledge of Vedic Sanskrit, the extent of their knowledge of the ancient Indian civilisation, culture, Vedic history and mythology.

Deeper Meaning of the Vedas

One who studies the Vedas will know that the Vedas contain profound secrets of the world besides their poetic imagery, prayers, rites, rituals and sacrifices. The different rituals have many apparent as well as deeper meanings of everlasting value. Only a person who has a deep knowledge of Vedic Sanskrit, Vedic history, Vedic civilisation and culture and Vedic mythology can correctly interpret the Vedas. It is also important that he should have read and understood all the *Samhitas, Brahmanas, Aranyakas* and *Upanishads*. This will give him the required knowledge and wisdom to understand the real meaning of the Vedas.

Sri Aurobindo wrote in his book, *An Essay on the Vedas* —

'*A criticism that ignores or belittles the significance of this unsurpassed record and this splendour of the self-expressing spirit and the creative intelligence, stands convicted at once of a blind malignity or an invincible prejudice and does not merit refutation.*'

In their literal sense, the Rig Vedic hymns are in praise of several Nature Gods, mainly for reaping material blessings on earth. The *Shrauta* kind of rituals and sacrifices were performed by the Vedic priests. On the outset, the sacrifice included the proper setting up of the sacrificial ground, the fire place, the raised platform, along with the necessary tools, articles and offerings for the performance of sacrifice amidst the chanting of the mantras.

In the *Shrauta* type of sacrifices, more attention was given to the external objects which were necessary for conducting the sacrifices like the arrangement of the enclosure, objects like wood sticks for kindling fire, spoons to be used for the offerings, logs that formed the fuel, the pressing stones for *Soma* stalks, the sacrificial vessel called *Chamasa* that held the offerings, the *Kunda* surrounding the pit, into which the offerings are put, the *Kusha* grass spread around the area, the water sprinkled on them, the oblations like milk, clarified butter, and so on. The priests of the Vedas performed the sacrifice. While the *Hota* priest chanted the Rig Vedic mantras, *Adhvarya* chanted the *Yajur Veda, Udghatri* chanted the Sama Vedic hymns, and the *Brahman* the priest of *Atharva Veda,* supervised the entire ceremony and chanted the hymns from *Atharva Veda.*

If the chants, sacrifices and rituals are interpreted in their inner meaning, then it becomes symbolic of the struggle between the spiritual powers of light and darkness, truth and falsehood, knowledge and ignorance, death and immortality. Then the offerings become symbolic. Sacrifice becomes the giving up of everything one possesses and ultimately surrendering oneself totally to the supreme power. The *Panis* and *Vritras* referred to the powers of darkness, evil and falsehood and not the actual demons as they are stated in the Vedas.

According to one interpretation, in the early times, the external form of worship was popular. As time passed, during the *Aranyaka* and *Upanishadic* periods, the external form of worship gave way to internalisation of the sacrifices and rituals. It is stated by some that this change from the external worship to internalisation amounted to spiritual progress. But spiritual progress cannot be correlated with periods of time. It is entirely subjective. The seers who composed the *Samhitas* could not have been any lesser in their wisdom than those who had composed the later sections of the Vedas. It may be that with the change of times, understanding of the true meaning of the Vedas might have become difficult for the people. Hence, the need was felt to give a detailed explanation of the *Samhitas* both in its outward form as well as in their internal form. A detailed account of the rituals and sacrifices with all its minutest details were dealt with along with their inner or mystic meanings in the *Brahmanas* for the benefit of the *Grihasthas* or householders. For the benefit of the *Vanaprasthas,* who resided in the forests and who could not perform the sacrifices as per their minutest details, the sacrifices were made mostly internal. Finally in *Upanishads,* the sacrifices are relegated to the background and in its place meditation and self-realisation are stressed for achieving the desired objective.

In another sense, while the objective of the householders is mostly to lead a happy and prosperous life on earth by obtaining the desired external objects, more importance was given to all external objects of sacrifice in the *Brahmanas.* The *Brahmanas* also reveal the true meaning of such sacrifices. The *vanaprasthis* who belonged to a stage in which although, they had come out of the stage of the *Grihasthas*, they still had not reached the stage of monks and were therefore in between the two stages of *Grihasthashrama* and *Sanyasa*. So *Aranyakas* dealt with sacrifices that were mostly internal. Finally, for the *Sanyasi* who sought the eternal, supreme truth, the imperishable *Brahman* alone and nothing else, the seers prescribed neither external nor inner sacrifices but they showed them the path of self-analysis through continuous and intense meditation as the paths for reaching their goal of liberation or *Mukti*.

The Vedas are so poetic, profound and complex that anyone who tries to interpret them can only touch their periphery.

This situation would be like the one where five blind people tried to explain how an elephant looked like by touching one or the other part of its body. They could only explain the part they felt and thought it to be the entire elephant. But truth was far from it. The elephant was huge and none could comprehensively and correctly interpret it. In the same way, the Vedas cannot be comprehended by a narrow view. Vedas themselves give ample scope for multiple interpretations. When the verses are taken in an isolated manner, they are bound to give wrong or incorrect meanings as they are interpreted out of context. Further, the ancient views are not to be interpreted in the modern context. Even the sages who were the pinnacles of wisdom and who revealed the Vedas were not categorical in their statements.

As hymn 10.129.7 of the *Rig Veda* puts it —

इयं विसृष्टिर्यत आबभूव यदि वा दधे यदि वा न।
यो अस्याध्यक्षः परमे व्योमन्तसो अंग वेद यदि वा न वेद।।
Iyaḿ visŗśtiryat ābabhūv yadi vā dadhe yadi vā na
yo asyādhyakşhaḥ parame vyomaṇtso aṇga
veda yadi vā na veda

'Who knows for certain about origin of the creation of the world and when creation took place; since no one knows about it. Only He who surveys from the lofty skies knows or perhaps even He may not know.'

As Sri Aurobindo has stated —

'Truth is what the soul has seen and experienced; the rest is appearance, prejudice, and opinion.'

There is an immortality to which the human soul has to ascend. We have to find our way to that and understand the true meaning of truth and immortality. This is true even of the real understanding of the Vedas. Vedic hymns can be comprehended properly if one has the required knowledge and understanding, and one can interpret the hymns according to its own spirit and vision because what is spiritually natural may look strange and supernatural for all ordinary human beings.

Criticisms of the Vedas

No great work can ever be accepted without criticism. Vedas being such vast treatises, were bound to evoke criticism from all sectors. Here are a few points which were taken up by the critics.

1. Number of Gods

In the first criticism, the critics point out that too many Gods are worshipped in the *Rig Veda.* No doubt many deities are mentioned in the *Rig Veda.* But one must understand that these deities are taken as manifestation of the single, supreme cosmic power. Different people have different desires. While one wants victory, the other wants prosperity, still another wants offspring and yet another desires all of these. The one who desires victory, worships the God of war, one who prays for splendour and brightness, worships the Sun, and so on. It only shows that the ancient seers had understood human nature very well. They never wanted to limit their worship to one deity. Depending upon one's desires, one was free to choose any deity of his choice. Everyone does not have same nature or aspirations. They differ in their nature, outlook, mental makeup etc. The *rishis* knew this fact very well, hence they gave the choice of worship to man. It only reveals the liberal attitude of ancient seers even with regard to spirituality.

Different Paths of Salvations

Hinduism offers many paths for salvation so that one can choose any path of one's choice that suits his temperament. Broadly, the scriptures based on the Vedas indicate three paths namely, *Bhakti yoga* for those who seek material and spiritual happiness with the firm faith that God the protector when invoked or prayed will definitely answer their call. Secondly, there is the path of *Karma yoga* for those who seek progress through performance of selfless actions. Finally, there is the *Jnana yoga* that leads to wisdom. It is further stated in the scriptures that the path suitable for many, especially in *Kaliyuga,* is the path of *Bhakti*. Even in the path of *Bhakti,* Hinduism is liberal. One can choose the deity of one's choice among the several manifestations of supreme power. There again, even in the case of the same God, one can view the God in any form or in any type of relationships. For example, Lord Krishna is worshipped by some people as a child with all his childish pranks and miraculous powers, there are others like Mirabai who desire to worship him in his role as a romantic lover and still there are others who pray to him in his form as a *karma* and *jnana yogi* who gave to mankind the essence of the *Upanishads* in the form of *Bhagavad Gita.*

Again one may believe in *Advaita* that speaks of the unity of the individual and cosmic soul and stresses the idea that 'God is in you'. There may be others who believe in other doctrines like *Dwaita.* The fundamental idea behind these varied ways is only to make man realise the ultimate truth that whatever means you adopt, the end result remains the same. The same truth holds good for all the religions of the world. Every religion only tries to make man divine. Man, in his ignorance, fails to understand this basic truth of all the religions. This is the reason for the religious and communal hatred and antagonism in the world. Once man realises this fundamental truth, then there will be peace and harmony in the whole world. In fact, the Vedas speak of the welfare of all humans.

सर्वे जना सुखिनो भवन्तु।
Sarve janā sukhino bhavaṇtu
(May the entire mankind live happily.)

The seers were fully aware of the fact that the superior power of the Universe can be only one and not many. At the same time, they also knew that the Supreme power is everywhere and in everything.

The verse 1.164.46 of the *Rig Veda* says, '*What is one, the sages call many.*'

The *Rig Veda* speaks of *Ekam Sat* meaning, the 'One Reality'.

It is also said in 10.129.2 of the *Rig Veda,* '*Tad Ekam*' which means 'That One' that one can see the divinity in anything. It all depends upon the viewer.

Again, 10.121.1 of the *Rig Veda* says —

हिरण्यगर्भः समवर्तताग्रे भूतस्य जातः पतिरेक आसीत्।
स दाधार पृथिवीं द्यामुतेमां कस्मै देवाय हविषा विधेम।।

Hiraṇyagarbhaḥ samavartatāgre bhūtasya jātaḥ patirek āsīt
Sa dādhār pṛthivīṁ dyāmutemāṁ kasmai devāya
haviṣā vidhema

(In the beginning rose Hiranyagarbha, born only Lord of all created beings, who is the sole ruler, He, whose commands all Gods acknowledge.)

The *Atharva Veda* says: '*He is the one, the one alone. In Him, all deities become one*'.

A stone is a mere stone for an ordinary person. Different people view the same stone differently. For a sculptor, the stone contains the shape of the image that he likes to carve. For one who is an atheist, an idol is nothing but a mere stone while for the one who worships it, it is an embodiment of divinity.

To the Vedic seers, Sri Aurobindo points out,

'*The physical worlds were to their eyes a manifestation and a two-fold diverse and yet connected and similar figure of cosmic Godheads, the inner and outer life of man, a divine communion with the Gods, and behind was the one spirit or being of which the Gods were names and personalities and powers. These Godheads were at once masters of physical nature and its principles and formed their bodies and inward divine powers with their corresponding states and energies born in our psychic-being because they are the soul powers of the cosmos, the guardians of truths and immortality, the children of the infinite, and each of them too is in his origin and his last reality, the supreme spirit putting in front, one of his aspects.*'

2. Form of God

The critics point out in the criticism that Vedas consider even water, wind, fire etc. as God. They feel this idea is ridiculous. But they forget the fact that a happy and peaceful life on earth is possible only when we respect and live in harmony with Nature and lead a life in accordance with the laws of Nature. Any conflict with Nature can bring only disaster to mankind. The one supreme power that governs the Universe has given innumerable natural gifts to mankind. It is only proper for the humans to be thankful to that Almighty for all his benevolent gifts by conserving them. The *rishis* of yore were fully aware that all that we find in the Universe including sun, moon, oceans, mountains and so on are the creations of that single Supreme Cosmic power. They had the necessary vision to accept that great Truth and in all humility, spread the message through their hymns. Even while praising the deities, they actually saw the power behind all the manifestations in the form of different deities. In Vedas, all physical forces are worshipped as the manifestations of God.

The verses of the *Rig Veda* speaks of everything as God. It says —

> *आ पशुं गासि पृथिवीं वनस्पतीनुषासा नक्तमोषधीः।*
> *विश्वे च नो वसवो विश्वेदसो धीनां भूत प्रावितारः ।।*
> Ā paśuṁ gāsi pṛthivīm vanaspatīnuṣāsā naktamos¸adhīḥ
> viśve ca no vasavo viśvavedaso dhīnaṁ bhuta prāvitāraḥ
>
> *(I sing to cattle, earth, to trees, to dawns, to night, to plants – o, all ye Vasus, ye possessors of all wealth, be ye the furtherer of our thoughts.)*
>
> Verse 8.27.2

> *तन्न इन्द्रो वरुणो मित्रो अग्निराप ओषधीर्वनिनो जुषन्त।*
> *शर्मन्त्स्याम मरुतामुपस्थे यूयं पात स्वस्तिभिः सदा नः।।*
> Tanna indro varuṇo mitro agnirāpa oṣadhīrvanino jus¸anta
> Śarmantsyām marutāmupasthe yuyaṁ
> pāta svastibhiḥ sadā naḥ
>
> *(May Indra, Varuna, Mitra, and Agni, Water, Herbs, Trees accept the praise we offer. May we get the dignified place among the Marutas. All, ye saviours, protect us always.)*
>
> Hymn 7.34

Every single gift of Nature is elevated to the position of deities. It only shows that the ancient seers of India even in those days were very much aware of the need for environmental protection that we talk to day. Further, there are also hidden meanings to which these deities refer. For example, *Agni* is the inner fire. In *Yajur Veda* the hymn 4.7 states, '*O Agni, thy highest name, the heart*'.

Hindu Gods are also associated with animals, birds, and flowers. The bull is associated with Lord Shiva. His abode is said to be Mount Kailash on the great Himalayas. Lord Vishnu has his abode in the ocean. Lord Ganesha, who is the God of knowledge and removes all ignorance and obstacles, is said to be seated on a rat symbolising ignorance. Lord Subramanya is associated with peacock. The Goddess Durga is shown riding a lion. Maha Lakshmi and Saraswati are said to be seated on the lotus flower. All these prove the age-old belief of Indians that everything on this earth is the creation of one Almighty and there is absolutely no difference among them although the outward appearances and qualities differ.

3. Material Gains

In third criticism, the critics point out that Vedas have many hymns, the purpose of which is to gain material happiness and there are also many rituals with the same objective. When that is the case, how can Vedas be considered as a sacred scripture that help man to elevate himself spiritually and finally liberate them? It is not as if the sages were not aware of that fact. Through the scriptures, the sages gave the necessary wisdom to mankind both for their material as well as for their spiritual progress.

The Vedas were intended for satisfying all the cravings of man. There is nothing that is not included in the Vedas. They contain everything including philosophy, theology, spirituality, material aspects, science, art, fine arts and so on. In the *Rig Veda* itself, there are more than 40 hymns about the everyday aspects of life like marriage, the life of people depending upon their stages in life, for people with different occupations, health, sickness, and death.

Vedas enable men to satisfy all the four kinds of human aspirations namely, *Dharma*, *Artha*, *Kama*, and *Moksha*. All men are not of the same calibre. There are only very few who aspire for spiritual wisdom. The majority of humans seek worldly pleasures for a happy living. The Vedas are meant not for the minority alone but for the entire humanity. Therefore, they also contain hymns seeking material pleasures of life, and hymns which express even the negative attitudes of man like praying to the deities for destruction of enemies. It is not because the ancient seers did not know the highest Truth or did not want to make all men realise that single truth by renouncing everything mundane and seek liberation. They knew that everything has to take place in the proper time. A child, for example, cannot be taught advanced things which are beyond his capacity to grasp. There are different levels of understanding for humans. There are those who crave for their individual material pleasures of life and there are those who are for their and for others' happiness. Still higher are those who are indifferent to any of the material pleasures of life but seek everlasting happiness for one and all through spiritual knowledge. In the last category are those who have surpassed all these and are always in blissful state and are one with the eternal Cosmic power. The intention of the sages might have been to elevate the minds of even the ordinary men by making them understand that the concentration through prayers and sacrifices will lead to the fulfilment of the desires either in the short run or in the long run. An ordinary man cannot understand the high philosophical truths directly. Hence the sages tried to elevate the minds of the people and bring the necessary maturity for understanding the lofty truths of the *Upanishads* step by step through the *Samhita, Brahmana* and *Aranyaka* portions of the Vedas. While the *Samhitas*, which consist of the hymns, are intended for the *Brahmacharis* who are in their first stage of life, the *Brahmanas* explaining the performance of sacrifices and rituals are intended for the *Grihasthas* who mainly seek worldly pleasures for a happy and prosperous worldly life. The *Aranyakas* that elaborate the philosophical and mystic meaning of the rites and sacrifices are intended for the *vanprasthis* who after discarding all worldly pleasures go to the forest for meditation in search of peace and knowledge. The *Upanishads* that deal with the real content of the Vedas are intended for the *sanyasis* who have come out of all worldly desires and seek nothing but the truth.

As a *brahmachari*, one is expected to lead a controlled life and chant the mantras. As a householder, one has to observe the rules and injunctions as laid down in the *Brahmanas.* As a forest dweller, one is supposed to understand and meditate upon the spiritual content behind the outward rituals and sacrifices as explained in the *Aranyakas* and practise austerity. With the maturity of mind attained during the three earlier stages one will be able to lead a life of a *sanyasi* and assimilate the highest truths contained in the *Upanishads.* In this manner, all humans are ultimately elevated to the highest level.

Apart from these, one must also understand that there are hidden meanings in the Vedic hymns. Only the one who is able to interpret the Vedas correctly can know their great value. The hidden meanings are very difficult to comprehend. They can be understood only by the enlightened souls. Along with the prayers for spiritual wisdom, we also find hymns advising people to refrain from acts that harm them. The following Rig Vedic verses prove this fact.

'Drive far from us each devouring fiend. Create the light for which we long.'

Verse 1.86

'Gods, may we with our ears listen to what is good, and with our eyes see what is good, ye, holy ones.'

Verse 1.90

'May Dadhikras prepare the way we travel! That we may pass along the path of order.'

Verse 7.44

'May we be free from bonds, Adityas.'

Verse 7.52

'Drive to a distance, oh, ye bulls, the darkness.'

Verse 7.58

'O, Varuna, whatever the offence may be which we as men commit against the heavenly host, when through our want of thought, we violate the laws, punish us not, O, God, for that inequity.'

Verse 1.89

'Open the paths for us to tread.'

Verse 8.5

'Each evil deed manifest and that which concealed, O, Gods, the whole of them remove from us.'

Verse 8.47

'Protect me from slipping away.'

Verse 8.48.5

'Give us clear sight and make us better.'

Verse 8.48.6

Further, the rituals are there for the physical and mental disciplines that are necessary for one in his spiritual growth. While some of the external acts bring about physical discipline, some of the other acts enable one to get absorbed in the act of worship. Both these acts gradually reduce all the negative tendencies in one and thus help him to improve himself spiritually. A tree cannot be expected to bear fruits in the beginning or the plant stage itself. The plant has to grow, then the buds have to appear, then the flowers, and it is only in the final stage that the fruit appears.

Similar is the case with ordinary human beings as far as the spiritual progress is concerned. The ancient *rishis* who were fully aware of this fact revealed the truths accordingly. The outward meaning of the hymns and rituals through the required physical and mental disciplines helped the ordinary humans to uplift themselves spiritually.

4. Offering of Soma Juice

The fourth criticism relates to the drinking and offering of the invigorating soma juice. Probably this act was not considered unholy during Vedic times. But this is not the only interpretation. Soma, in many of the hymns of *Rig Veda* also means, the moon that is worshipped as a deity. In its hidden meaning, the soma juice refers to the blissful state, the divine ecstasy of the seer, who reveled in the realisation of the Ultimate Truth in which he becomes one with the Ultimate.

It indicates that stage where the total surrender leads to total unification between man and God. It can also be interpreted in another way. To attain such a stage, the seers used their mind as pressing stones, with which their thoughts referring to soma are pressed and squeezed, that means, contemplated upon, and finally only the juice, that is, the essence of wisdom is retained.

5. Animal Sacrifice

The fifth criticism relates to animal sacrifices, which are viewed as barbaric by many critics. But in the outward act of sacrifice, the priests might have used a symbolic animal made of straw or any other material as an offering. Symbolic offerings and rituals form an important part of Hinduism even today. The verses relating to animal sacrifices can also be interpreted as the poetical expressions of the seers.

The poets make use of expressions where two unrelated concepts or things are taken as similar and are compared with each other. For example, it is common for a poet to describe the curly, dark hair of a woman as the dark cloud of the sky, or mention a man as a lion just to emphasise his strength. Similarly, the expression 'hard-hearted person' does not mean a man having hard, stone-like muscles in his heart. It only refers to the hard and unsympathetic attitude of the person. Again, a man of steel only means a man of grit, strength and firm will. However, it is very difficult to understand the hidden meanings of the Vedic Sanskrit poetic expressions. The verses indicate the sacrifice of the animalistic tendencies, not the actual slaughtering of animals. We can find the symbolism of the sacrifices from the *Brahmanas.* The following verses from *Yajur Veda* prove it —

'Food is cattle and he piles it with cattle.'

Verse 5.7.1

'The white horse is the form of a day, the black of night, the bricks are the form of day, the mortar of night.'

Verse 5.7.1

'The bricks are cattle, in each layer he puts down a bull (a brick).'

Verse 5.7.2

'The immortal Agni who hath entered into us mortals within the heart, may we enclose him in ourselves.'

Verse 5.7.9

'The heads of animals are bricks' and also, *'the fire is an animal, animals are food, the heads of animals are this fire.'*

Verse 5.7.10

'Agni was the animal, with it they sacrificed; Vayu was the animal with it they sacrificed; Aditya was the animal, with it they sacrificed.'

Verse 5.7.25

The true meaning of the concept of Vedic sacrifice is that Gods must be invoked by means of the sacrifice of the animal in us and bring forth the *Agni* by chanting the powerful mantras.

'Vritra is the belly, hunger is man's enemy and he who knows this slays the enemy hunger.'

Verse 2.4.12

Also, during the later period, the external form of sacrifices and *yajna* lost their importance and the internalisation of sacrifices dominated the *Aranyakas* and *Upanishads* of the Vedas.

The *Brihad Aranyaka Upanishad* gives the hidden meaning of the horse in horse sacrifice, where various parts of a horse correspond to different aspects. A chart elucidating the same is given below —

S. No.	Part of the Horse	Corresponding Aspect
1.	Head	Dawn
2.	Eyes	Sun
3.	Vital Force	Air
4.	Open mouth	*Agni* or *Vaishvanara*
5.	Body	Year
6.	Back	Heaven
7.	Belly	Sky
8.	Hoofs	Earth
9.	Sides	Four quarters
10.	Ribs	Immediate quarters
11.	Membranes	Seasons
12.	Joints	Months and fortnights
13.	Feet	Days and nights
14.	Bones	Stars
15.	Flesh	Clouds
16.	Half-digested food	Sand
17.	Blood vessels	Rivers
18.	Liver and spleen	Mountains
19.	Hair	Herbs and trees
20.	Forepart	Ascending Sun
21.	Hinder part	Descending Sun
22.	Yawn	Lightning
23.	Shaking body	Thundering

The *Garbha Upanishad* points out that a person can perform sacrifice within one's own body as the body has all the necessary articles and items that are required for the sacrifice. This *Upanishad* also states that all human beings are sacrificers. This body of ours itself has its origin in *yajna*, and changes according to *yajna*. Sacrifice also means *Atmarpana* or giving up oneself completely for higher truth or total surrender of oneself to the divine.

The *Pranagni Hotra Upanishad,* after explaining the external form of sacrifice, elaborates on the sacrifice performed in one's own body that has within itself all divinities. In the inner or mystic sense, in the sacrifice that is performed in one's body, lust is the sacrificial animal.

6. Rebirth and Karma

The sixth criticism is against the idea of rebirth by those who view that there is no rebirth. We cannot find many verses relating to this belief in the Vedas. But this basic idea that forms one of the strongest beliefs of the theory of *Karma* in Hinduism, is found in the later Epics and *Puranas*. However, there are a few verses about rebirth in the *Rig Veda* though in its rudimentary form.

'*Those who died yesterday, today are living.*'

Verse 4.1.4

'*Leave sin and evil, seek anew thy dwelling, and bright with glory another body.*'

Verse 10.14.8

'*Wearing a new life, let him increase his offspring; let him rejoin a body.*'

Verse 10.16.5

The only satisfactory explanation that we can give for the various types of disparities that we see among people in many aspects at best can be explained only through rebirth based upon the precept '*As you sow, so shall you reap*' which in other words is destiny or fate.

If that is the case, then the atheists ask, "*Why believe in Gods and prayers?*"

The only answer for this can be that, God or the Supreme power is mere witness. Prayers help us in bettering and improving ourselves that will shape our future after we exhaust all our *karmas* of the past. A person who has saved immensely can live luxuriously even if he does not undertake any work until all that he had saved gets exhausted. Similarly the one, who has incurred a huge debt and has to clear the debt, cannot lead a luxurious life until he clears off all his debts, even though in the present he works hard and earns a lot. Similar is the case with bad and good deeds. One who has done bad things in life incurs sin and he reaps the consequences for his deeds after he has exhausted the results of his past *karmas*. It is in this sense that sages induce a man to be good in thoughts, words and deeds. They also point out that one can shape one's destiny according to one's will. It all depends upon the load of his good as well as bad *karmas* of the past. The sages also point out that the past *karmas* are like arrows that are released from the bow. Howsoever efficient the archer may be, he cannot change the direction or force of the released arrows. Such is the power of thought, word and deed. Prayer enables one to become humble and reduce his ego that helps him to acquire all good qualities and become good in thought, word and deed. This helps him in shaping his future destiny. When he shows good, he reaps well. Probably the great saints and incarnations burn up all the past *karmas* within no time. But even they, though they can, never wish to change their destiny. They, too, undergo sufferings due to the traces of their past *karmas* that are remaining, because they know that it is against the natural or cosmic law to try and change their destiny.

It is said that the great sage Maharshi Ramana of Tiruvannamalai in Tamil Nadu was suffering from cancer. With his will, he could have easily got over the illness. But he did not do so as it amounted to postponing the reaping of the effects of his past *karma*.

7. Varnashrama

The seventh criticism relates to the caste system found in the Vedas. *Varnashrama,* as told in the Vedas, did not indicate any division based on birth. It was meant only for the purpose of division of labour. In Hinduism, division of labour to an extent is also found among the Gods. For example, worshipping Lord Ganesha for removing all impediments in life, worshipping Goddesses Saraswati, Lakshmi and Durga for knowledge, prosperity and courage respectively is traditionally followed by the Hindus. However, in later years this concept lost its original meaning and began to be misinterpreted. There is no hymn in the *Rig Veda* that bars Vedas for any class of society based on birth or even *Varnas.*

The *Vajra Suchlike Upanishad* answers the question as to who is a Brahmin. It says one cannot be a Brahmin on account of his birth, body, or colour. This *Upanishad* says, that a Brahmin is the one who has realised the *Atman* that is beyond knowledge through the experience of continuous meditation.

Witchcraft

The eighth criticism relates to the knowledge of witchcraft that is considered as evil. But it can be stated that the word *Mantrikam* in Sanskrit contained mantras meant for driving away the evil forces, which do harm to others and it was not meant originally to harm others. They were used for defense and not for offence.

9. Origin of Vedas

According to the ninth criticism, certain critics believed that Vedas were not written by the natives of India. According to them, the Aryans who either invaded or migrated to India wrote the Vedas. But the Aryan invasion and the Aryan migration theories are refuted today. The critics point out the similarities of the Gods mentioned in the Vedas, particularly in the *Rig Veda.* But in reply to this, it can be pointed out that, *Rig Veda* 1.25.7 tells about the knowledge of sea routes. The ancient Indians had carried on sea trade and had followed maritime activities with distant lands ever since early times. The Indian products found in other lands provide ample proof for this claim.This might have resulted in the spreading of knowledge, culture and values among different land areas. It is found that for full 30 centuries in the past, India was at the top of the world commercially, culturally, intellectually and spiritually at the same time.

Sir Aurel Stein wrote —

"*The vast extent of Indian cultural influences from Central Asia in the north to tropical Indonesia in the south and from the borderlands of Persia to China and Japan, has shown that ancient India was a radiating centre of a civilisation which by its religious thought, its arts and literature, was destined to leave its deep mark on the races wholly diverse and scattered over the greater part of Asia.*"

10. Different Deities

According to some critics, the innumerable scriptures talk about innumerable deities as well as different methods of worship, resulting in confusion. Some also feel that there are also contradictions in the different teachings. It is like too many cooks spoiling the broth. This can be taken as the tenth criticism. But it has to be stated that the scriptures provide innumerable paths and deities so that man can choose a path or a deity of his liking. All the scriptures also point out that the various deities are only the personification of the one and the only superior power. Further, all the scriptures are not meant for all. The *Upanishads* that give the highest wisdom are meant only for one who can understand their content properly. They are not meant for the ordinary men. The *rishis* who gave *Upanishads* categorically state that they are to be taught only to those who are keen to know the ultimate truth, and also who are matured enough to understand their contents. For all the others who want to know the Vedic teachings on which Hinduism is based there are *Itihasas* and *Puranas,* which make available the great spiritual truths of the Vedas in a simple manner through stories and episodes.

11. Virtues

The eleventh criticism is related to the virtues that one has to follow. It is felt by some that it is the outward rituals rather than the virtues like empathy, sympathy, compassion that one should possess. But it is a mistaken view.

The first two steps of yoga namely *Yama* and *Niyama* relate to physical and mental cleanliness.

Yama relates to practice of non-violence, truth, non-stealing, celibacy, mercy, charity, sympathy, empathy, compassion, honesty, patience, stability, food discipline, external cleanliness etc.

Niyama refers to perseverance, joy, charity, fear from bad actions, austerity etc.

The final stage of every yoga is *Samadhi.* It is at this stage when the entire world appears as one to the *yogi* without any demarcation between '**I**' or '**YOU**'.

If the food is not tasty, one cannot blame the ingredients, which are of high quality. It only reveals the lack of adequate knowledge on the part of the cook. The same ingredients, in the hands of an excellent cook will result in tasty food. The same is true with knowledge as well. Those who have not understood the contents of the ancient Hindu scriptures are bound to have such doubts.

12. Vedas as Primitive

Finally, there are a few critics who consider Vedas as containing primitive and monstrous concepts. They consider Vedas to be tedious, low and commonplace, representing human nature on a low level of selfishness except for a very few rare sentiments here and there that may be claimed to have come from the depth of the soul.

Max Mueller who had immense admiration and appreciation for the Vedas opines that there are a large number of Vedic hymns which are extremely childish, tedious and commonplace, although they contain many ideas that are modern.

But it can be stated for certain that Max Mueller, a great scholar, would not have made such a comment if only he had tried to go deep into the Vedas to find the real inner meaning of those hymns which seemed childish and tedious to him.

As an answer to those who viewed Vedic hymns as childish, primitive and barbaric, Sri Aurobindo vividly gave the following explanation —

'*The poet has to express a spiritual and psychical knowledge and experience and he cannot do it altogether or in the abstract language of a philosophical thinker, for he has to bring out, not just the naked idea of it, but also its very life and the most intimate touches as vividly as possible. He has to reveal in one way or another a whole world within him and the quiet inner and spiritual significances of the world around him and also, it may well be, the Godheads, powers, visions, and experiences of planes of consciousness other than the one that our normal minds are familiar with. He uses or starts with the images taken from his own normal and outward life and that of humanity and from visible nature, and though they do not of themselves actually express, yet obliges them to express by implication or to figure the spiritual and psychic idea and experience. He takes them selecting freely his notation of images according to his insight or imagination and transmutes them into instruments of another significance and at the same time pours a direct spiritual meaning into the nature and life to which they belong, applies outward figures nearest to the inward experience, its material counterpart is taken throughout and used with such realism and consistency that while it indicates to those who possess it the spiritual experience, it means only the external thing to others.'*

One Vedic hymn describes Indra as the son of earth and heaven and that he recreated his own parents. This may, in its outward meaning, sound ridiculous and silly. But when one goes into the depths of the meaning of the hymn, then one will be able to understand its real meaning that Indra is the supreme spirit, the creator of earth and heaven, a cosmic Godhead, between the mental and physical worlds, recreating their powers in humans. It shows that the ancient *rishis* went to the extent of outraging the physical imagination for expressing the great mystic truths.

In the Vedic verses, as Sri Aurobindo had noted —

'*The physical melted its shades into the lustre of the psychic, the psychic deepened into the light of the spiritual and there was no sharp dividing line in the transition, but a natural blending and intershading of their suggestions and colours.*'

Even Yaska, the earliest commentator of the Vedas, who belonged to 2000 BC stated that the *Rig Veda*, the basis for all the other three Vedas, can be interpreted at several different levels. It shows that depending on the aptitude, skill and knowledge possessed by a person, Vedas may be interpreted in their outward meaning or the spiritual or symbolic meaning.

It must be pointed out that criticism for the sake of criticising is not a mark of scholarship. One should pronounce judgement only after a thorough understanding of the subject. So anyone who ventures to condemn anything totally should always assess his capacity first for such an act. A mere outward understanding of the Vedas cannot make a person knowledgeable enough to condemn the scriptures, which are considered the priceless and immortal treasures of mankind as a whole.

Vedas were written in Vedic Sanskrit. They were written in very ancient days and they were all written in poetic language. The sages who wrote them had a very high level of spiritual wisdom which was a result of their intense and continuous meditation.

So, anyone who condemns the Vedas in an outright manner should first take into account all these factors before pronouncing his final verdict.

It is said, that beauty lies in the eyes of the beholder. But the beauty and grandeur of the Vedas does not lie only in the eyes but also in the heart and the thought process of the beholder. A person who wears dark glasses will see everything as dark. Again, a sculptor who looks at a stone sees the image that he is carving in that stone. But for an ordinary person, it is a mere stone. The ancient sages of India gave the essence of their knowledge in the form of scriptures for the benefit of mankind as a whole. It is up to us to make use of it.

Symbolism in the Vedas

As Sri Aurobindo pointed out, the Vedas are the ancient psychological and spiritual wisdom of India. While the outer meaning is meant for the ordinary men who seek material pleasures of life, while living on earth and thereafter, the inner meaning are meant for the illumined souls. Particularly, the *Upanishads* that form the final section of the Vedas are intended only for the illumined souls, who understand the innermost meanings of the Vedas through intense meditation or *tapasya*. The inner meaning of the Vedas is primary. The external meaning is only secondary. The Vedic seers used the words both in their general and derived sense. It has been rightly pointed out that taking the outer meaning alone is like taking the body and allowing the soul of knowledge to flee.

According to Sri Aurobindo, the Gods mentioned in the Vedas are not just personification of abstract ideas or psychological and physical functions of nature, but the living realities.

The Vedic deities represent not only the forces of Nature but also the forces present in the physical body. For achieving spiritual perfection, one has to strengthen the divine forces in oneself. At the same time, the evil forces symbolised by the demons are to be slaughtered.

Sri Aurobindo in his book on *The Secrets of the Vedas* says —

'*The Vedic deities represent the various cosmic powers. The Gods are forces of Nature as well as the forces found in the physical body. Anyone who desires to progress spiritually and attain spiritual perfection has to strive towards the development of these*

Godheads in himself. The external rituals found in the Vedas have a corresponding inner ritual for a spiritual aspirant who wants to elevate himself.'

Symbolic Gods

The Vedic rituals and sacrifices are not to be understood as mere outward rituals. They constitute the inner ritual, that is, a sacrifice, at the innermost level of man. *Agni*, is supposed to be the fire god. But for the enlightened, it refers to the inner divine spark within oneself, the strong, bright force, the brilliance, and the illumined energy that elevates man spiritually. Similarly, the names of Gods are epithets and they are descriptions of the *Saguna Brahman*. For example, *Mitra* symbolises the Lord of love and harmony, *Bhaga*, the Lord of enjoyment, *Surya*, the Lord of illumination, and *Varuna*, the Lord of expansiveness supporting the world. *Indra* is to be interpreted as the Lord of senses, *Vayu* represents the life force, and *Soma* refers to the divine bliss that intoxicates the one who experiences it. It is the Vedic symbol for *Ananda* or Bliss.

Agni as we discussed is the divine spark in humans. The sacrificial fire, thus, relates to sacrificing one's ego to the divine spark.

Devas refer to the power of truth and light and *Asuras* symbolise the negative forces in man.

The offering of *ghee* or clarified butter constitute the mind of man. The sacrificial food is nothing but the physical body that is composed of food. The hidden inner energies that are the divine powers or the deities are woken up once *Agni* or the hidden energies in the physical body are invoked along with the offerings (surrendering oneself completely) to Gods. This results in spiritual awakening, transformation, purification and evolution resulting in liberation or *Mukti*.

Lord Indra in Vedic hymns, considered as the Lord of Heavens, is to be understood as the Lord of the senses. He corresponds to the enlightened mind. *Vratra*, stated to be the snake demon in the hymns representing the negative energies in man.

Dhenu means nourisher, so it is denoted as a cow.

Chamas means food. But it also means enjoyment or pleasure.

Indra (the awakened mind) destroys Vratra, (the negative energies) that hides the cows (the rays of truth) inside the cave of *Panis* (the sense dominated life of humans). In this war, *Rudra* and *Marutas* that are the positive forces help Indra, the God of Heavens who fights against the demons and eventually wins over them. In its mystic sense, it represents the continuous efforts of the spiritual seeker for overpowering the dark and the negative forces in him and finally winning over these negative tendencies. The Gods, who help Indra in this task, represent the will, the perseverance, and the disciplines that help the spiritual seeker in his efforts in achieving the spiritual goal.

The various stages in the spiritual transformation and progress are represented by *Ribhus*, the seasons. When, all the dark forces, the *Asuras* (the negative energies) are overpowered, *Usha*, the Dawn (awakening or enlightenment) comes along with *Ashwins* (the spiritual energies).

Once the *Usha* comes (awakening of the inner consciousness), *Surya*, the God of light and brightness reveals himself (enlightenment) first as *Savitar*, early morning sun rays (the divine grace), and then *Mitra*, the friend of Indra ((the divine comrade of the awakened mind). He is followed by *Rita* (truth in action) and *Ritachit* (truth consciousness), *Ila* (truth, vision or revelation), the Goddesses *Saraswati*, *Mahi* and *Bharati* (knowledge and wisdom), *Sarama* (the intuitive mind), *Dakshina* (the discretionary ability), *Varuna* (the ocean of infinite truth) and the other deities (the divine powers).

All this means that when the divine grace falls on the spiritual aspirant, the supreme knowledge dawns upon him spontaneously and automatically with all its brightness. At that stage, the liberated one drinks the nectar of soma (gets dissolved in the spiritual bliss or divine ecstasy). Again, *Agni* is said to represent the fire of transformation. After burning the inner demons, *Agni* lights the way for enlightenment. Similarly, soma represents the divine bliss that one experiences when one realises the *Brahman* and feels Him in all the creations. Saraswati is taken to mean the river of Knowledge.

In the *Aranyakas* and *Upanishads* we find the internalisation of the Vedic rituals into the microcosmic world of the human body. The *Upanishads* especially state the interconnectivity of macro and micro

Universe for purpose of liberation through knowledge. The external world is equated with the seeker's internal organs. For example, the organ of speech is associated with fire, the eye with the sun, the vital force with the air, the mind with the moon, and the self with the heart. The one who performs sacrifice is identified with the spiritual aspirant who seeks *Brahman* – the supreme truth.

Further the internal world of the aspirant also reflects the external world. For example, the organ of speech represents the earth. Similarly, the mind is the sky, the vital force is the heaven. Even the four Vedic priests are also internalised; the speech with the *Hotri* priest, the eye with *Adhvarya*, the breath with *Udgatri*, and the mind with *Brahman* priest.

In *Rig Veda*, verse 1.179 is about the complaints of Lopamudra to her husband Sage Agastya about his negligence to her. Lopamundra symbolises the fervent prayer. Agastya represents the celestial power. The inner meaning of this verse is that fervent prayers succeed in drawing the celestial powers after long effort.

The Rig Vedic verse 1.191 deals with poison from poisonous unseen insects infecting a person and Gods removing the poison and protecting the person. The mystical meaning of this is that man is infected by sins, but with God's help, the sins can be removed.

Verse 2.29, hymn to *Visvadevas* says —

'*Protect us, God, from the wolf that destroys us. Save us, you holy, from the pit and falling.*'

The wolf mentioned here is the dark or the negative forces. The falling into the pit is symbolic of slipping into the evil acts.

The verse 6.5 states —

'*Now we have stepped on the road that leads to bliss, without foe, the road where a man escapes all enemies and gathers wealth.*'

In this verse, the wealth means spiritual treasure, enemies refer to the negative qualities and paths indicate good thoughts, words and deeds.

The Rig Vedic verse 7.103 is in praise of frogs. In its true sense, frogs here refer to the priests who utter the hymns in chorus giving the sound effect produced by ecstatic frogs during the rainy season.

It is seen from the Vedas that the ancient saints were even aware of the concepts of modern psychology. It is found that the psychoanalytical approach, behavioural approach, physiological psychology, psychophysical analysis, that are practised by modern psychologists are made use of in the Vedic theory of mind.

Symbolic Rituals

The sacrifice of animals mentioned in the Vedas can be interpreted in its mystic sense. According to one interpretation, they mean that the sacrifice of the animals like goat, horse etc. is better rather than allowing them to die with disease and starvation.

A barren cow is mentioned as an important offering and the sacrifice of such a cow might be because of the fact that a barren cow neither gives milk nor offspring.

A Vedic ritual is interpreted in three ways in the *Brahmanas.*

1. The cosmological interpretation where man is taken in relation to nature, time and space
2. The interpretation based on the individual's relationship with other human beings in the family, society and political setup.
3. Interpretation based on individual's physiological, psychological, intellectual and spiritual level of existence when a person stands in relation with his own self

The *Brahmanas* explain the possibility of various interpretations of the Vedic Gods, rituals and sacrifices. The sacrifices are taken as symbolic actions only. For example, in *Ashvamedha yajna* the sun is referred to as *Ashvamedha*, while in another place it has reference to the moon. In some places in the Vedas, the king who performs the sacrifice is mentioned as *Ashvamedha*, while at some places Dawn, Sun, Wind, Fire, Year, Sky, Space, Earth, Stars are all equated with the different parts of the horse.

The *Shatapatha Brahmana* says that if a person performs the sacrifice without knowing its true meaning and pours the oblation into the fire, it is like pouring oblations into the ashes.

The tenth chapter of *Sankhayana Aranyaka* describes the inner oblation to fire and states that all divine forces are inside the man. Fire is found in speech, wind in the vital breath, sun in the eyes, moon in the mind, directions in the ears, and water in the semen. Thus, all the divine personalities are inherent in the *Purusha.* The *Chandogya Upanishad* says, man truly is the sacrifice.

The microcosmic and the macrocosmic powers can also be linked to each other. The speech with fire, fire with earth, earth with vital energy, the vital energy with wind, wind with mind region, and mind region with all that pervades. It amounts to the fact that sacrifice to *Agni* is all-pervasive and all-encompassing. Every element in the Cosmos participates in the sacrifice as each is related to the other.

In the *Sankhayana Aranyaka,* oblation to fire is interpreted as diving deep into the human psyche. It is said that a man should perform the *yajna* throughout his life. At every moment of his life, he has to invoke the fire in him according to the energy principle. Fire represents physical as well as mental energy. A synchronisation of all the elements, energies and function is all that what is meant by a Vedic sacrifice.

In *Atmarpana,* one gives up oneself to the divine —

'The working of the hands becomes the mudra, the gesture of praise, the divine talking, Japa or uttering the sacred verses becomes yajna, the offering to the divine and breathing becomes the Agnihotra.'

Many verses and hymns from the *Yajur Veda* reinforce this argument.

'*In the spring, early morning, one should offer the beast with black neck to Agni; in summer at mid-day, offer the beast of different colours to Indra; in autumn, in the afternoon, one should offer a beast to Brihaspati. These represent the brilliance of the Sun in the spring in the morning, in summer at mid-day, in the autumn in the afternoon.'*

Verse 1.2

'*Offer a dwarf to Vishnu when one is engaged in a struggle. He then becomes Vishnu and conquers the worlds.'*

Verse 1.3

Similarly the animals are to be offered to Indra, by one who is engaged in a contest or the one who desires a village and prosperity.

The animals to be sacrificed refer to the power of senses that are offered in sacrifices for the desired benefits. It is stated, '*Indra to be offered a beast with a spot on the forehead and horns bent forward for getting a kingdom.*' The animal represented here corresponds to the shape of the thunderbolt of Indra.

'*The days and nights are cattle, the soma drink represents power.*'

Hymn 1.5

'*He who desires food should offer to all Gods a beast of many forms. It refers to offerings of many forms of food.*'

Hymn 1.6

'*The cow is the sap of the metres with which he wins the sap which is splendour. He who desires rain and offspring should offer to Mitra and Varuna a cow of two forms. It represents day connected with Mitra and night with Varuna. By the sap of the metres one wins rain and offspring, by the sap of metres one wins food.*'

Hymn 1.7

Again, it is stated —

'*One who desires splendour should offer to Brihaspati a bull and a cow. The bull grazes at will, and also splendour. It means by will one wins will that is splendour.*'

'*Honey is the body of man; in that he offers honey on the fire, verily thus the sacrificer places his body in the fire.*'

Hymn 3.2

As Sri Aurobindo has stated that *Rig Veda* is a psychological book and inspires people to move towards God. *Rig Veda* invokes Indra, the God of senses and Varuna, the God of life force for drinking the soma juice.

Dr David Frawley describes Indra as a brave soul, the inner spirit, fighting evil in us to become free from the shackles of ego. *Agni* refers to *Kundalini* and soma juice to *Sahasra Chakra*. *Savitar* should be taken as the Sun that dispels darkness.

Greatness of the Vedas

'The oldest literary sources we have from the ancient Greek World are the works of Homer (C.700 BC). The oldest books from the Middle East are the Hebrew Bible. The parts of Old Testament are of course much older, much of which was done after 500 BC. The Gathas of Zoroaster date before the founding of the ancient Persian Empire that is around 525 BC. But they all come after Vedas.'

— David Frawley

These comments clearly indicate the antiquity of the Vedas. Further, he says, that from China, the oldest book is *I ching,* written around 1000 BC or even earlier. The Egyptian book of the dead is much older than these, around 3000 BC, for which there is no living records available now. Even by the most conservative estimates, the four Vedas date back from 1500 to 5000 BC. If not all, at least some survive even today in a tropical country like India where everything decays fast. We are fortunate that even after so many invasions, India could still retain the Vedas, though not fully, yet a part of them.

The period that is mentioned here, that is 1500 BC-5000 BC, is to be understood as the period when the Vedas were brought out in written form. Vedas existed in India for thousand of years before that and they were passed on to the successive generations orally from the teacher to his disciples. It is a matter of great pride for India, for having the oldest and the greatest treasure of mankind and to have preserved them over the years.

Sri Aurobindo remarks —

'The early mind of India in the magnificent youth of the nation, when a fathomless spiritual insight was at work, a subtle intuitive vision and a deep clear and greatly outlined intellectual and ethical thinking and heroic action and creation which founded and traced the plan and made the permanent structure of her unique culture and civilisation, is represented by four of the supreme productions of her genius, the Vedas, the Upanishads and the two vast epics, Ramayana and Mahabharata. Each of them is of a kind, a form and an intention not easily paralleled in any other literature.'

Modern Science & Vedas

It is stated that some areas of Vedic literature like Cosmology and Quantum Physics can still be found in modern science. The Vedic literature shows that Indians knew about atoms, Quantum Physics and other scientific theories even in those times. The Vedas mention Atomic Energy and Nuclear growth. The complete atomic structure is explained in the *RigVeda* in the hymn 1.164. It is even felt that the Greek ideas about atoms might have been the result of Indian influence over Persian civilisation. It shows that the findings of the modern science date back to the Vedic insights. With the development of Atomic Science, it has been proved that all elements have the same source of energy. The sages of yore called it *Chaitanya*. While the modern scientists state that the invisible energy is seen through several objects (like the electrical energy is seen through the lighted bulb), the Vedic *rishis* stated that the *Chaitanya* that is not visible is perceived through several of its manifestations that can be seen through our naked eye.

The Theory of Relativity of Space and Time given by the great scientist Einstein can also be traced back to the Vedic wisdom. The Vedas point out that one must go beyond Space and Time to understand the ultimate Truth. For an ordinary human being, this is possible only in a state of enlightened sleep. A *jnani*, even when he is awake, realises this truth in his meditative state. In that meditative state, there is no Space and Time for him as he transcends both and attains unison with *Brahman,* the eternal truth.

In the Vedas, *Kalpas* describe the cyclical process of the beginning and end of the Universe. This is in conformity with the findings of modern Physics. It is even observed that the term 'light years' for measuring time was known even in the distant past in India as *Kalpa*. The term *Kalpa* signifies the inconceivable duration of the period that is between the beginning and the end of the world.

Many of the western critics have accepted the Indian sages of the Vedic era as the precursors in the field of science and cosmology.

'*They came closest to modern ideas of atomism, Quantum Physics and other current theories. India developed very early, enduring atomic theories of matter. Possibly, Greek atomistic thought was influenced by India, via the Persian civilisation.*'

— Dick Teresi

'The Hindu revelation which proclaims the slow and gradual formation of worlds is of all revelations, the only one whose ideas are in complete harmony with modern Physics.'

'Name any modern discovery and we venture to say that Indian History need not long be searched before the prototype will be found on record.'

— Louis Jacolloit

'Ages before Lamark and Darwin, it was held in India that man has passed through 84 lakhs of births as plants, animals or as an inferior species of man and then took birth as the ancestor of the developed type existing today.'

— Sir John Woodroffe

Frederic Spiegelberg in his book *Spiritual Practices of India* observed that while the theory of relativity was applied in the making of atom bombs elsewhere in the world, in India, the same knowledge was applied to the development of the new state of consciousness, that too, even in the distant past.

'While the West was still thinking of 6000 years old Universe, India was already envisaging ages and eons and galaxies as numerous as the sands of the Ganges — the Universe so vast that modern astronomy slips into its folds without a ripple.'

— Fluston Smith

(The Mystic Journey – India and the Infinite – The Soul of People)

Indian Cosmologists were the first to estimate the age of the earth at more than four billion years.

'Many of India's ancient theories about the Universe are startlingly modern in scope and worthy of people who are credited with the invention of the zero, as well as Algebra and its application of Astronomy and Geometry, people who so carefully observed the heavens that, in the opinion of Monier-Williams, they determined the moon's revolution much more correctly than the Greeks'.

— Nancy Wilson Ross

The Big Bang Theory

The cosmic dance of Shiva accompanied by the beating of the *damaru* probably suggested the sudden energetic impulses that could have propelled the Big Bang. In his book *The Wishing Tree*, Subhash Kak points out that the *Puranas* which were written with Vedas as the basis mention the creation and destruction of the Universe in cycles of 8.64 billion years that is quite close to currently accepted value regarding the time of Big Bang. Contrary to the existing linear theory of time, the modern scientists have advanced a recent theory that confirms the alternative expansion and contraction of the Universe. This modern theory too finds place in the Vedas where it is stated that the world is created and destroyed at periodical intervals of time through the concepts of *Kalpas* and *Manvantaras*.

The Vedas also give knowledge about the formation of matter and even the chemical makeup of minerals. The Vedas state that Universe is self-created. So the matter contained in the Universe was also not created. Since nothing was created, it cannot be destroyed.

Dick Teresi, in his book *Lost Discoveries – the Ancient Roots of Modern Science* reveals the fact that even several thousands of years before Aristotle, the Vedas had declared that the earth was round and it revolved around the Sun. The hymns also mention that the Sun is the centre of the Solar System and that the earth is held in Space by the Sun. Even 2000 years before Pythagorus, the Vedas had declared that the Solar system was held together by the gravitational pull. The knowledge about the gravitational pull found in the Vedas was twenty-four centuries before Newton discovered the laws of gravity.

Vedic Concepts in Modern Times

While the Greeks spoke of a flat earth, the Vedas had long ago stated that the earth was spherical. The seven horses tied by the snakes which draw the chariot of *Surya* (Sun) mentioned in the *Rig Veda* represent the seven columns forming light and the movement of the Sun's rays. Modern Physics has proved that the sunrays travel in a curved manner. The snakes with which the seven horses are tied to the chariot represent the curved movement of the rays of the Sun. Even before the time of Galileo and Copernicus, the sages of Vedic period pointed out that there is no real sunrise or sunset and that these are only to indicate the beginning and end of a day.

Rig Veda has hymns about advanced concepts like eclipse cycles through its references to the zodiacal signs. Alexander Duff, a British historian pointed out, that many inventions and discoveries of modern Science that are considered to have emerged from Europe were actually made in India several centuries ago.

In Vedic literature, there are references and descriptions of flying machines called *vimanas*. The *Yajur Veda* and *Atharva Veda* mention sailing in the ocean, and flying in the air in the *vimanas*. It is said that the art of navigation was born in India and the word 'navigation' probably has its root in the Sanskrit word '*navgetih*'. Several modern ideas relating to Geography, Geology, Medical Sciences including surgeries, Physical and Chemical Sciences, Arts and Fine Arts, Economic development, Psychology, Metaphysics, Spirituality can be traced back to the Vedas.

Ayurveda, the Indian system of treatment of diseases, was the earliest school of medicines known to mankind as a whole.

There are even descriptions of weapons in the *Atharva Veda*, which had similar amounts of energy as found in the modern atom bombs. The great epic *Ramayana* also has a reference about a super weapon that could destroy the earth in an instant.

Indian Music

The classical Indian music that is based on the seven *svara* (notes) originated from the *Sama Veda*. In the Vedas, we find highly sophisticated and complex science of music where the metre and tones are linked to specific modes and times of the day, revealing the fact that the ancient Indians had understood the effects of sound vibrations on humans even in those times. The Indian classical dance also has the Vedas as the basis. The approaches of modern psychology like the Behavioural, Psychoanalysis, Cognative, Statistical, Physiological Psychology, Psycho-physical Analysis are found in the Vedas, although, they are viewed from a different angle and expressed in a different language pertaining to that time and period.

Vedic Mathematics

It is also said by the researchers that the Vedic Mathematics is found to be more advanced than the one found in Greek, Babylonia, Egypt or in Chinese civilisations. The decimal system, trigonometry and calculus originated in India. Sage Bhadarayana was the first to mention trigonometry and to give the theory on right angle triangles. This later became the Pythagorus Theorem. The Indians invented 'zero'. While the largest number used by the Greeks and Romans during the early times was only 106, in India even during the Vedic period, it was 1053.

Albert Einstein had once remarked —

'We owe a lot to the Indians who taught us how to count, without which no worthwhile scientific discovery could have been made.'

Status of Women

It is a matter of great pride for the Indians that even during the Vedic age, in the very distant past, women were treated at par with men. There was no need for women's liberation in India even in the distant past. We find the names of Goddesses like Ila, Saraswati, Usha, Aditi and many women sages mentioned even in the earliest *Rig Veda*. The *Sukta* in 10.85 of the *Rig Veda* states that the daughter-in-law should be treated like a queen.

Rishis of Yore

Further, the *rishis* of yore were fully aware of the concept of environmental protection which is the talk of the day in these times. All natural resources were considered as Gods and they were worshipped for their contribution in supporting life and the entire Universe.

As Sri Aurobindo had mentioned —

'The Vedas and Vedanta have stood the test of time and have been the source of almost all profound philosophies and religions of India.'

At the international level, he says —

'The ideas of the Upanishads can be rediscovered in much of the thought of Pythagorus and Plato that form the most part of Neo-Platonism, and Gnosticism. Sufism only repeats them in another religious language.'

Kurt Schildmann, a German linguist claims that his study of the ancient inscriptions discovered in the caves of Peru and the United States shows that they are similar to Indus Valley Sanskrit. It suggests that sea fares from India might have reached America thousands of years. Even the oldest preserved Iranian language *Avestan* is related to Vedic Sanskrit. Some of the names of the *Rig Vedic* deities closely resemble the deities of other regions of the world. For example, *Dyaus* is cognate to Greek Zeus, Latin Jupiter, and Germanic Tyr., *Mitra* might be Persian Mithra, *Usha* might be the Greek Eros and Latin Aurora, and *Agni* corresponds to Latin Ignis. It is also believed by some that the Vedic religion itself is closely associated with the pre-Zoroastrian Persian religion.

Max Muller in his lecture on 'India – What Can it Teach Us' says —

'If I were asked under what sky the human mind has most fully developed some of its choicest gifts, has most deeply pondered over the greatest problems of life and has found solutions of some of them which well deserve the attention even of those who have been nurtured almost exclusively on the thoughts of Greeks and Romans and of the Semitic race, the Jewish, may draw the corrective which is most wanted in order to make our inner life more perfect, more comprehensive, more universal – again, I should point to India.'

About *Upanishads,* he remarks —

'The Upanishads are the sources of Vedanta philosophy, a system in which human speculation seems to me to have reached its very acme.'

Schopenhauer remarked —

'*In the whole world, there is no study so beneficial and so elevating as that of the Upanishads. They are the products of the highest wisdom.*'

All these prove beyond doubt that Vedas are all comprehensive and that there is nothing on earth that is not found in the Vedas.

The concepts of *Viswaneedam*, the global family, and *Vasudhaiva kutumbakam*, the whole world as one family, originated from the Vedas. These concepts reveal the universal outlook of the ancient seers of India. The *Rig Veda* ends with this hymn —

समानी व आकूतिः समाना हृदयानि व।
समानमस्तु वो मनो यथा वः सुसहासति।।
Samāni va ākūtiḥ samānā hṛdyāni vaḥ
Samānamastu vo mano yathā vaḥ susahāsati

'May the whole of mankind be of one mind, have a common goal and the hearts with united love and may the mind and goal be one and the same for all to live a life of happiness.'

This universal prayer for the universal welfare with the basic knowledge that all beings are one as revealed in the earliest of all the Vedas is valid and is the greatest proof of the grand and the broad outlook and the inherent nature of the Indian blood.

'The ancient and classical creations of the Sanskrit tongue, both in quality and in body and abundance of excellence, in their potent originality and force and beauty, in their substance and art and structure, in grandeur and justice and charm of speech and in the height and width of the reach of their spirit stand very evidently in the front rank among the world's great literatures. The language itself, as has been universally recognised by those competent to form a judgement, is one of the most magnificent, the most perfect and wonderfully sufficient literary instruments developed by the human mind, at once majestic and sweet and flexible, strong and clearly formed and full and vibrant and subtle, and its quality and character would be of itself, a sufficient evidence of the character and quality of the race whose mind it expressed and the culture of which it was the reflecting medium.'

— Sri Aurobindo
(An Essay on the Vedas)

4

Rig Veda

Rig Veda Samhita

The *Rig Veda* is supposed to be the oldest and the most magnificent of all the Vedas. It is considered to be the most ancient text in Sanskrit language and the oldest religious scripture in the whole world. It is the oldest collection of ideas known to mankind.

The date of this Veda cannot be stated for certain as there are different opinions regarding its origin. Many sages who believed to have belonged to different periods of time had composed the hymns. It is, therefore, the result of the efforts of generation of poets of many centuries. According to some scholars, the *Rig Veda* was written even before 5000 BC. Some others claim that it was written around 1700 BC-100 BC. Western scholars date it around 1500 BC. To some others this Veda was supposed to have been composed between 1500 BC and 900 BC but the archaeological findings indicate a much earlier date.

The language used in the *Rig Veda* is Vedic Sanskrit. This is an earlier version of Sanskrit. But it is very different from classical Sanskrit of the later period. It is said that its language and style are beautiful, poetic and mysterious. The mantras contain the greatest truths of existence. All the other three Vedas are based on *Rig Veda*.

The word *Rig* is derived from the verb root '*Ri*' meaning 'to praise'. The feminine noun '*Ri*' refers to praise or verse, essentially a sacred verse in praise of deities.

The priest who chanted the Rig Vedic hymns was known as '*Ritwik*'.

The metrical hymns are to be chanted loudly with proper pronunciation and as per the tune already set. It is the Veda adoring deities. The hymns contain the names of the *rishis* who composed it.

In *Yajur Veda* and *Sama Veda,* we come across many of the *Rig Veda* hymns.

A very early commentator of *Rig Veda* was **Yaska**. Later, in 14th century, an exhaustive commentary on the *Rig Veda* was written by **Sayana**.

Hymns of Rig Veda

The early hymns of the *Rig Veda*, though considered as poetic marvels but very difficult to understand, are in the form of beautiful statements, praising the Nature Gods, and their personifications like Agni, Varuna, Surya etc. The later hymns are in praise of the Supreme Being. They are sung by the priests for obtaining the blessings from Gods for themselves, for the princes and patrons on behalf of whom the sacrifice was conducted, and also for friends and others. The hymns contain both outward and inner meanings. While the outward meaning satisfies those who crave for material happiness in this world, the inward meaning expresses the craving for the higher spiritual wealth desired by the sages. Two-third of this Veda is about God of Agni and Indra. Nearly 500 hymns are addressed to Indra and Agni.

Agni occupies an important place in this Veda. He is considered as the link between God and man. He is also referred to as the Lord of the Sacrifice and a messenger, who carries the oblations to Gods.

Indra, the Lord of thunder, rainfall and war is the chief deity in the *Rig Veda*. His favourite weapon is the thunderbolt. There are hymns that praise and describe the greatness, heroic exploits, generosity and powers, and mysterious nature of the deities. In the external sense, there are prayers for various favours and gifts like health, cattle and wealth, long life, progeny, victory in war, destruction of enemies and demons, glory, brilliance, protection and guidance. The hymns were sung during the rituals as per the prescribed rules and were expected to bring the desired result by pleasing the deities and powers that are both outside as well as inside the man. This form of worship might have been the earliest form of worship known to humans.

This Veda contains several hymns relating to the various aspects of Vedic Science including the practice of yoga, meditation, mantra, and so on. The earliest mention of Ayurveda, Astrology and Astronomy are found here. It also deals with other subjects such as the procedure of wedding and the evils of gambling. The hymns mention different kinds of weapons used in warfare like, spears and bows, arrows, iron weapons and also the use of horses, and chariots with spokes.

Beyond the outward interpretation, the spiritual, the psychological and the symbolic interpretations of this Veda are considered the most important. The central teachings of the Vedas include, the search of the truth that is higher and deeper than the truth of the outer existence, and immortality towards which the human soul should rise with the ultimate objective of uniting with the supreme Godhead. Although there are other worlds, the highest is the world of truth and light, the Great Heaven. The true knowledge is *Rta-Chit*, the truth-consciousness.

Our life in the material world is a war between the *devas* and *asuras*. The *devas* or Gods represent truth, light and immortality whereas the *asuras* represent darkness. We should seek the blessings of Gods by uttering the all-powerful mantras and offerings, to overpower the *asuras*. Non-material welfare, internal happiness, piousness, duty, service, benevolence are given importance along with material happiness in seeking the divine blessings.

It is also stated in the hymns that one supreme order binds all gods. It reveals the fundamental oneness of everything. The Gods mentioned in this Veda are also considered as subordinates to that supreme power.

We can roughly divide the subject dealt within this Veda into three groups —

- The hymns which are in praise of the deities.
- The hymns dealing with the philosophical speculations about the origin of the Universe and nature of people.
- The hymns dealing with social, political and secular subjects like marriage, wars, greatness of generosity and so on.

The 10th *mandala* of *Rig Veda* especially deals with several spiritual topics relating to cosmogony and other miscellaneous subjects.

Shakhas of Rig Veda

It is said that the *Rig Veda Samhita* originally had 21 branches or *shakhas* but at present only two *shakhas* are available. They are —

- *Shakala shakha*
- *Bhashkala shakha*

The *Rig Veda* is divided as per two methods —

In the first method, it is divided into 8 *ashtakas*. Each *ashtaka* gets subdivided into *vargas* that contain *mantras*. There are 10552 *mantras* spread over 2024 *vargas* in the 64 *adhyayas* in the entire 8 *ashtakas*.

In the second method, there are 10 *mandalas* or sections. They are divided into *anuvakas*. The *anuvakas* are in turn divided into *suktas* and the *suktas* in *mantras*.

The following chart makes all these divisions clear.

Divisions of Rig Veda

Mandala	Suktas	Mantras	Gods Praised
1	191	2006	Agni, Indra, Vishnu
2	43	429	Agni, Indra
3	62	617	Agni, Indra
4	58	589	Agni, Indra
5	87	727	Agni, Indra, Vishwadevas, Marutas, Mitra-Varuna, Ashwins, Usha, Savitar
6	75	765	Agni, Indra
7	104	841	Agni, Indra, Vishwadevas, Marutas, Mitra-Varuna, Ashwins, Usha, Indra-Varuna, Vayus Saraswati, Vishnu, and other deities
8	103	1716	Different Gods, Indra (hymns 5-59)
9	114	1108	Soma plants
10	191	1754	Agni and other Gods, Creation (hymns 129-130)
Total	**1028**	**10,552**	

The *Rig Veda* has long collection of short hymns. Arranged as per length, the 2-7 *mandalas* that are considered the oldest parts form 38% of the text, 8th and 9th *mandalas* account for 15% and 9% of the text respectively, and 1st and the 10th *mandalas*, which are considered as latter texts, cover 37% of the text.

The Gods in Rig Veda

We find three major categories of Gods in the *Rig Veda*. They are the Gods who are associated with heaven, the air, and the earth.

1. The Gods of **Heaven** are Dyaus, Varuna, Mitra, Surya, Pushan, and Ashwins and the Goddesses are Usha, the dawn and Ratri, the night.
2. Gods associated with **Air** are Indra, Apam Napat, Rudra, the Marutas,Vayu, Paranjanya, and the ocean.
3. Prithvi, Agni and Soma are associated with **Earth**.

References to other Gods like Trita, the lightning form of fire, and Matarisvan, the one who brought fire to mankind, the legendary river Saraswati are also found in *Rig Veda*. In addition, we also find Gods associated with certain abstract concepts, namely Dhatr, the creator of Sun, the Moon and the Earth, Tvastar who is the artisan of Gods and who preceded Vishvakarma, his daughter Saranu, the wife of Vivasvant and the mother of the twins Yama and Yami, Savitar, Prajapati, Aditi, and the Apsaras, particularly Urvashi, and Gandharvas. Soma, a plant, the juice of which is an energiser and is offered to Gods as oblation is considered as a deity. Soma is also referred to as the Moon God.

Finally the demons or *asuras* like Vritra, Vala, Arbuda, Visvarya, and Svarbhanu so on also find place in the *Rig Veda*.

Indra

Indra is the chief God who is regarded as the most powerful. He is the Lord of heavens, sky, war, thunder and rainfall. He is supposed to ride on a white elephant called *Iravata*. His weapon is called *Vajrayuta* or the thunderbolt made by the deity Tvastar. He destroyed Vratasura and Vala and released the cows that were kept in captivity by the Panis.

Agni or Jatadevas

Agni is the Lord of sacrifices and messenger of Gods who dispels darkness. He is supposed to be the one who carries the sacrificial offerings to the Gods. He is as important as Indra. He was brought from heaven by Matariswan and was given to Bhrigus. In its inner meaning, Agni refers to the inner fire of man.

Rudras

These are the Gods of storms and lightning who provide the required medicines.

Surya

He is the chief of solar deities. He is extremely brilliant and bright. He is the giver of power, strength, health and brilliance.

Savitar

Savitar is the Sun of very early morning hidden by dark night. He is also known as Aditya. He upholds law, drives away sickness and pardons sins committed. The famous Gayatri mantra is addressed to Savitar for enlightenment.

Aryaman

Aryaman is a solar deity.

Ribhus

Ribhu, Vaja and Vibhvan are collectively known as Ribhus. They are three semi-divine beings, wise and skilful craftsmen. They also possess special expertise in chariot-making and fire-making.

Varuna

He is the chief of Adityas and the compassionate ruler of the earth and heaven. He is the God of the sky and rain. He is considered as the Lord enforcing natural order. He is the upholder of moral law providing justice to all. He is regarded as the son of Aditi and brother of Mitra. He punishes those who deviate from the natural law and commit sin, but pardons them when they repent for their misdeeds. He is considered as the knower and controller of one and all. In later hymns, he is considered as the Lord of the oceans, waters, night sky and underworld. He is considered to be an *asura* or demon.

Aditi

She represents the concept of wholeness. She is also the queen of the eternal order.

Daksha

He is the *Prajapati*, Lord of men, one of the sons of Brahma.

Ansa

Ansa is a solar deity.

Mitra

He is the Lord of heaven, divinity, honesty, friendship, contracts and meetings. He guards the world and is the upholder of natural order. He is the protector of oaths. He stirs men to action. He is one among the Adityas. In later hymns, Mitra is associated with the morning light.

Usha

She is regarded as the daughter of the sky and the Goddess of early morning who brings hope, happiness, riches, light, beauty and all good things in life.

Vayu

He is the Lord of thought. He is swift as mind. He is intelligent, invisible, and also the vital breath. He is the protector, Lord of medicines, and is the one who illumines the earth and heaven.

Vishnu

He is the Lord of all the three worlds. He is a minor God in the *Rig Veda* and is one of the Adityas.

Pushan

He is a pastoral God. He is the Lord of all paths, prosperity, marriages, journeys, roads, guardian of cattle who drives away enemies and is responsible for inducing thoughts. He also protects people from wild animals and helps them to tread on the path without any difficulty.

Soma or Soma Pavamana

It is a plant, whose juice is invigorating, also considered as the Lord of speech and Moon. It is the God of inspiration and also speech inspiring the mind. It lures the Gods with its juice and brings them to the sacrifice. It also brings joy, bliss, strength, and immortality and cures all ailments.

The Apris

The Apris constitute objects connected to the fire sacrifice like the fuel, the sacred grass, the enclosure and so on. They are supposed to be the various manifestations of Agni.

Vasus

They are the attendants of Indra. They are *Dhara*, the earth, *Anala,* the fire, *Apa*, the water, *Anala,* the wind, *Dhruva* the pole star, *Soma,* the moon, and *Prabhasa,* the light.

Nasatya and Dasra – The Two Ashwins

They are the twin horsemen and sons of Saranya, the Goddess of clouds. They are the brothers of *Usha*, the dawn. They symbolise shining of sunrise and sunset. They are the deities of Ayurvedic medicines. They have healing and curative powers. They are supposed to descend on the earth thrice a day to cure diseases of people.

Adityas

These are solar deities. They personify the Universal law and are 12 in number. They are described as the 12 spokes of a wheel that corresponds to the 12 months in a year. They are namely Mitra, Varuna, Aryaman, Daksha, Bhaga, Amsa, Tvastar, Savitar, Pushan,

Sakra, Vivasvat, and Vishnu. They uphold law of nature, illumine the world, drive away darkness, and nourish all living beings. They are the sons of Aditi and Kashyapa.

The Marutas

They are Storm Gods and progeny of Rudra. They are the lords of wind, lightning and rain. They give strength, wealth, progeny and longevity.

Parjanya

He is the ferocious Rain God, the God of the sky and the slayer of demons.

Rta

He is the self-regulating world order or the rhythmic pattern of the Universe and is the lord of the universal order of the seasons, longevity, rain and yield of milk in cattle. He determines the path of heavenly objects like the sun, moon, stars and planets.

Vishwadevas

All the lords of the Universe including all Vedic Gods, namely Bhaga, Daksha, Mitra, Aditi, Aryaman, Varuna, Soma, Pushan, Indra, Tarksya, Marutas, Agni, Rta.

Vishvakarma

He is the chief architect of the Universe. He is the son of Brahma, designer of the palaces, weapons and flying chariots of the Gods.

Tvastar

He is the builder of divine implements, particularly the *Vajrayuta* of Indra.

Bhaga

He is one among the Adityas, and the son of Aditi. He is the lord of bright light who gives support, bliss, gifts and wealth.

Vashishtha

He is a great sage born to the celestial nymph Urvashi and Varuna-Mitra.

Atri

He is a sage and the son of Brahma.

Brihaspati or Brahmanaspati

He is the giver of wisdom, wealth, power, strength, victory in wars and agricultural produce, healer of diseases, protector, Lord of all sacred prayers, and is the maker of law. He is also the *Guru* or teacher of the *Devas*.

Saraswati

She is the Goddess of knowledge and river. She is supposed to have seven sisters. She gives knowledge, health, wealth, and strength, provides water and helps God in destroying enemies.

Aranyayi

She is the Goddess of forests.

Rathi

She is the Goddess of love.

Manyu

He is the God of war and thunder who destroys demons and other enemies. He is sometimes referred to as Indra.

Purusha

He is the supreme Godhead, the Universal self.

Dyaus

He is the God of the sky and the husband of *Prithvi* or earth.

Prithvi

She is the Goddess of earth.

Dadhikravan

He is the mighty stallion who is the giver of many gifts. He was given by Gods to Puru.

Kapinjala

He is the mystic bird of good omen with a beautiful voice.

Yama

He is the God of the dead and departed and also the God of justice.

Apam Napat

He is the God of freshwater of rivers and lakes and also Fire God originating in water.

Nirtri

They are the guardians of directions representing south-west direction.

Vena

He is a divine horse.

Purusha and Prakriti

The two represent *Heaven* and *Earth*. The Sun is supposed to move between them. They give prosperity.

Saranyu

She is the Goddess of clouds, the daughter of Tvastar and the wife of Surya.

The other deities mentioned in the *Rig Veda* include **Manas, Dakshina, Jnanam, Vasukra, Kshetropathi, Ghrta, Asamathi, Pururvasas, Mayabheda, Tarksya**.

Rishis in Rig Veda

The total number of *rishis* in *Rig Veda* is supposed to be 407, out of which 21 are supposed to be women sages. It is believed that the sages belonged to ten families. The hymns in this Veda are believed to have been written by generations of different sages belonging to different eras. The names of different *rishis* are mostly associated with each of the ten *mandalas* of the *Rig Veda*.

It is believed that *mandala* 1 and 10 were written by sages belonging to different families, whereas *mandala* 2 to 8 are considered as the works of a *rishi* and his descendants.

The table given below shows which family of seers is associated with which *mandala*.

Mandala	Associated Family
2	Gritsamada and his family, the Bhrigus
3	Vishwamitra and his family
4	Vamadeva and the Gotama family
5	Atre and his family
6	Barhaspatya and his family, the Angirasas
7	Vashishtha and his family
8	Kanva and his family
9	Kashtapa and his family

It is believed that Vyasa taught *Rig Veda* to Paila, one of his disciples and he in turn collected and arranged the *Rig Veda Samhita*. The oldest portions of the *Rig Veda* are from 2 to 7 *mandalas*. It is said that the others were added later. The 1 and 10 *mandalas* are also considered the later additions.

Brahmanas of Rig Veda

The *Rig Veda* has three *Brahmanas* – *Aitareya Brahmana, Shankhayana Brahmana* and *Kaushitaki Brahmana.*

1. Aitareya Brahmana

This *Brahmana* belongs both to the *Shakala* and *Ashvalayana* schools of *Rig Veda.* It is also known as *Ashvalayana Brahmana.* It is believed to have been composed around 600 BC and is probably the oldest prose written in any Indo-European language. It deals mainly with the Soma sacrifice, worship and royal ceremonies.

This *Brahmana* has 8 *Panchikas* or groups. Each group has 5 chapters. Altogether there are 40 chapters.

It deals with the duties of the *Hotri* priest, explains about the various sacrifices performed by the *kshatriyas* and the mutual relationship between *brahmins* and *kshatriyas.*

It is believed that Rishi Mahidasa Aitareya composed the first 30 chapters and Rishi Shaunaka added the last 10 chapters to it later.

The contents of this *Brahmana* include —

- **Chapters 1-13** — *The duties of the Hotri priest in the Agnishtoma sacrifice*
- **Chapter 14** — *The meaning of Agnishtoma and related topics*
- **Chapters 15-17** — *Description of Ukthya, Shadasha, Atiratra and other sacrifices*
- **Chapter 18** — *The rules for the Hotri priest*
- **Chapters 19-24** — *The duties of the Hotri priest at the twelve minor sacrifices*
- **Chapter 25** — *Expiations to be performed by the sacrificer, the proper time for performing Agnishtoma, duties of Brahma priest*
- **Chapters 26-30** — *Duties of Gravastuta, Subrahmanya and 6 other minor priests involved in the sacrifice.*
- **Chapters 31-40** — *Sacrifices performed by the Kshatriyas like Vajapeya and Rajasuya and the mutal relationships of brahmins and kshatriyas*

2. Shankhayana Brahmana

This *Brahmana* belongs to *Bhashkala Shakha* of *Rig Veda*. It mainly deals with sacrifices or *yajnas*. It has 30 chapters. Its content is similar to that of the *Aitareya Brahmana,* but it is arranged in a more systematic manner.

3. Kaushitaki Brahmana

This *Brahmana* is also associated with the *Bhashkala Shakha* of *Rig Veda*. It differs from *Shankhayana*, in a few words and syllables at some places. In this *Brahmana*, the sentences are also enumerated. It mainly deals with sacrifices or *yajnas*.

Aranyakas of Rig Veda

Rig Veda has *Aitareya Aranyaka*, *Shankhayana Aranyaka* and *Taittiriya Aranyaka*.

1. Aitareya Aranyaka

It has five *Aranyakas* that are subdivided into 18 chapters.These are composed by different sages.

Aranyaka - 1

It contains *Mahavratas* of the fundamental dutics along with *Saman* songs that are to be sung on particular days. It gives both the ritualistic as well as mystical explanations.

The first three chapters relate to *Prana Vidya*. According to this, the vital breath that forms the life breath is the same for all living beings.

Thus, *prana* is to be worshipped in the form of *rishis*. The one who follows the Vedic rules and procedures and performs the *yajna* would become the God of fire or sun or air and the one who goes against this, will fall into the category of lower level creatures.

Aranyaka - 2

It explains *Uktha*. The fourth, fifth, and the sixth chapters of this *Aranyaka* form the *Aitareya Upanishad*.

Aranyaka - 3

This *Aranyaka* is the *Samhitopanishad.*

Aranyaka - 4

It contains a collection of *Mahanamni* verses. It is technical and deals with mantras.

Aranyaka - 5

It is like a *sutra* text and is technical in nature. It deals with *Nishkevalya Shastra* that is recited during the afternoon ceremony portion of the *Mahavrata* ritual.

2. Shankhayana Aranyaka

There are 15 chapters in this *Aranyaka.* The contents here is similar to that in *Aitareya Aranyaka.* The first two chapters are similar to *Brahmana* and the last chapter is said to be a later addition.

- **Chapters 1** and **2** deal with *Mahavrata.*
- **Chapters 3** to **6** form the *Kaushitaki Upanishad.*
- **Chapters 7** and **8** constitute the *Samhitopanishad.*
- **Chapter 9** discusses the greatness of *prana.*
- **Chapter 10** gives the esoteric implications of the *Agnihotra* ritual.
- **Chapter 11** explains about rituals that are the antidotes for warding off death, and sickness. It also explains the effects of dreams.
- **Chapter 12** is about the benefits of prayer.
- **Chapter 13** discusses philosophical aspects. It indicates that one should give up bodily attachments and carry on *shravanam* and *manana,* and should practise all disciplines of penance, faith, self control and so on.
- **Chapter 14** gives the two mantras, namely, 'I am Brahman', and the second one about the teaching that one who does not understand the meaning of mantras but only recites Vedic hymns is like an animal that does not know the weight it carries.
- **Chapter 15** gives a long list of the names of spiritual teachers starting from Brahma to Gunasankhayana.

3. Taittiriya Aranyaka

It contains 10 *Prapathikas* or chapters. The first half of the text is called *Kathakam*, which is believed to have been borrowed from the *Kataka Shakha* of *Yajur Veda*.

- **Chapter 1** is about *Surya Namaskar*.
- **Chapter 2** deals with a description of 5 *Mahayajnas* that every *brahmin* should perform daily.
- **Chapters 3** tell us about further technicalities of other *yajnas* and *homas*.
- **Chapters 4** has a section dealing with mantras that avert havoc.
- **Chapter 5** is an academic treatise on *yajna*. It deals with *pravargya* rites.
- **Chapter 6** deals with *Pitra-medha* mantras. These mantras are used at rituals for the disposal of the dead body.
- **Chapters 7, 8 and 9** form the *Taittiriya Upanishad*.
- **Chapter 10** forms the *Maha Narayana Upanishad* or the *Yajnika Upanishad*. It contains several important mantras taken from the three Vedas.

Upanishads of Rig Veda

There are 10 *Upanishads* associated with *Rig Veda*. They are —

1. Aitareya Upanishad

Aitareya Upanishad is considered as one of the earliest *Upanishads*. It is a part of *Aitareya Aranyaka*. This *Upanishad* is associated with Sage Aitareya, who made this *Upanishad* widely known. It consists of 3 chapters with 33 verses. The *Upanishad* begins from the fourth chapter of the second *Aranyaka* of *Rig Veda* and continues till the fourth, fifth and the sixth chapters.

The earlier parts discuss the sacrificial ceremonies like *Mahavrata* and its interpretations. It gives the deeper meaning of the sacrifices with the aim to elevate the mind of man from outer ceremonial acts of worship through external sacrifices to the inner or inward sacrifice. The *Aitareya Upanishad* teaches about creation.

The first chapter discusses the creation of *Purusha*. In the beginning there was only the Absolute Self and nothing else. He, that one spirit, out of His own will, created the entire Universe. To guard the Universe, He created the various deities and human being and everything else including water, which is awareness and consciousness, light rays, which represent the elements of divinity, and death that is inevitable on earth.

Then, the sense organs were created, from which powers and aspects emerged.

Organ	Power or Aspect Created
Mouth	Speech
Nostrils	Breath
Eyes	Fight
Ears	Hearing
Skin	Hair
Heart	Mind
Hair	Plants and Trees
Reproductive Organs	Power to reproduce
Navel	Outgoing Breath

The eight directions are said to have emerged from death.

Later, He created hunger and thirst, food, cow and horse and all other beings as well. They were given different duties to perform. The Self asked them to enter the respective parts of man.

Aspect	Part it entered
Fire	Mouth as speech
Air	Nostrils as breath
Sun	Eyes as rays of sight
Directions of Space	Ears
Plants and Trees	Skin
Moon	Heart through mind
Outgoing Breath	Navel as death
Water	Reproductive organs as semen

In this manner, the various divinities entered man and the man became divine. Hunger and thirst seemed to have pleaded to the Self for a place. The Self, therefore, created a place for them in man and meditated for water and food which were created to satisfy the hunger and thirst.

Later the Self tried to seize the beings through sense organs but failed although the Self is the one by whom we are able to use the sense organs. So ultimately the Self could seize the being only through breath. The inherent meaning is that, desire of life cannot be stopped through sense organs, or mind, or thought. It can be stopped only by death which results by the departure of breath. The air, which is of the nature of soul, represents the soul here. The *jiva* or the individual soul originates from the father and enters the womb of the mother. The man is born in this world and goes through his life. In this way, he is born again and again until he knows the *Atman* or Self. Once he realises the *Atman*, he gets release from the bondage of repeated births and deaths. This *Upanishad* points out that everything in the Universe is guided by and is also based on this consciousness that is *Brahman*.

The second chapter deals with the three births of the Self and the third chapter describes the qualities of Self or *Brahman*.

Three classes of men who aspire wisdom are mentioned in this *Upanishad* —

1. Those who are detached from the world and whose minds are free belong to the highest class.
2. To the second category belong all those who worship *Prana* or the life breath and attain knowledge gradually.
3. In the third group are men who care for worldly possessions. For them, the meditative worship as shown in the *Samhita* is suitable.

This *Upanishad* is also known for its philosophy of *Atman* as the intellect. According to this *Upanishad*, intelligence is *Brahman*, and all living creatures and the five elements namely, **earth, wind, space, water** and **fire** are the creation of that intelligence that is *Brahman*. The entire *Upanishad* is written in symbolic language and, therefore, it is very difficult to interpret the meanings contained in this *Upanishad*.

2. Akshamalika Upanishad

This *Upanishad* is about the question put up by Prajapati to Guha about the rosary beads and Guha's reply stating that the cleaning and worshipping of the rosary represents everything including the various forms of God. Guha then explains the effects of rosary worship in destroying sins.

3. Atmaboda Upanishad

This *Upanishad* explains at length about the sacred mantra, *AUM* that is considered as the innermost *Brahman* and about Lord Narayana who exists in all. It says that *Brahman* exists as knowledge in the middle of the heart and the knowledge of *Aham Brahmasmi* (I am *Brahman*) is going beyond *maya*.

4. Bahvricha Upanishad

This *Upanishad* is about the Supreme power, the Goddess who alone existed in the beginning of creation. From Her being, *Brahman* was born and later everything else was born. She is the consciousness within and is the *Maha Tripura Sundari*. She is the *Atman*, she is *Brahman*, she is Consciousness, and everything that assumes various forms.

5. Kaushitaki Brahmana Upanishad

This *Upanishad*, which is one of the oldest *Upanishads*, has come down in fragments. It has four chapters, and is about the question on existence of Supreme power, put by Chitra Gargyayani to Svetaketu, the priest sent by Chitra Gargyayani's Guru and father Aruni and the reply to the question about Existence by the priest to his disciple.

This *Upanishad* stresses that the path to *Mukti* is through knowledge. The soul that departs from the body goes to the moon and takes birth again in another body as per one's deeds and knowledge. Ultimately one realises *Brahman* and transcends the good and bad *Karmas* and all pairs of opposites. This *Upanishad* considers the vital breath or *Prana* as the prime mover or *Brahman*.

Prana is also identified with the *Prajnatman* or the intelligent self, which is ageless, immortal bliss. It explains about getting that highest treasure, about meditating on *Brahman*, about worship of Sun, Moon, and other deities, the superior excellence of the vital breath, the Self and rituals performed by the son for the father.

6. Mudgala Upanishad

The summary of *Purusha sukta* is given in this *Upanishad.*

Lord Vishnu pervading the Space and Time and giving liberation, the nature and glory of Lord Vishnu, Aniruddha, origin of *Prakriti* and *Purusha* from Hari or Vishnu, creation, rebirth, *moksha* or liberation, the supreme mystery of *Purusha sukta*, the greatness of *Purusha sukta*, instruction of *Purusha sukta* by Vasudeva to Indra, the single God becoming many, the nature of *Brahman*, to whom the *Purusha sukta* is to be imparted, how to impart this knowledge — all these form the subject matter of this *Upanishad.*

7. Nadabindu Upanishad

The contents of this *Upanishad* include an explanation of what is the mantra *AUM*, the benefit of reciting this mantra, about the nature of rebirth of a person who dies in different *matras* having different deities as *Devatas* or Gods, knowledge of *Para Brahman* that is pure and beyond space and time. According to this *Upanishad*, the bliss or supreme happiness is obtained by the one who meditates on *Para Brahman.*

It also explains meditation and *Atma Jnana*, absence of rebirth for a *Tattva Jnani*, illusory nature of the world, about one who practises *Vishnu Mudra*, concentration of *chitta* (mind) on sound that proceeds from *Pranava* which is *Brahman*, and the state of *Para Brahman* or *Paramatman*, that is beyond this state, the existence of the mind till the sound lasts and beyond this the state of no mind, when a *jnani* becomes liberated or *mukta* at this stage of *Samadhi*, which is beyond the three stages of waking, dreaming, and dreamless sleep and attaining his true original state by becoming *Brahma-Pranava.*

8. Nirvana Upanishad

The *Paramahamsa* in whom the Self is destroyed and who wears the garland of bliss that includes the freedom from all the three qualities of *Sattva*, *Rajas* and *Tamas* and who demonstrates that *Brahman* is present in one and all.

According to the *Nirvana Upanishad*, knowledge results in the burning up of the notion of existence or non-existence of casual, subtle, gross bodies and egoistic feelings, when one becomes the very *Brahman*, the eternal form.

9. Sowbhagyalakshmi Upanishad

This *Upanishad* deals with the Gods asking Lord Narayana to impart the knowledge about the Goddess of prosperity. It includes meditation on *Sri* – the Goddess of prosperity. Also, these are hymns on *Sri* and hymns about *Maha Lakshmi* who is the Goddess of prosperity.

Sowbhagyalakshmi Upanishad gives details of Lord Narayana's reply to Gods about *Maya*, meditation by yogis, the dissolution of mind, concentration, and the attainment of bliss. In this *Upanishad,* Lord Narayana explains to Gods about the nine wheels, namely, the basic wheel or *chakra* of *Brahman*, the wheel of *Swadishtana*, the wheel of the navel, the wheel of the heart, the wheel of throat, the wheel of palate, the wheel of brow, the wheel of *nirvana,* and the wheel of Space.

The benefits of studying *Sowbhagyalakshmi Upanishad* in the form of all blessings is also one of the subjects dealt with in this *Upanishad.*

10. Tripura Upanishad

This *Upanishad* tells about the dwellings of Gods in the three *lokas*, the nine sources, deities, gestures, planets, the foremost dwelling of God of Love with Fortune's Goddess, the power of consciousness, the principal wisdom, and the worship of Goddesses *Saraswati*, *Lakshmi* and *Gowri*.

5

Sama Veda

Sama Veda Samhita

Sama Veda is the wisdom of chants and is considered the book of songs. It is a collection of melodies and is considered as the Veda of holy songs representing the ecstasy of spiritual knowledge and the power of devotion. Many of the mantras of *Rig Veda* are arranged here to suit *soma* sacrifice.

Sama is derived from the word *saman* that literally means 'destroying sin'. *Sama* also refers to that which brings equipoise and tranquillity to the mind. It is said that the singing of *sama* makes the mind stable and the sound waves of *sama* give peace to the vagrant mind. The singing of *sama* begins with a high pitch which is lowered gradually. *Sama Veda* consists of many *richas* or *slokas* from *Rig Veda* that are highly lyrical and musical. The hymns in the *Samhita* part of this Veda are sung using the seven notes or *swaras* by the Sama Vedic priests called *Udagatri* during the performance of sacrifices to please the deities. Such songs are called *Sama gana.* This Veda is highly poetic and ritualistic. It is particularly known for its precise meter of the poetry. The Indian classical music based on the *sapta swaras* has its roots in *Sama Veda*.

Almost all verses in this Veda are traceable to the *Rig Veda*, especially taken from 8th and 9th *mandala* of *Rig Veda* and is almost a reduced version of *Rig Veda* set to tune and rhythm. Nearly 1800 of the Rig Vedic mantras are repeated here. In addition, 1 *Yajur Veda* mantra, and 2 of the Sama Vedic mantras are also repeated here. However, the method of pronunciation of *Sama Veda* and Rig Vedic hymns are different since even one syllable entirely changes the meaning and the context of the mantras. It clearly explains how the hymns must be sung by giving emphasis to the sounds of the mantras that have effect on the environment and the person who sings them. Some of the ways in which *Sama gana* can be sung are *Brahat*, *Rathantar*, *Gayatra*, *Vairoop* and *Rajat*. It is believed that originally there were many rituals that became intricate and elaborate as time passed on. Thus emerged the need for compilation of all the rituals and chants in a separate book, as a guide to the priests who sung them. His complitation eventually become the *Sama Veda.* As per the legend, Vyasa taught this Veda to Jaimini, his disciple. This Veda is said to have been composed around 1300 BC-1000 BC.

Hymns of Sama Veda

These hymns are mostly addressed to deities like Agni, Indra, and Soma. Agni is prayed for guidance, for destroying darkness by giving light, for blessing one with wealth and happiness, and to protect one by destroying one's enemies.

Sama Veda also stresses the importance of soft speech, cleanliness, fulfilling one's vows, performing good deeds, perseverance, giving away things and imparting knowledge to others.

It also mentions the importance of control over senses, yoga, hard work, good actions, speaking truth, good company, engaging oneself in pious and religious activities, noble deeds and meditation.

Shakhas of Sama Veda

Sama Veda has the largest number of *shakhas,* numbering about 1000. Around 13 names are found in the records. They are *Ranayana, Shatyamukhya, Vyasa, Bhaguri, Onlundi, Goulgulvi, Bhanumanoupamayava, Karati, Mashaka Argya, Varsgagavya, Kuthuma, Shakugitre,* and *Jaimini.* But only three *shakhas* of the *Samhitas* are available now. They are, *Kauthuma*, *Jaiminiya* and *Ranayaniya*.

There are 1875 verses in this Veda. This Veda is in two parts. The first part is the *Purvarchaka* or the first adoration and the second part is *Uttararchaka* or the later adoration.

The *Purvarchaka* has got 6 chapters with 650 mantras. The melodies here are on the basis of single verse. The *Purvarchaka* is further subdivided in to four sections or *Kands* namely, *Agneya*, *Acindra*, *Pavman*, and *Aranya Kands*. *Agneya* contains 114 mantras, *Acindra* contains 352 mantras, *Pavman* has 119 mantras, and *Aranya* has 55 mantras. In between these two is *Mahanamnayarchik*. It contains 10 incantations. Altogether there are 650 mantras.

The *Uttararchaka* has got 21 chapters with 1225 mantras. The melodies here are on the basis of units of three verses.

Brahmanas of Sama Veda

There are 10 *Brahmanas* in this Veda. They are —

1. Tandya Brahmana

This *Brahmana* has 25 chapters divided into 347 sections. It is also called *Panchvimsha Brahmana* and also *Adbhut Brahmana*, since it contains many miraculous stories. This *Brahmana* deals with general information about *yajnas* like, the employment of various *samans* in different Vedic rituals, detailed explanation of the *soma* sacrifices and legends about various sages to whom the *samans* were revealed. It also enumerates the *Vratyastoma* ritual by which non-Aryans were admitted into Aryan fold. It is the main *Brahmana* of both the *Kauthuma* and the *Ranayaniya* branches. Its 25 chapters are —

- **Chapter 1:** Collection of mantras
- **Chapters 2 to 3:** *Vistutis*
- **Chapters 4 to 9.3:** Rites like *Jyotishtoma*, *Ukthya*, *Atiratra*, *Prakritis* of *Ekahasand Ahinas*
- **Chapters 9.3 to 9.10:** *Soma Praya chittas*
- **Chapters 10 to 15:** *Dvadasha* rites
- **Chapters 16 to 19:** One day rites
- **Chapters 20 to 22:** *Ahina* rites
- **Chapters 23 to 25:** Longer rites like *Sattras*

2. Shadavimsha Brahmana

It literally means twenty-six. It has 5 sections and deals with one day *Abhichara* or sorcery rite. It constitutes the 26th section of the *Prauda Brahmana* and was added to it later.

3. Sama Vidhana Brahmana

It deals with the recitation of *samans* for obtaining specific result. It is devoted to magic and explains the chants to be sung for various spells. It has three *Prapathikas*.

4. Arsheya Brahmana

It contains an index of sages connected with the *Gramageya* and *Aranya Samans*. It is divided into three *Prapathikas*.

5. Devatadhyaya Brahmana

This *Brahmana* lays down the criterion for deciding the deities of *Sama ganas*.

6. Chandogya Upanishad Brahmana

This *Brahmana* has 10 divisions and there are two parts in this.

***Prapathikas* 1 and 2** form the *Mantra Brahmana* or the *Mantra Parvan* containing mantras used for *Grihya* rites. Each of these two *Prapathikas* is further subdivided into 8 *Kands*. There are 268 mantras including 11 additional formulae in this.

The ***Prapathikas* 3 to 10** form the *Chandogya Upanishad.*

7. Samhitopanishad Brahmana

It deals with the secret aspects of *Samhitas*, the fees that must be paid to the religious teachers, and the responsibilities of the great tradition of *Sama Veda*.

8. Vamsha Brahmana

It is a short *Brahmana* containing a list of ancient Sama Vedic teachers.

9. Jaiminiya Brahmana

After *Shatapatha Brahmana*, *Jaiminiya Brahmana* is next in importance. *Jaiminiya Brahmana* is fairly long and contains several Vedic legends and stories. In the last *Kand* of this *Brahmana*, geographical and historical information is given. It is seen that in many ways it runs parallel to *Tandya Brahmana*. But it gives a more detailed treatment of the subject. The ritual section deals with —

- *Agnihotra* and *Agnishtoma* in the first *Kand*
- The *Gavayamana* and *Ekahas* containing one day *soma* sacrifices, 12 days sacrifices called *Ahinas*, and longer sacrifices called *Sattras* in the second *Kand*
- The *Gavayamana* and *Dvadashaha* in the third *Kand*

10. Jaiminiya Arsheya Brahmana

Of all the above *Brahmanas*, *Tandya Brahmana* is the biggest and the most important one. Its content is similar to that of *Kauthuma Arsheya Brahmana*. These two *Brahmanas* are also quite similar, except for the fact that *Jaiminiya Arsheya Brahmana* gives only one name of a sage for each *Saman*, whereas the *Kauthuma Arsheya Brahmana* gives the names of more than one sage.

Aranyakas and Upanishads of Sama Veda

Aranyakas

Only *Jaiminiya Aranyaka* of *Sama Veda* is available now.

Upanishads

The two well-known *Upanishads* of this Veda are *Chandogya* and *Kena*. They are also called as *Talavakropanishad*. However, sixteen *Upanishads* are associated with this Veda. They are —

1. Aruneyi Upanishad

Aruna's son went to Brahma and asked him how he could give up all work and Brahma replied, "One should give up all his relations, all his possessions and mantras, the holy thread, all the worlds, and should live like a *sanyasi* with minimum clothes, bathe three times a day, concentrate on his unity with *Atman*, and repeat only the *Aranyakas* and the *Upanishads*."

Later, this *Upanishad* explains how one should become a monk.

2. Avyakta Upanishad

This *Upanishad* explains the states of evolution in the beginning, namely, *Avyakta* that is indeterminate, *Maha Tattva* that is determined indeterminate, *Ahamkara* or determinate and the *Nasadeeya Sukta* that says about the beginning of creation when nothing was clear or determinate and when even Gods were not born.

It further states that no one can disclose this truth, as to when the world sprang up and whether it was framed by divine hand or not.

Only the Lord in heaven can tell, if he wants.

3. Chandogya Upanishad

This *Upanishad* is one of the oldest and longest of all *Upanishads*. The name of this *Upanishad* comes from '*Samans*', the singer of songs who are called '*Chandoga*'. It is a part of *Chandogya Brahmana* that has 10 chapters.

Most of the passages of *Brahma Sutra* are from *Chandogya Upanishad*. The teachings of a number of sages are given here.

The first two chapters of the *Brahmana* deal with worship and Vedic sacrifices. The other eight chapters constitute *Chandogya Upanishad*. This *Upanishad* says that the one who is not conscious of his body, will not be affected either by desire or anger. A number of truths are explained in this *Upanishad* in the form of stories. The initial chapters of this *Upanishad* explain the rituals involved in Vedic sacrifices. The later chapters are concerned with the origin and profundity of the concept of *AUM*. The importance of chanting the sacred mantra *AUM*, that is associated with the life breath or *Prana* is explained here.

The doctrine of reincarnation is also stated here as an ethical consequence of one's good or bad *Karmas* or actions. This *Upanishad* also points the importance of sacrifice, austerity, charity, and the study of the Vedas under the guidance of a Guru. Further, it explains the value of speech, thought, meditation, understanding, strength, memory and hope.

Three parts of religious life are discussed in this *Upanishad.* They are —

- Performance of Vedic sacrifices
- Study of Vedas
- Alms-giving and Austerity

A well-known passage in this *Upanishad* is the dialogue between Satyakama Jabala and his mother. This passage asserts that the status of a Brahmin comes from character, not by birth. For the one who realises the soul that is free of evil, age, death, sorrow and thirst, there is freedom in all the worlds.

This *Upanishad* also suggests '*Tat Tvam Asi*' or 'That is what you are' or 'You are that' denoting the identity of *Brahman* and the *Atman* or Self. The '*Omkara*' or the syllable *AUM* is called '*Udgitha*'. It is the Supreme. Knowing this, he who meditates upon this syllable, becomes a fulfiller of all desirable ends.

Meditation on *Prana*, connected with nose, tongue, eye, ear, mind and so on results in both good as well as bad feelings. The nose smells both good and bad smells. So does the tongue, ear, eyes and mind in a corresponding manner. When the *devas* finally meditated upon *Prana* in the mouth as *Udgitha,* the *asuras* could not overpower them. *Prana* in mouth is pure and is free from sin.

Angiras, Brihaspathi and Ayasya meditated on that *Prana* as *Udgitha*. He who meditates on the *Udgitha* as the syllable *AUM*, looking upon it as *Prana*, gets all his desires fulfilled. This is meditation with reference to body. Then this *Upanishad* explains about meditation with reference to Gods. One who meditates upon Sun becomes a dispeller of darkness as *Udgitha*.

This *Upanishad* also explains about the meditation on the syllables of *Udgitha* —

- '*Ud'*, that is *prana*, heaven, sun, and *Sama Veda*
- '*Gi'*, that is speech, sky, air and *Yajur Veda*
- '*Tha'*, that is food, the earth, fire, and *Rig Veda*

About the meditation for the fulfilment of wishes, this *Upanishad* says that one should meditate upon the objects contemplated and reflect upon *Saman*, *Rik*, the sage, the deity, meter, hymn, and heaven. Having meditated upon *AUM* the deities became immortal and fearless. *Udgitha* is *Pranava* and vice-versa. The Sun is *Udgitha*. *Upanishad* also provides explanation on *Rik* and *Saman* and the greatness of the knowledge and meditation upon *Udgitha* through *Saman* and the process in the performance of the various Vedic sacrifices. The one who knows *Brahman* as the all-pervading and unchanging *Akasha* gets unchanging prosperity.

When *Brahman* as *Prana* which is the eastern and one of the five doors of the heart, is meditated upon as brightness, and the source of food, then one becomes resplendent and an eater of food.

When the *Brahman* as *Vyana* that is ear, moon, and the southern door of the heart is meditated upon as prosperity and fame, one becomes prosperous and famous.

The one who meditates upon *Brahman* as *Apana*, the western door of the heart, that is speech and fire, as the holy effulgence, born of sacred wisdom, and as the source of food, he becomes radiant with sacred wisdom and eater of food.

One who meditates upon *Brahman* as *Samana*, the northern door of the heart, that is mind, *Parjanya* or Rain God as fame and grace, he becomes famous and graceful.

The one who meditates on *Brahman* as *Udana*, the upper door of the heart, which is also air, and *Akasha* as strength and nobility, he becomes strong and noble. The person who perceives it reaches the heavenly world.

The light of *Brahman* that shines above is in the body of man. One can see and hear this *Brahman*. One who meditates on this light becomes beautiful and bright. Man's life is filled with three sacrifices—

- His first 24 years are the morning oblation, for the *Gayatri mantra* related to morning oblation has 24 syllables.
- The next 44 years are his mid-day oblations, *Tristubh mantra* related to this oblation is made up of 44 syllables.
- The next 48 years are the third oblation as the *Jagati mantra* associated with this has 48 syllables.

He who knows this doctrine of sacrifice will live in vigour for 116 years.

Then this *Upanishad* says about reaching the Supreme light – *Brahman*. Many stories relating to meditation on *Brahman* are also given in this *Upanishad.*

It also talks about the doctrine of *Prana*.

4. Jabala Darshana Upanishad

Sankriti, a great sage, an expert in yoga, was a devotee and disciple of Dattatreya, who was the incarnation of Lord Vishnu. He approached his teacher Dattatreya and requested him to impart the knowledge of the science of yoga to him, for attaining salvation. Dattatreya explained the eight *angas* or parts of yoga as *Yama, Niyama, Asana, Pranayama, Pratyahara, Dharana, Dhyana* and *Samadhi*.

Yama relates to the practice of non-violence, truth, non-stealing, celibacy, mercy, honesty, patience, stability, food discipline and cleanliness.

Niyama is perseverance, joy, charity, worshipping God, listening to philosophy, fear of bad actions, clear intellect, chanting and austerities.

The nine important *asanas* or postures are namely, Swastika, Gomukha, Padma, Veera or valour, Simha, Badra or safe, Muktha, Mayura and Sukha.

The yogi should fix a proper *asana* to practise *pranayama*. For this a clean, even, and pleasant place without any disturbance should be selected. The yogi should face east or north. The body should be kept erect and one must concentrate on the tip of the nose. Then he should practise *pranayama*. One should practise this exercise three to four days a week at dawn, noon and dusk. This cleans the *Nadis*.

Then the yogi should practise *pratyahara*. It is diverting the sensory organs by force. Then *dharana* should be practised. The yogi should hold on what he is meditating upon. *Dharana* destroys all sins. This *Upanishad* explains the five types of *Dharana*. One should practise *Dharana* that destroys sorrows.

Then *Dhyana* should be practised on Lord Shiva who is the form of *Para Brahman*. Then one should practise *dhyana* of Him who is beyond the reach of meditation, the *Sachidananda*, for attaining salvation.

Then comes *Samadhi,* which destroys the ills of birth and death. In this stage, one realises that *Jeevatma* and *Paramatma* are one and the same, although due to illusion different. When the entire world appears as one, he is cured of all sorrows.

After attaining this knowledge, Sankriti lost all his fear and attained the blissful state.

5. Jabala Upanishad

Sage Pippalada approached Sage Jabali and asked him to teach him the secret of the absolute philosophy as to what is *Sattva* or Principle, *Jiva* or being, *Ishwara*, and the method for salvation.

Jabali replied, "*Jiva* is God acting as Ego. This *Jiva* is *Pashu*, or *Pashupati*, Shiva, the Lord of all beings who knows everything. To acquire the knowledge, one should take holy ash, recite the five *Brahma Mantras*, mix it with water, and apply three lines on the forehead and shoulders chanting the three mantras."

The **first** line is *Garhapatya* or the domestic fire, *Rajas*, earth, *Jivatma*, power of creation, *Rig Veda*, dawn and Brahma.

The **second** line is *Dakshinagni* or fire of the south, *Sattva*, atmosphere, soul, desire, *Yajur Veda*, noon, and Lord Vishnu.

The **third** line is *Ahavaneya Agni* or the fire of Sun, *Tamas*, *Paramatma*, place of Gods, power of knowledge, *Sama Veda*, dusk and Lord Shiva.

The one who applies the holy ash with this knowledge gets rid of all sins and has no rebirth.

6. Kenopanishad

Kena means 'by whom'. This *Upanishad* is one of the oldest ones and is also known as *Talavakara* since it belongs to the *Talavakara Brahmana* of the *Jaimini Shakha* of the *Sama Veda*. There are two sections of prose and two sections of poetry in this *Upanishad*. The verses deal with the Absolute principle, the Supreme unqualified *Brahman*, that is behind the world of phenomenon and the prose deals with the Supreme as *Ishwara* or God.

In this *Upanishad* we find Goddess Ambika or Amba or Uma appearing as *Jnanambika* or the Goddess of *jnana* or Supreme knowledge. Ambika appears to give instructions about the doctrine of *Brahman*, knowledge or Supreme reality to Indra, the King of the *devas*, when the *devas* in their arrogance failed to recognise the Supreme Being. This *Upanishad* says that the knowledge of *Ishwara* would reveal the path to self-realisation. The *devas*, once after defeating the demons, showed extreme vanity with the thought that there is none above them. They forgot that their success was due to God's divine grace. In order to destroy their vanity, *Brahman* appeared before them as a *Yaksha*. But the *devas* did not know who the *Yaksha* was. *Devas* went to Vayu and Agni to find out about the *Yaksha*. Agni and Vayu were made to understand that Agni cannot burn even a grass and Vayu cannot blow away even a small blade of grass by themselves. Then Indra, the king of *devas* went near *Yaksha* and the *Yaksha* disappeared. Indra then went to Himavati, the daughter of Himavan and asked her who the *Yaksha* was. She revealed to them his true identity who was nothing but *Brahman*. She explained to Indra that all power emanated from the one Great power. It is *Brahman* the one, which the mind cannot grasp. It is not seen or heard, or smelt. On the contrary, it is the power by which man sees, hears and smells. The one who realises *Brahman* and withdraws from the world attains immortality.

The knowledge of *Ishwara* or *Saguna Brahman*, that is *Apara Vidya*, places one on the pathway that leads to *Karma Mukti* or deliverance from actions performed. Gradually, the soul acquires the higher wisdom, the knowledge of the Absolute or *Nirguna Brahman* that is *Para Vidya* that results in the consciousness of its identity with the Supreme *Brahman* and leads to liberation. Austerity, restraint, and work are the foundation of the mystical doctrine, the Vedas are its limbs, truth is its home. He who knows this Truth achieves unison with the infinite, blissful and supreme *Brahman*.

7. Kundika Upanishad

After studying *Upanishads* during *Brahmacharya*, the *brahmachari* marries a suitable girl with the permission of the teacher. Then he takes up *Grihasthashrama* or the life of a householder. At the end of this second stage, he has to kindle a sacred fire to become a forest-dweller or *Vanaprastha*, and perform a sacrifice for one day and night. Then he has to divide his property among his sons in a proper manner, give up all sensory pleasures and should proceed to sacred places as a *Vanaprastha* along with his wife as a friend. He should take minimum food, mainly fruits and water. He should practise self-restraint.

After some time, he should take up *Sanyasa* or renunciation. At this stage, there is no need for mantras as the individual crosses that stage. He should dress as a monk, and should have no permanent abode. He should ponder over Vedanta and meditate on *Brahman*. He should sleep on sand or outside a temple. He should always remain calm under all circumstances and should maintain even mindedness. Then he would realise the identity of individual self with the Universal Self, which is the meaning of *AUM*.

With the practice of yoga, the ascetic realises *Brahman*. The sages who attain the transcendental state never return to worldly life. They are unaffected by everything that goes around them as they know that they are experiencing bliss. Such people attain the final liberation.

8. Mahopanishad

In the beginning of creation, when Lord Narayana was alone, he could not be happy. From the desire of the *Paramatman*, the *Yajnastoma*, that is the hymn known as *Avyakta* arose. From it arose fourteen *Purusha* like Brahma, Vishnu, Rudra and so on, one maiden called *Mula Prakriti*, ten organs pertaining to perception and action, the mind, bright intellect, ego, *Prana, Atma, Buddhi* or intelligence, *Kama* or passion, *Karma* or work and *Tamas*, five *Tanmantras*, along with gross elements, then the Being.

The *Paramatman* employed Being in creation and he himself remained detached. Again, from Vishnu, a person with Trident arose with three eyes and with all the best qualities along with *Pranava*, *Rik*, and the other Vedas, and all meters. Again from the sweat on the forehead of the Supreme Being came waters. From it a bright golden egg was born. That was the four-headed Brahma facing east. Narayana then became everything, facing all the four directions and upwards. Thus, the Cosmos is the manifestation of that Being. He exists and at the same time does not exist because He is existence itself. The dissolution and creation of the Universe are due to the contraction and expansion of that Power. It is reality, bliss, knowledge and nothing else.

Sukha, the son of Vyasa, knew all this by his subtle intellect. Once he asked his father about how the wordly life was created and how it gets dissolved. Vyasa imparted the knowledge to his son. But he had already known it. So Vyasa asked him to approach Janaka, the king of Mithila to obtain this knowledge and so Sukha went to Janaka.

There he was made to wait for seven days and later Janaka gave him all the pleasures of the world, but Sukha was unmindful of these pleasures. Janaka, after making sure of Sukha's nature, asked him what he wanted from him. Sukha then put the same questions to Janaka that he had put to his father, Vyasa. He asked Janaka to tell the Truth.

Then Janaka gave him all details of knowledge, the essence of wisdom, by knowing which, one gets liberated while living. The joy of liberation or *Nirvana* arises when the mind detaches itself from all the materialistic objects. Brooding over objects is bondage. Rejection of them is liberation. The one who is liberated while living will have no taste for enjoyment. He is untouched by exaltation, anger, fear, lust, and meanness. He is free from all kinds of desire. He performs without expectations, likes and dislikes, joy and grief, virtue and vice, success and failure. He is egoless, prideless, silent, has no jealousy, and is calm. He exists like a detached onlooker and functions without any attachment or desire. He has no *Dharma* or *Adharma*, thought, joy, grief, desire, birth or death. All tastes are the same for him. He does not hanker after worldly pleasures. Although he has a mind, he is like the one who has no mind. At the time of death, this *Jivan Mukta* enters the state of *Adeha Mukta* and is liberated without body.

After gathering this knowledge, Sukha went to the peak of the Meru Mountain for trance. There he remained in trance for thousands of years. This *Upanishad* then narrates the story of Niadha, a lad, who after visiting more than 3 crores of sacred places told Ribhu that after bathing in so many places, a question as to how to get out of sorrow which is the consequence of all worldly pleasures has arisen in his mind.

This *Upanishad* then tells about the knowledge that was imparted by Ribhu.

9. Maitrayani Upanishad

This Upanishad is comparatively a later one. In this, Maitri is the principal teacher and Maitrayana is the *shakha* to which this *Upanishad* belongs. It is divided into four *prapathikas* or divisions. It advocates meditation on the soul.

The **first** *prapathika* tells about the boon asked by King Brihadratha who after becoming detached, retired to the forest after crowning his eldest son as the king. The king performed great penance for about 1000 years and finally Sage Shakhayana came to him and told him to ask for a boon. The king bowed to the sage in great reverence and asked him to impart the knowledge of the Self. But the sage tried to persuade the king to ask for some other boon, as this knowledge, which many others sought in the past was impossible to impart. But the king had only one desire and that was to know about Self. So he requested the sage to uplift him with that knowledge which he had asked.

In the **second** *prapathika,* the reply of Sage Shakhayana is told. He said that the body is like a cart without intelligence. The reins are the five organs of perception, the steeds are the organs of action and the charioteer is the mind. The soul cannot be described. It is immortal, unmanifested, subtle, imperceptible, incomprehensible, selfless, pure, steadfast, stainless, desireless, fearless and self-abiding, and it dispels darkness. The elemental Self due to ignorance on account of results of good and bad actions does not comprehend the soul that is within oneself. By knowledge, yoga and meditation, God is realised and one attains union with the soul that is identical with various Gods and powers. Then the sage taught *Brahma Vidya* imparted by Sage Maitreya.

Once, the radiant and chaste Valakhilyas requested *Prajapati* to tell them about the cause that drives the body. Then *Prajapati* said, the one who is beyond speech, is pure, holy, independent, endless, unchangeable, eternal and so on is the driver of the body. The Self that is subtle is the *Purusha*. The conscious part of this *Purusha* is the knower of the body in each person. When *Prajapati* alone was there, before creation, he was not happy. Through his desire, all creatures were born. They were unaware of this supreme power. So to kindle their awareness He entered into them, by making himself five-fold air, namely, *Prana, Apana, Vyana, Udana* and *Samana*. *Prana Vayu* moves upward, *Apana Vayu* moves downward. *Samana* causes the food to settle and circulate to all parts of the body equally, *Udana* sends down the liquid and food, and *Vyana* pervades all the nerves. The fire within, the cosmic fire and the inner fire digests the food that is eaten. The Supreme Being established himself in the cave of the heart. He makes the body revolve like a wheel. This Self depends on the non-Self by the fruit of actions according to which one is born.

The **third** *prapathika* tells about the other Self that experiences both birth as well as death according to past good or bad *Karmas*. This Self that is like a drop of water on a lotus leaf is overwhelmed by *prakriti* and is, therefore, in a state of delusion. It does not see the Lord in itself. This Self binds itself, as in a net due to ignorance.

In the **fourth** *prapathika*, the delusion caused by *maya* is explained. Attached to the sense objects, the Self forgets itself and this results in repeated births and deaths. The remedy lies in following one's own *Dharma*. It is said, that by *Satvic* qualities, the mind is refined and from the refined mind, the spirit is got, which stops the transmigration. When a person makes his mind free from delusion, he reaches the mindless state. This is the knowledge and also liberation. Mind is the cause for bondage and also liberation. When it is attached to objects, it causes bondage, and when it is detached from objects liberation is obtained.

10. Maitreya Upanishad

This *Upanishad* advocates that by the purity of mind, one is able to destroy the effects of good and bad actions. One enjoys unlimited bliss, when one remains in the Self with a pure mind. Those who discard worldly life and happiness achieve the bliss of the Self and get merged in *Brahman*.

Sage Maitreya went to Kailasha and requested Lord Shiva to impart to him the secret of the supreme Truth and the Lord replied.

The body is the temple and the individual self is Shiva. One should worship God with the belief that **'He and I are one'**. Bathing is removing the impurity of the mind, and cleansing is controlling the senses. One should live on alms and become devoted to Him. Such a person attains liberation. Mental cleanliness is the discarding of the three inborn tendencies namely —

- *Loka vasana*, or the worldly desires
- *Shastra vasana,* or the desire for the scriptures
- *Deha vasana,* or the desire of the body

The alms is the feeling of non-duality. After embracing renunciation, one should live far away from all his people. When one moves away from the son of ego, who is the brother of wealth, and the wife, the home of delusion, one is liberated. For such person, there is no need to go to a hermitage or interior of forest, for performing meditation. True renunciation does not consist in discarding action or by reciting mantras. It is the oneness of the *Jiva* or the individual self with *Atman*, or the Universal Self. Only when dispassion for all worldly objects arises in one's mind, one should think of renunciation. This *Upanishad* says, the wisest ones take up to contemplation of *Brahman*, the middle ones contemplate on scriptures, low people think of mantras and the lowest are deluded by the effectiveness of holy places. The worship of idols results in repeated births and deaths. Hence the sage should perform worship in his heart only, contemplating on *Brahman* that is enshrined in one's heart, that is not different from the Self. The one who fully understands what is *Brahman*, without any delusion, the one who listens to this knowledge with supreme faith, becomes merged with *Brahman*.

11. Rudraksha Jabala Upanishad

Bhusunda asked Lord Kalagni Rudra about the beginning of Rudraksha beads and the benefit of wearing them on the body. Lord Kalagni Rudra replied, "Once I closed my eyes for 1000 celestial years for destroying Tripura demon. From the closed eyes, teardrops fell on the earth blessing the devotees and they became Rudraksha beads. By mere utterance of the name Rudraksha, one gets the benefit of giving ten cows in charity and by seeing and touching it one attains double that benefit. By wearing it, one gets rid of all the sins. When one meditates with Rudraksha band, then their powers are immense. Among Rudrakshas, one which is as big as the *amlaka* is the best; one as big as the berry is considered the middle sort and the Rudraksha that is as big as a Bengal gram belongs to the lowest of all categories. One should use Rudrakshas of good quality only. The Rudrakshas that are eaten by worms or broken or are without thorn, should be avoided. The self-holed Rudraksha is the best variety. A devotee should wear Rudraksha all over his body. Wearing 1000 beads is the best of all. The devotee should utter the mantras while wearing Rudrakshas."

Then Bhusunda asked Lord Kalagni Rudra about the different forms and effects of Rudraksha beads, their various faces, and the means of getting rid of all evils. Lord Kalagni Rudra replied, "The bead with one face is of the form of Supreme Truth. This is the best. The one with two faces is of the form of *Ardhanareeshvara* or Lord Shiva as the right half of the body along with Parvati who is the left part of the body. The bead with three faces is the form of three fires. That with four faces is a manifestation of the four headed Brahma, the one with five faces symbolises *Pancha Brahmas* or the five-faced Shiva, that with six faces is the form of Kartikeya or Ganesha, that with seven faces is of the form of seven Mother Goddesses. The Rudraksha with eight faces is of the form of the eight-fold nature, namely, the five elements, mind, ego and matter, that with nine faces is of the form of the *Nava Shaktis* or nine powers, that with ten faces is of the form of ten *yamas* or the means used by yogis to attain peace, that with eleven faces is of the form of eleven Rudras, that with twelve faces is of the form of Maha Vishnu, that with thirteen faces is of the form of *Kama* or God of Love, and that with fourteen faces is of the form of Rudra. The devotee who wears any of these gets the corresponding blessings. One who wears Rudrakshas should take only *Satvic* food. He should avoid intoxicants. Wearing Rudrakshas during eclipses, on Makara Sankranti day, new moon, full moon and other auspicious days frees one from all sins.

The base of the Rudraksha bead is **Brahma**, navel is **Vishnu**, its face is **Rudra** and its hole symbolises **all the Gods**.

One day Sanat Kumara asked Kalagni Rudra to tell him about the method of wearing Rudraksha beads. At that time, many sages also came there and told Kalagni Rudra that they all had come there to know about the method of wearing Rudraksha, Then Kalagni Rudra elaborated on the good effects of wearing Rudrakshas and imparted the knowledge which they sought from him.

This *Upanishad* ends by telling the great effects of studying and reciting the *Rudraksha Jabala Upanishad*.

12. Sanyasa Upanishad

There are two *adhyayas* or chapters in this *Upanishad*.

The **first** chapter is a short one. It tells about how one has to enter into *Sanyasa* and how the *sanyasi* should live, eat and so on.

The **second** chapter tells about the one who is entitled to renunciation, its rules, who can renounce, how the *sanyasi* should behave, the six kinds of renunciation, the nature and appearance of six kinds of *sanyasis*, namely the *Kutichaka, Bahudaka, Hamsa, Parama Hamsa, Turiyatitha* and *Avadhuta*, the alms received by the *sanyasi*, and how he should speak, and so on. The ascetic has to practise meditation on the nature of Self only. For a *sanyasi*, the study of scriptures, yoga, *Sankhya*, rituals with mantra, *tantras*, study of any other religious texts, are all useless. When he becomes old and weak, he should repeat the mantra *AUM*, 12000 times a day as it destroys sins. In such a *sanyasi*, the Supreme *Brahman* shines within a period of one year.

13. Savitri Upanishad

Agni is *Savitar*, and earth is *Savitri*. *Agni* and earth are seen together. In the same way, *Varuna* is *Savitar* and water is *Savitri*, air is *Savitar* and ether is *Savitri*, sacrifice is *Savitar* and meter is *Savitri*, thunder is *Savitar* and lightning is *Savitri*, moon is *Savitar* and the stars are *Savitri*, man is *Savitar* and the woman *Savitri*, mind is *Savitar* and the world is *Savitri*.

The first foot of *Savitri* is the earth, the second is the mind region, and the third foot is firmament or sky that inspires our thoughts. He who knows this to be *Savitri*, conquers death.

The *Upanishad* then tells about the two mantras, *Bala* and *Ati bala* for which *Virat Purusha* is the seer, *Gayatri* the meter, and the deity is *AUM*. These mantras remove hunger and fatigue. The one who knows and meditates on these mantras accomplishes all his tasks and shares the realm with *Savitri*.

14. Vajra Suchika Upanishad

This *Upanishad* tells about *Vajra suchi* or the diamond needle that pierces ignorance, rebukes the ignorant and praises those who have wisdom. It answers the question as to who is a Brahmin. The soul is not a Brahmin as it is the same in all beings. No single colour can characterise a Brahmin. The body is also not the criteria as it is the same for everyone being is made up of the five elements. It does not depend upon birth either as there, as there had been many sages who did not have a noble birth.

Sage Rishya Shringa was born of a deer, Kaushika of reed, Jambuka of a jackal, Valmiki of an anthill, Vyasa of a fisherwoman, Gautama of a hare's back, Vashishtha of Urvashi and Agastya from a pot. They became Brahmins on account of their knowledge. Also *Karma* is not the mark of a Brahmin because *Karma* is found in all creatures. Only the one who has realised the *Atman* or *Brahman*, which is beyond knowledge, and which is realised by his experience after prolonged meditation can alone be called as a Brahmin.

This *Upanishad* says, that this is the intention of the Vedas etc. The others cannot be considered as Brahmins.

15. Vasudeva Upanishad

Sage Narada requested Lord Narayana to teach him the rules of *Urdhva Pundra,* that is, the religious marks which are vertical and point upwards in those who follow Vaishnavism.

Lord Narayana replied, "After worshipping Vishnu, the *Brahmachari* and the *Grihastha* should apply *Urdhva Pundra* on his forehead and other twelve places of his body with his ring finger, reciting either the *Vishnu Gayatri* or the twelve names of Lord Vishnu. The *sanyasi* should apply the *Urdhva Pundra* with his fourth finger on the head, forehead and chest chanting the *Pranava Mantra*, *AUM*. The *Urdhva Pundras* like the *Trimurtis*, the three states of mind, the three worlds that are *Bhur, Bhuva, Suva*, are three namely, '*Aa*', '*Uu*', and '*Ma*'. These *Urdhva Pundras* are full of *Prana* and full of letter *AUM*, that becomes many. The Lord of *AUM* takes one above and hence the need to apply *Urdhva Pundra*. The sage, who wears the four things upwards, namely, the stick, bravery, yoga and *Urdhva Pundra* attains Salvation."

16. Yoga Choodamani Upanishad

This *Upanishad* is given with a view to do good to yogis. The *Jeevatma* is under the control of *Prana*, which goes up and down. *Apana* pulls *Prana* and vice-versa. The one, who realises this mutual pull of *Prana* and *Apana* from top to bottom, understands yoga. The *Vayu* goes out with the sound '*Ha*', and inward with the sound '*Sa*'. Together the beings keep on chanting this mantra as '*Hamsa*' each day and night. Each being keeps on chanting this mantra for 21,100 times. This mantra that is called *Ajapa Gayatri* gives salvation to all yogis. Even the very thought of this mantra helps one to get rid of all sins. It is the holiest of all practices, the greatest of all chantings and it is the highest wisdom.

The *Ajapa Gayatri* rises from *Kundalini* and supports the soul. The one who knows this will know the Vedas. The power of *Kundalini* located above *Mooladhara* is in eight-studded form. It covers the mouth of *Sushumna*, which is the gate of *Brahman*. This Kundalini Parameshwari, the Goddess of the Universe who should pass through the gate of *Brahman*, closes this gate with her mouth and sleeps. The heat generated by the practice of yoga, the speed of wind and her mental power make her stand up. With her needle-shaped body, she goes upwards through the *Sushumna Nadi*. The yogi should open the gate of salvation by using the key of *Kundalini*.

Para Brahman is *AUM* that is the *Turiya*, the one without a second, that cannot be described. From that *Para Brahman* emerges *Para Shakti*, the female aspect, that is the soul. From soul ether arose, from ether wind arose, from wind fire arose, from fire arose water and from water arose the earth. The five Godheads namely, Sadashiva, Ishwara, Rudra, Vishnu and Brahma rule over these five elements.

Brahma who was the first of the *devas* became the Creator. **Vishnu** upkeeps and **Rudra** destroys.

This *Upanishad* explains about the organs of wisdom, the organs of action, *Linga Shareera*, the three properties of the body, and the four states of the body. The *Atma* in the form of *AUM* resides in the body.

Then this *Upanishad* elaborates upon the three letters of '*Aa*', '*Uu*', and '*Ma*'. *Pranava* is the ultimate God or *Para Brahman*. It is upward looking in the case of people with wisdom. In others, it is downward looking. The sound of *Pranava* is continuous and its peak is *Brahman*. The organs tie up the living being but *Paramatma* is not.

AUM is the ethereal light and it has to be meditated upon by the mind. The one who continuously chants *Pranava* is able to destroy his sins.

Pranayama is twelve repetitions of *AUM* called *Pooraka*, followed by sixteen repetitions of *AUM* called *Kumbhaka* and then followed by ten repetitions of *AUM* called *Rechaka*. Chanting of *Pranayama* 12 times only with the sign of sweating is poor, 24 times with the sign of trembling is medium, and 36 times is the best. With this, the objective is attained. A yogi should salute his teacher and Lord Shiva and sit alone in Lotus position, concentrate his sight on the tip of his nose and practise *Pranayama*. A proper posture leads to avoidance of diseases. *Pranayama* avoids sins.

With *Pratyahara*, where the sensory organs are turned inward, one is able to control his mental activity.

Samadhi gives knowledge and helps in achieving salvation.

6

Yajur Veda

Yajur Veda Samhita

Yajur Veda is the book of rituals and contains the wisdom of sacrifices or *yajna*. It applies to the entire sacrificial rites. It refers to the actual conduct and acts of worship such as oblations offered to *Agni*. It deals with different types of *yajnas*. It is devoted to rituals and rites and explains the acts and wisdom of worship. It meets the demand for ceremonial religion. This Veda has various chants to pray and pay respect to the various instruments involved in sacrifice. The instruments are believed to symbolise aspects of *Brahman*. There are also a few hymns addressed to various Gods although the main emphasis is on the theory of rituals. In a deeper sense, this Veda explains the yogic practices to be followed for purifying the mind and awakening the inner consciousness of man. The rituals are meant for recreating the Universe within oneself and also to achieve union with the Universe.

Lord Vishnu and Lord Shiva are mentioned in this Veda. *Prajapati*, the Creator of the world is identified with *Vishvakarma*, the chief architect of the Universe. *Brahman* signifies the creative principle of the world. This Veda is used as a guide by the Yajur Vedic priest called *Adhvaryu* who recites the hymns in low voice explaining the rites in *yajnas*.

The hymns are largely taken from *Rig Veda*. Nearly 581 Rig Vedic mantras are repeated in this Veda. Here we find the practical application of the Rig Vedic hymns in *yajna*. Most part of this

Veda is in prose and describes the actual conduct of the rites. These priests execute the sacrificial acts in the *yajnas* by simultaneously muttering the prose prayers and the sacrificial formulae. This Veda is the smallest of all the Vedas.

Yajur is derived from the word *Yajus* meaning reverence, veneration or sacrifice. The mantras in this Veda are also called *Yajus*. It contains the famous *Gayatri mantra* too. It discusses the concept of numeric infinity. This Veda also states that if you subtract *purna* from *purna*, then only *purna* remains. This Veda is believed to have been written around the 10th century BC which corresponds to the Iron Age.

Hymns of Yajur Veda

The hymns found in *Yajur Veda* are prayers to the Creator to inspire us to perform good deeds and not become wicked. One is asked to follow and protect truth and perform all his duties fearlessly. The hymns comprise the prayers for knowledge, for following the path of truth fearlessly and to perform the duties of the family religiously.

Fire or *Agni* is prayed for protecting the body, for long life, for radiance, for soft and sweet speech, for liberation and to discourage wrongdoings and actions, for the inspiration and encouragement to do good actions, to walk on that path that gives happiness and where there is no destruction and unhappiness and chance to go astray, to make the mind stable, to be egalitarian, and destroy illusion, for good food, for long life and for protection from sins.

Sun or *Surya* is prayed for his blessings.

Rudra is worshipped for annihilation of ailments, liberation from death and for cessation of all attachments and for constructive and good thinking.

The husband and wife are advised in *Yajur Veda* to destroy the fear and instability in the mind and make the *Atma* strong, full of enthusiasm and optimism for engaging in good actions that will result in domestic happiness and all comforts.

By following *Yama* (non-violence, truthfulness, abstinence from stealing, celibacy, and abstinence from amassing unnecessary wealth) and *Niyama* (cleanliness, contentment, penance, and devotion), one can protect all the internal energies which help in destroying all miseries and achieving prosperity. There are prayers for good health, stable mind and energy. Humans are asked to lead a disciplined and orderly life. The scholars are asked to impart their knowledge to others who are ignorant. This will ensure their development of the self and spiritual progress simultaneously. The *Agni* within should always be kindled. All knowledge is to be acquired from one's heart, mind and senses. The source of knowledge is not outside us but within us.

At the outset, this Veda seems to be the Veda of rituals and sacrifices. Inwardly, this Veda provides a yogic system for purifying the mind and awakening of the inner consciousness of man. The external act of ritual is only to recreate the Universe within our own psyche with the aim of uniting the individual with the universal. The culmination of the sacrifice is nothing but sacrifice of the self and that is *Atmajnana* (knowledge of self) where one's ego is offered to the divine.

The lesser sacrifices that are materialistic win the lesser worlds. Whereas the sacrifice of the self wins all the worlds and gives the greatest gift of immortality. Thus the mystical or the inner meaning of this Veda is the purification and elevation of consciousness through rituals that are meant to uncover the higher self, rising above man's ego and the material life. In this way, this Veda systemises the *Karma Yoga* or the path of deeds.

The Krishna and Shukla Yajur Veda

Originally there was only one *Yajur Veda*. Later it got divided into two branches —

- *Krishna Yajur Veda*
- *Shukla Yajur Veda*

The *Krishna* or *Taittiriya* is the older *Yajur Veda* and the *Shukla Yajur Veda*, is the latter one. The *Samhitas* of both these branches of *Yajur Vedas* were originally compiled by Vaishampayana. He taught this Veda to his disciple Yajnavalkya who was also his nephew. Later there were serious differences of opinion between the two of them regarding the interpretation of the Veda. The Guru then bade his disciple to throw out all that he had taught him. Yajnavalkya obeyed his Guru's commands. The other disciples of Vaishampayana were believed to have assumed the form of *teetar* birds and they ate all the knowledge that Yajnavalkya had vomited. Yajnavalkya then went to the Sun God, Surya. Surya taught him a new Veda that later came to be known as the *Shukla Yajur Veda*. The earlier Veda came to be known as the *Krishna Yajur Veda*.

In the *Krishna Yajur Veda*, the explanations and directions that follow the verses are incorporated in the work. Hence there are explanatory portions in this. The Krishna Yajur Veda has 7 *Kands*. Each *Kand* is divided into several *prapathikas* that are further subdivided in to *anuvakas*. The *Krishna Yajur Veda* deals with rituals. The *Brahmana* passages are mixed here. In this, each *anuvaka* is assigned with a title. Some of the hymns in this *Samhita* namely, *Sri Rudram, Chamakam*, and *Shaivite Trayambakam mantra* have gained great importance. The terms *Bhur, Bhuva, Suva* that are prefixed to the *Gayatri mantra* of the *Rig Veda* are found in the *Yajur Veda* four times.

Sri Aurobindo remark that the content of this Veda can be taken either as a poetical and legendary description of the happenings in Vedic times or it can be interpreted in its inner meaning as symbolic of the struggle between the spiritual powers on the one side and darkness on the other side, truth and falsehood, knowledge and ignorance death and immortality. For example, *Panis* and *Vratras* that are mentioned in the Veda are the human enemies in their outer sense. But in its inner meaning, represent the powers of darkness and evil. Similarly the seven *Angirasas* are symbolic of the powers of *Agni* or the divine flame representing the will. Sacrifice is symbolic of giving up everything that one possesses to the Divine. Again the offerings are also symbolic. However to comprehend the inner meaning is extremely difficult.

The *Shukla Yajur Veda* contains only mantras necessary for the sacrifices. The explanations are given separately. There are branches or *shakhas* in both the *Yajur Veda*. However there are differences of opinion regarding the number of *shakhas* and mantras.

Shakhas of Krishna Yajur Veda

The *Krishna Yajur Veda* originally had 101 *shakhas* but only 4 of them are known now. They are —

1. *Taittiriya Samhita* of Panchala (*Apasthambi Samhita*)
2. *Maitrayani Samhita*
3. *Karaka Katha Samhita* of Madraand
4. *Kapisthala Katha Samhita* of Bahika

The best known is the *Taittiriya Samhita*. It is named after Tittiri, a pupil of Yaska. The *Taittariya shakha* is practised all over South India now. Previously it was said to have existed in North India only.

The *Maitrayani Shakha* is found in Gujarat and Maharashtra.

The *Karaka Katha* is found in interior Maharashtra.

The *Kapisthala Yajur Veda* was once found in West Punjab, and Gujarat, but only fragmentary texts are available now.

The *Taittiriya Samhita* deals specifically with the detailed description of sacrifices like *Paurodasa, Yajamana, Agnishtoma, Jyothishtoma, Vajpeya, Rajasuya, Dasapurnamasa,* and *Soma yagas* and so on. This *Samhita* consists of 7 books or *Kands*. It is further subdivided into 5 to 8 *prapathikas* or chapters each and has a total of 44 *prapathikas* and 651 *anuvakas* or mantras. The other three *Samhitas* are not well-known though they deal with similar sacrifices like that found in the *Taittiriya Samhita.*

Brahmanas of Krishna Yajur Veda

In this Veda, the *Brahmanas* are not separate as they are appended to the *Samhitas*. They are two in number —

1. *Taittiriya Brahmana*
2. *Vadhula* or *Anuvakhyana Brahmana*

In the *Taittiriya Brahmana* there are three *Kands*. The first two Kands are divided into eight chapters each and the third *Kand* is divided into twelve *adhyayas*. The *Brahmana* is also divided into

Anuvakas or sections, sometimes containing sentences on a particular topic. This *Brahmana* contains 17480 sentences in total.

- The **first** *Kand* deals with the *Agnyadana, Govamayana, Vajpeya, Soma, Nakshatreshti* and *Rajasuya.*
- The **second** *Kand* deals with *Agnihotra, Upahomas, Sautramani* and *Vaisyasava.*
- The **third** and final *Kand* gives some additional details on the *Nakshatreshti*, the *Ashvamedha* and some parables of Bharadwaja along with *Purushamedha yajna.*

The second *Brahmana,* the *Vadhula Brahmana* or the *Anuvakhyana Brahmana,* is a minor *Brahmana* and is in the *Vadhula Shrautasutra.* It is in the form of a manuscript.

Aranyakas of Krishna Yajur Veda

There are three *Aranyakas* of *Krishna Yajur Veda*. They are —

Taittiriya Aranyaka

It has ten chapters.

- The **first** chapter deals with *Surya Namaskar.*
- The **second** chapter describes in all minute details the five *mahayajna* that every Brahmin should perform daily.
- The **third** and the **fourth** chapters are concerned with further technicalities of the other *homas* and *yajnas*. The fourth chapter has a section on the mantras that are used to avert or cause havoc.
- The **fifth** is an academic treatise on *yajna.*
- The **sixth** deals with the *Pitramedha* mantras and is chanted at rituals for disposing the dead body.
- The **seventh**, **eighth**, and **ninth** chapters form the *Taittiriya Upanishad.*
- The **tenth** chapter is the *Mahanarayana Upanishad* containing several important mantras taken from the other Vedas.

Maitrayaniya Aranyaka

There are seven *prapathikas* in this. The major portion contains *Maitrayaniya Upanishad.*

Katha Aranyaka

It has three *prapathikas*. The second and the third *prapathikas* deal with *parvargya* rites.

Upanishads of Krishna Yajur Veda

There are 32 *Upanishads* belonging to *Krishna Yajur Veda*. They are —

1. Akshi Upanishad

This *Upanishad* is in two parts.

- The **first** part starts with the glorification of Sun by Rishi Samkriti and his request to God for leading him from the unreal to the Real, from darkness to Light, and from death to Immortality.
- In the **second** part, Samkriti asks the Sun God to teach him *Brahma-vidya* and the Sun in turn imparted the knowledge of Reality to Samkriti for liberation. He emphasised performing actions rooted in yoga only, studying *shastras* and attaining the first stage of yoga.

  Then he talks about the next stage of yoga called *Vichara*.
- The **third** stage of non-attachment is general, concerned with non-involvement in objects, and also specific and which is superior namely, the silence, repose, and motionless where non-duality is established.
- About the **fourth** stage, he describes that it is achieved by the exercise of the earlier three stages.
- The **fifth** stage is the dissolution of the mind, where one survives but only as a being.
- Then there is a mention of attaining the **sixth** stage in which there is neither existence nor non-existence, neither 'I' nor 'Non-I'.

- Finally comes the **seventh** stage which is the state of embodied liberation and where everything is nothing but *AUM.* It also provides the explanation of *AUM.*

2. Amrita Bindu Upanishad

This *Upanishad* discusses about the pure and impure mind. It says that the pure mind is without desires and the impure mind is with desires. The mind attached to sensual objects leads to bondage, while the mind that is devoid of attachments leads to liberation. Pure mind is needed for the one who seeks liberation. In the supreme state of mind, the impure mind is destroyed and is brought under control within the heart. The supreme state is nothing but the eternal Bliss. The *Upanishad* also advocates meditation on *AUM* and the realisation of **'I am that *Brahman*'**. It also says that the one who has transcended the three states of waking, dreaming and dreamless sleep gets freed from the cycle of rebirth. The one and the only Universal Soul is present in all beings, and meditating on the imperishable *Brahman* leads to the attainment of the highest state of *Brahman. Amrita Bindu Upanishad* stresses that the Vedas are not only for reading, but also for proper understanding and realisation of the Supreme *Brahman.*

3. Amrita Nada Upanishad

This *Upanishad* tells about the need for a wise one to abandon all *shastras* after knowing the *Brahman*. It also tells us about the six parts of yoga. They are —

- *Pratyahara* – subjugating the mind
- *Dhyana* – contemplation
- *Pranayama* – control of breath
- *Dharana* – concentration
- *Dhyana* – meditation
- *Samadhi* – state of bliss

The explanation of each of these parts is given in this *Upanishad.*

It also talks about practising of yoga, about things that are to be avoided in yoga for spiritual wisdom namely, fear, anger, laziness, too much of sleep or waking, too much of food and fasting. The *Upanishad* also discusses about absence of rebirth for the one whose breath goes out of the head and is purified through the pineal gland.

4. Avadhuta Upanishad

This *Upanishad* deals with the questions put by Samkriti to Dattatreya about who is an *Avadhuta*, what is his condition, what are his characteristic features, what is his worldly existence, and Dattatreya answering the questions.

"*Avadhuta*," Dattareya says, "is the one who is immortal and the greatest, who is above *varnas* and *ashrams*, beyond all good and bad. He performs *Ashvamedha Yajna* within himself, has no worldly duties, and does not identify the body with the self. He needs neither concentration nor contemplation as he has no distraction. He does not need separate experience as he is eternal experience itself and has gained everything. He is the mere witness for everything, in whom bliss shines brightly and is in union with the God."

5. Brahma Upanishad

This *Upanishad* starts with questions put up by Shounaka to Pippalada as to with whose glory is the creation of the body, the divine city wherein *Brahman* is installed and who that glory is.

Pippalada imparts the supreme wisdom of *Brahman* to Shounaka. The *Prana* and the *Atman* constitutes the glory, and the *Brahman* who shines within the body as the faultless one, self-luminous, all-pervading, controls the *Jiva*.

Just as a spider projects and withdraws the web by means of one thread, similarly *Prana* returns by drawing back. *Prana* belongs to the *nadis* or subtle nerve-chords as the indwelling deity. Like a falcon goes to its nest, the one in dreamless sleep goes through one's own abode. Just as a child enjoys itself without any motive, or desiring any result, similarly the one who is in that state enjoys happiness.

The Self or the Being is the indwelling controller and everything including the cause and effect, the *Brahman* and the *Atman*.

Brahman shines forth from four seats, namely, the navel, the heart, the throat, and the head. In these, he shines with four aspects namely, the state of wakefulness, the state of dream, the state of dreamless sleep and the transcendental state.

- In the **wakeful** state, he is Brahma.
- In the **dreaming** state, he is Vishnu.
- In the **dreamless** sleep state, he is Rudra.
- In the **transcendental** state, he is indescribable.

He is also everything – the Sun, Vishnu, *Ishvara*, *Purusha*, *Prana*, *Jiva*, Fire and so on. The *Brahman* that is transcendental shines within all these. He has no mind, ears, hands, feet, light, worlds, Vedas, *devas*, sacrifices, relationships, and differences existing except the one *Brahman* that is always shining. Within the space of the heart lies the sky of Consciousness in which all this Universe evolves and moves about. For one who knows this need not wear any external sacred thread. For he wears the thread constituted by the awareness of *Brahman*, and the greatest *jnana* or wisdom that is the greatest purifier.

The one Lord who is self-luminous remains hidden in all beings, pervading as the self of all beings, controlling and watching over all works. He exists in all creatures and is the mere witness, the supreme intelligence, one without a second, with no attributes. Eternal peace is for that wise one who realises this. Through truthful and austere practice of meditation, one can realise that.

At that stage, speech falls back with mind and that wise one is released from all kinds of bondage. The centre of wakeful state is in the eyes, for the dreaming state it is in the throat, for the state of dreamless sleep it is the heart and for the transcendental state it is in the crown of the head.

6. Brahma Vidya Upanishad

This *Upanishad* explains the body of the sound *AUM*, the location of the sound *AUM*, the terminus or ending of the sound *AUM*, and the vanishing or fading away of the sound *AUM* in silence.

7. Dakshinamurty Upanishad

Several sages including Shounaka had assembled under a banyan tree called *Maha Bandira* in the land of Brahma for performing fire sacrifice. They approached Sage Markandeya who was wearing the dried twigs of banyan tree and asked him how he had managed to be a *chiranjeevi*, the deathless one, and how he was always in a happy state. For this, Markandeya answered stating that it is because of the knowledge of the most secret philosophy of Lord Shiva, who is *Dakshinamurti*, the one who at the time of the final deluge, keeps everything in himself and shines because of the bliss of his own spirit.

In his secret mantra, Brahma is the sage, Gayatri is the meter, and the God is Dakshinamurti.

The **first** mantra is of 24 letters. It is —

ऊँ नमोभगवते दक्षिणमूर्त्ये मह्यम् मेधां प्रज्ञां प्रयच्छ स्वः ।
Auṁ namo bhagavate dakşinmurtaye
mahyaṁ medhām′ pragyām′ prayaccha swaḥ

The *Upanishad* says that one should perform *dhyana*, mentally saluting him, who is white like a crystal, who holds in his hand a chain of pearl beads, the pot of nectar, that is, knowledge, and the *jnana mudra* symbol of wisdom and who entangles himself with a snake, wears the moon on his head and wears different types of ornaments.

The **second** mantra consists of 9 letters. It is —

ऊँ नम असिवयनं ऊँ।
Auṁ nam asivayanam′ Aum′

One should perform *dhyana*, thinking about the three-eyed God who has the sign of protection in his three hands, and the fourth hand is kept on his knee, who has tied a snake around his body, who shines like white milk, who sits below a banyan tree and who is surrounded by sages like Shuka for giving all pure thoughts.

The **third** mantra is —

ऊँ ब्रूं नमो ह्रीं इं दक्षिणमूर्त्ये ज्ञानं देहि स्वः ।
Auṁ brūm′ namo hṛṁ im′ dakşinamurtaye gyānaṁ dehi swaḥ

Then the *dhyana* is performed thinking ‘let God Dakshinamurti whose body is white due to the application of holy ash, who wears the crystal moon on his head, who holds *jnana mudra* or the symbol of wisdom in his hand with beads of rosary, *veena*, books and ornaments, wearing the hide of elephant, resembling the meditating Rama, sitting on the throne, surrounded by sages, protect all.’

Lord Brahma obtained the wisdom of Creation and became happy, after praying to *Dakshinamurti*. The *Upanishad* ends with a statement that one who reads and understands this secret philosophy of Shiva will get rid of all sins and will attain salvation.

8. Dhyanabindu Upanishad

This *Upanishad* says, that *Dhyana Yoga* destroys even the accumulated sins that one has committed over many *yugas*. When the *Nada* or the spiritual sound stops along with *Beejakshara*, the seed letter, the *Nada,* less supreme state, is obtained. For a yogi, who reaches this stage, all doubts get destroyed. One who is of a firm mind without delusion and ever remaining in *Brahman* should see all creatures like a string in the rosary of beads existing in *Atman* that is everywhere.

The *Purusha* depends on the body for its existence. One who aspires *mukti* or liberation should contemplate on the mantra *AUM* as *Brahman.*

This *Pranava Mantra* is the bow, *Atman* is the arrow and *Brahman* is the aim.

One who aims at it with great care becomes one with it. When that *Brahman* is realised, no *karma* or action affects him. *Omkar* or the mantra *AUM* should be contemplated upon as *Ishvara* or God that resembles an unshaken light, with the size of a thumb, and motionless present in the middlemost part of the Lotus of the Heart with *Pranayama* or regulation and restraint of breath.

One can see God only through *dhyana*. The mind or the *manas* gets absorbed in the Supreme one through *dhyana*. One should meditate upon Lord Vasudeva being in the centre and meditate upon Maha Vishnu as staying in the navel. Then, through expiation, he should meditate on the three-eyed Lord Shiva, between the two eyebrows. Then one should meditate upon Sun, Moon, and *Agni* one above the other. The middle of the eyebrows in the forehead, which is the root of the nose is the seat of nector, where *Brahman* is located.

This *Upanishad* also tells about the six parts of yoga, the yoga postures, about the *Chakras* having twelve spokes and 72,000 *nadis*. Out of these, ten *nadis* are carrying *Prana*. Even out of these, three *nadis* are most important in carrying the *Prana*.

They are, namely, *Ida* on the left, *Pingala* on the right, and *Sushumna*, that is known as the path of the *Prana*, having their *devatas* (the Sun, Moon, and *Agni*) located in the middle.

Jiva is always tossed by *Prana* and *Apana* and is never at rest. *Prana* always draws itself from *Apana* and vice-versa. The *Jiva* comes out with '*Ha*' and gets in with '*Sa*', that is, with the mantra '*Hamsa*'. The *Jiva* utters this mantra 21,600 times in one single day and night. This is called *Ajapa Gayatri*.

The yogi should open the door, which is shut, with great effort, since, *Parameshwari*, or the *Kundalani Shakti* sleeps shutting the door, the door that leads to the everlasting *Brahman-randhra*, with her mouth. The yogi will have to pierce through the door to salvation by means of the *Kundalani Shakti*. This *Upanishad* then discusses about the qualities to be followed by a *yogi.* These qualities are celibacy, moderation in eating and so on for becoming a *Siddha* in little more than a year. The yogi gets *Siddhi* or powers when the *Kundalini Shakti* is up in the throat.

Through *Moola Bandha,* one maintains youth even in old age. The *Upanishad* also tells about *Uddiyana Bandha, Jalandhara Bandha, Mudra Khechari* that prevents disease, death, sleep, hunger and thirst, *Maha-Mudra* that destroys sins.

This *Upanishad* gives a description of *Atman*, its location, its nature during dreamless sleep, about *Prana* that stays everywhere in the body, travelling through the 72,000 *nadis*, and staying in the 28 crores of hair pores, and is yet the same everywhere. It is called *Jiva.*

This *Upanishad* concludes after explaining how to perform yoga and describing about the *Brahman-randhra* that is located between the two eyebrows.

9. Ekakshara Upanishad

This *Upanishad* is a prayer to the Lord of all beings, the *Hiranyagarbha*, the protector of the world, imminent in all, the first born, the omnipresent, the ancient, the principle of life, the manifested world. He is the love in all beings, the supporter, the imperishable, the source from which Vedas proceed, and the divinities and hosts of demons. He is the birthless *Prajapati*, the one whom the sages who perform Vedic sacrifices adore, the eternal dweller in the heart, the supreme goal of the wise, the one transcending all forms of wisdom for protecting and nourishing everyone.

10. Garbha Upanishad

This *Upanishad* points out that the body comprises the five elements of nature, namely, earth, water, fire, wind and ether. It also describes the six tastes of food, six qualities, seven *dhatus*, three impurities, three organs of excretion, and four kinds of food.

It describes about reproduction, the growth of an embryo until it gains complete human form in the eighth month, the birth of male and female babies and eunuchs, the qualities of parents at the time of impregnation which have effect on the child yet to be born, and also the birth of twins. It also highlights the knowledge about past birth and the knowledge of the imperishable *AUM* to the foetus in the eighth month while in mother's womb, the body becoming compete in the ninth month and recognising the good and bad deeds done in the past birth, taking determination not to commit the same mistake of past bad deeds again and resolving to resort to *Sankhya Yoga* that destroys misery, and forgetting all that recognised in the womb by the foteus once it is born in this world.

After explaining all these, the *Upanishad* that is called the scripture of liberation expounded by Pippalada, ends.

11. Kaivalya Upanishad

This *Upanishad* is about Ashvalayana approaching Lord Brahma, and requesting Lord Brahma to teach him the knowledge of *Brahman* that is the highest, cultivated by the good and by which a wise one drives away all the sins and reaches the highest, that is, *Purusha*. This *Upanishad* stresses the importance of renunciation for liberation.

The three states of consciousness namely, waking, dreaming and the dreamless sleep are the compared to earth, heaven and the world of *Brahman*.

This *Upanishad* says that by meditating on Lord Shiva who has three eyes, blue neck, who is ever peaceful, who is the source of all creation, who is the witness of all and who is beyond all darkness, one gets liberated, overcomes death and attains immortality. Some attain immortality by means of faith, devotion and meditation. The self-controlled ones, through the knowledge of Vedanta and *sanyasa* or renunciation realise this reality.

It says that the 'I' is the only witness, the pure consciousness and the eternal God. It is different from the enjoyable, the one who enjoys and the enjoyment. In that 'I' everything is born, rests and gets dissolved. That 'I' is the *Brahman* which is the minutest, the greatest, the manifold Universe, the ancient, and the effulgent one.

The Vedas teach about this *Brahman*, who has revealed the Vedas and *Upanishads*. He is the knower of the Vedas, without merit or demerit, without distinction, without birth, without any self-identity with the body or organs.

There is no earth, water or fire for *Brahman*. One attains pure *Paramatman* by residing in the heart. One who studies *Shatarudriya* gets purified by the fire, and gets absolved from the sin of drinking, from the sin of killing a Brahmin, from evil deeds done knowingly or otherwise, and attains the knowledge for destroying repeated births and deaths and thereby attains *Kaivalya* or liberation.

12. Kalagni Rudra Upanishad

Once Sanat Kumar asked *Kalagni Rudra* to teach him the truth in the three streak marks called *Tripundram* that stretches from the forehead down to the eyes and goes from the centre of one eyebrow to the other.

Kalagni Rudra told him that the material for this *Tripundaram*, should be the ash of fires. Then he explained about the importance of each of the three lines. Finally, it is stated in this *Upanishad*, that one who knows this truth is purified of all sins and he becomes the blessed one.

13. Kalisantarana Upanishad

Towards the end of *Dwapar Yuga*, Narad approached Brahma and asked him whether he, Narad, will be able to go beyond the mundane existence of *Kali Yuga*, and if so, how and what the rules would be.

In reply, Brahma told Narad that he will be able to do so by uttering the name of Lord Narayana who is the primeval *Purusha* in the following manner —

हरे राम हरे राम राम राम हरे हरे।
हरे कृष्ण हरे कृष्ण कृष्ण कृष्ण हरे हरे।।
Hare Rāma hare Rāma Rāma Rāma hare hare
Hare Kṛṣna hare Kṛṣna Kṛṣna Kṛṣna hare hare

Brahma said, "These sixteen words, which form the mantra, will destroy all evil effects of *Kali* in the next *yuga* and finally *Para Brahman* alone will shine." For uttering these names, there are no rules. Whosoever utters this mantra consisting of sixteen words, three and a half crore times, will be able to cross over all sins and will attain *mukti*.

14. Katha Upanishad

This *Upanishad* is in the *Katha Shakha* of *Krishna Yajur Veda*. It tells the story of Nachiketa, the son of Vajashrava, and the teachings imparted by Yama to Nachiketa. Though this *Upanishad* begins as a story, it leads to the exposition of the profound philosophical truths. This story was first mentioned in *Rig Veda*.

This *Upanishad* has two chapters. Each one of these chapters has three *vallis* or sections. Some passages of this *Upanishad* are found in *Bhagavad Gita*. It says, that desire, anger, hatred, and fear pertain to the mind but not to the Self. Hunger, thirst and so on pertain to the body, but not to the Soul. One should try to view things objectively and not subjectively. Then one will realise that he is not just the body and mind. Once that realisation comes, then one can exist as the imperishable Self without any of the impurities of mind and body affecting him. Even while living, one should treat the body and mind as not his own. When the desires are reduced to the minimum, gradually, they will be rooted out completely. When the desires are eradicated completely, consciousness of the body will also cease and the Self alone will shine. This *Upanishad* says that for such a person there is no death because death is only for the body and not for the soul. The one who lives in this world without the awareness of the body is called *Jivan Mukta*.

The supreme goal of the Vedas is to make man *Jivan Mukta*.

Story of Nachiketa

In Nachiketa's story, his father Vajashrava performs a sacrifice and after the completion of the sacrifice, he gives old and feeble cows to the priests as *dakshina*. This act disturbs Nachiketa and he offers himself as *dakshina* to the priests. Nachiketa's words anger his father and in a fit of rage, he says that he should donate himself to Yama, the God of Death.

Nachiketa goes to the abode of Yama and waits for him for three days and nights. Yama, on his return finds the young Nachiketa waiting for him. Being pleased with the boy, he offers three boons to him to compensate for the delay and discomfort caused to Nachiketa.

This *Upanishad* reveals the truths of this world and the other world that is beyond our comprehension. Though quite young, Nachiketa was full of wisdom.

The **first boon** that he asked from Lord Yama was to relieve his father of all anxieties and make him calm in mind. Yama granted this boon.

For **second boon**, Nachiketa requested Lord Yama to enlighten him about the sacrifice, by performing which he could enter Heaven and be freed from hunger, thirst, fear and sorrow. Lord Yama told him that the sacrificial fire is the source of the worlds. Pleased with him, Yama also told him that the sacrificial fire would be known by his name Nachiketa and whoever kindled that fire thrice, would become united with the three lords and attain liberation. Then Yama told him to ask for the third boon.

The **third boon** Nachiketa asked for was to enlighten him as to what happens to a man after his death. To this, Yama replied by saying that even Gods entertained this question. The answer to this question, being very subtle, is highly complicated and therefore very difficult to comprehend. Yama tried to dissuade Nachiketa from asking this question. He, therefore, asked Nachiketa to ask for any other boon like wealth, gold, horses, cattle, elephants, vast extent of earth and tried to tempt him with all such material pleasures of the world. But Nachiketa was adamant on knowing the answer to this question. He did not want any other boon or any other material gifts from Lord Yama except the knowledge about death. He regarded all the worldly pleasures as temporary and insisted on getting the eternal knowledge.

Lord Yama was greatly impressed by Nachiketa. It proved that Nachiketa was beyond all pleasures and aspirations and craved for knowledge alone. The central theme of this *Upanishad* is the dialogue between Lord Yama and Nachiketa about the third boon. Yama told him that the ignorant who thinks that he is intelligent and enlightened goes through the cycle of birth and death again and again. Only the knower of the Self can impart the knowledge of Self. It cannot be obtained through arguments. The wise one, through concentration of mind, knows the Self lodged in the innermost self, that is very hard to perceive. He abandons joy and grief. He, after knowing and grasping the Truth, attains the subtle Self and rejoices. *AUM* is the goal of all Vedas and all austerities. This syllable *AUM* is *Brahman*, both lower and higher. Whoever knows this, attains all that he desires. There is no birth and death for the intelligent self. It is unborn, eternal, everlasting, ancient, and is not slain even when the body is slain. This Self, that is the subtlest, is seated in the heart of all. One who is free from desires is able to see the glory of the Self and becomes free from grief. It is far, near and everywhere. It is joyful as well as joyless. It is bodyless, great and all pervading. It is smaller than the smallest and greater than the greatest. It cannot be known by studying Vedas or by mere intelligence. It can be known only if one restrains from bad conduct. The one who has an unrestrained mind, is impure and gets immersed in worldly pleasures, such a person goes after material pleasures of life and gets caught in the cycle of birth and death. He does not attain *Brahman*. But the one who lives in the opposite way becomes immortal, reaches the end of the path and attains that supreme state of Vishnu. The senses are to be controlled by the mind and the mind has to be controlled by the greater Self. Through yoga, the senses are held back.

Purusha is the subtlest. It is subtler than the senses, sensory objects, mind, intellect and even *mahat*, which is the *Hiranyagarbha* and is *avyakta* or unmanifested. This Self is hidden in all beings. The path is hard and one has to learn that Truth from the exalted ones. Man gets liberated from death by knowing that Self, which is soundless, formless, imperishable, tasteless, odourless, eternal, constant, all pervading, subtlest, omniscient, and omnipotent. Its light is greater than that of the Sun, Moon, stars, lightning and fire.

This Lord of the past and future is of the size of a thumb. He is a smokeless flame, the one who is always awake like consciousness. The metaphor of an uprooted tree is given here to explain that Heaven is the root of all life. When the *Prana* goes out, what remains is the Self. It is not seen, but by its light everything shines. When all longings disappear, *Brahman* or the Self is attained. The highest state is when all the five senses are at rest together with the mind and when the intellect is not active.

The heart has 101 nerves. Of these, one goes out piercing the head. Going up through that one attains immortality. He, who hears this story, attains glory in the world of *Brahman*. One who sees immortality sees only the inner Self. It is only the unintelligent who go after material objects and outward pleasures and fall prey to death. But the wise attain immortality by knowing the Self or *Brahman*. When all the desires disappear, then a mortal becomes immortal. This knowledge can be received not by reasoning, thought, intuition or intellect, but by entering one's own heart. The wise ones look within and understand the soul and get liberated.

After acquiring this knowledge, Nachiketa attained immortality.

15. Katha Rudra Upanishad

Gods requested Brahma to impart the spiritual knowledge to them. Brahma replied, "After going through all the earlier three stages of life, one should take up *Sanyas* after getting the necessary permission from elders and relatives. One should depart from material life, after removing the sacred thread and discarding hair. He should look at his son and utter words 'thou art scripture, thou art the syllable *AUM*.' His son should say, "I am the scripture, I am AUM." Then without shedding tears, circumambulating his village, and not looking at anything, one should depart.

After reaching the forest, he should perform *Agnihotra Yajna* for twelve nights by pouring oblations of milk into the sacred fire. During this period, he should survive on milk. At the end of twelve nights, the wooden vessels that contain milk should be offered to the fire with a mantra. The clay pots are to be immersed in water and the metal pots are to be given to the teacher with a mantra. He should prostrate before the three fires, namely, the household fire, the southern fire, and the fire into which the oblations are offered. He should abandon the sacred thread in the waters with a mantra. Then he can resume his journey or end himself.

If he resumes his journey, he should subsist on alms thereafter. He has to renounce everything including garment that covers his body for protection. He should bathe in and drink pure water. He should become even minded. Ultimately, he would become *Brahman* by knowing 'I am *Brahman* alone' from Self.

By realising *Brahman* that is Truth, knowledge, non-duality, essence, eternal joy, one attains happiness. Total fearlessness is attained when the great ascetic realises his unity with the Self. Fear is the result of duality between the one and the Self within. One who realises this never suffers by the impact of good or bad actions. Consciousness without *maya* is pure *Brahman*.

This *Upanishad* ends with the true essence of the teachings of all *Vedanta* —

'Dying oneself, becoming oneself, one yet remains oneself.'

16. Kshurika Upanishad

Kshurika refers to knife. This *Upanishad* talks about the means to cut attachment using the knife of wisdom and shows the way to *mukti* or liberation. Using the mind and with wisdom, one should meditate. One should use the path of sharp mind, yoga should also be practised continuously to reach the secret place called *Indra Vajram* which is located above the knees and cut it through meditation and yoga. The life power which lies in between the union of thighs must be released by practising skilful yoga and then one should go upward. Then the group of *nadis* or nerves near the neck should be reached and all the 101 *nadis* located there must be realised and the best three *nadis* namely, the *Ida nadi* that is the protector on the left side, the *Pingala nadi* on the right should be identified, and one should understand the real position of *Sushumna nadi* that is in the centre. The one who identifies this, understands the secret of the Vedas.

Sushumna nadi is the form of Brahma. It makes one merge with Brahma. There are 72,000 *nadis* in the body and in each *nadi* there is an oil-like substance. By meditation, this oil-like material is taken out from all the nerves, except in the case of *Sushumna nadi,* where it is not possible to separate the oily material. This *nadi* has good or bad smell depending upon the good or bad deeds performed by the person. One should meditate upon this *nadi*. Then, one should sit in a silent place, become detached with no desires, and realise the philosophy of yoga and should withdraw within himself. Through intense practice of *Pranayama* and meditation on *AUM*, one is able to cut off all family bonds with a sharp mind that gets further sharpened by renunciation. Such a person gets freedom from bondage and attains immortality.

17. Maha-Narayana Upanishad

The Lord of all creations, who is found everywhere, enters the creatures in seed-form and grows to become a living being. In him is the entire Universe and unto him everything dissolves. He envelops the whole space. In him, all creatures abide. *Prakriti* was born from him. He created living beings out of the five elements. He enters into them as the inner controller, who is greater than the greatest, higher than the highest, the imperishable, and the one having unlimited forms. He is the Universe, ancient, and lives beyond *Prakriti*. His name is Great Glory. No one knows the beginning or end of this *Paramatman*.

No one can see him with the eyes. He can only be realised by meditating on him with a detached mind fixed in the heart. Such people who meditate on him become immortal.

This *Upanishad* gives the secret knowledge contained in the *Paramatma Sukta* from the *Yajur Veda Samhita*, the hymn to *Hiranyagarbha* from *Taittiriya Brahmana*.

18. Panchabrahma Upanishad

Sage Pippalada asked the God (*Ishwara*) as to who came first.

For this, *Ishwara* replied, "*Parabrahma* took five shapes in stages."

The **first** one was *Satyojata*, which is the aspect of the earth and includes the Sun, Goddess Lakshmi, Brahma, the *Pranava* mantra *AUM*, *Rig Veda*, *Garhapatyagni* or the household fire, *mantras*, *Sapta Swaras* or the seven notes and yellow colour. This gives all that is wished for.

Secondly, the *Parabrahma* took the shape of *Aghora*, which is the aspect of water and includes the Moon, Goddess Parvati, *Yajur Veda*, blue colour of the cloud, *Dakshinagni* or the southern fire and the fifty letters. This drives away all sins, destroys all evil and grants riches.

Thirdly, *Parabrahma* took the shape of *Vamadeva*, which is the fifth aspect of fire, which includes the illumination of crores of Suns, *Sama Veda*, eight types of songs, and courageous tone. It is *Ashvaneeyagni*, which is the power of knowledge, destroys all sins, has power and is slightly blackish white in colour. It gives full consciousness, rules over all the three worlds, grants good luck, and results for the actions performed by one.

The **fourth** shape of *Parabrahma* is the *Tatta Purusha* with eight letters of *Aa, Ka, Cha,Ta, Tha, Pa, Ya, Sa*. It is in the eight-petalled lotus and is surrounded by air. It has five fires, protects the effects of mantras, is the personification of the fifty consonants. It is *Atharva Veda*, chief of several crores of *Ganas*, big-shaped, red in colour, gives whatever is asked for, is the medicine to cure worry and anxiety, and diseases, and the root of all creations, the basis of all strengths. It is the *Turiya* state that is beyond the three stages of waking, dreaming and dreamless sleep and is therefore *Brahman*. It is worshipped by Brahma, Vishnu and Maheshwara. It is the basic philosophy from which all others emerge.

Ishwara is the **fifth** and the final stage and shape of *Paramatman*. It is the witness for intelligence and activates the brain. It is the aspect of sky and is decorated by *Pranava Mantra AUM.* It has the shape of all *devas*, is peaceful and beyond sound. It is the letter *Aa* and is the first among vowels. It is the form of *Pancha Brahma* that exists everywhere. It activates the actions of creation, upkeep, destruction, disappearance and blessing. It hides *Pancha Brahma* within itself. It exists as itself. It shines beyond the *Pancha Brahma* by its own light. It shines throughout – in the beginning, middle and end. This *Ishana* aspect forms the upper boundary of peace. The emergence of Truth and all that is heard, seen or exists is *Parabrahma*. After one understands this *Brahma karya*, or the existence of the five shapes, *Ishana* is understood. After knowing that all originates from *Parabrahma* in one's soul, the wise man experiences the truth that 'It Is Me' or 'I Am Brahman'. He, who realises this, is liberated.

This *Upanishad* says that one should chant the *Panchakshara* or the five-letter mantra, starting with '*Na*', and ending with '*Ya*', that is, '*Namah Shivaya*', which is the body of Lord Siva.

After one understands the philosophy of the soul of *Parabrahma*, one realises that each form is nothing but the form of those five shapes. The one, who realises this, shines like *Pancha Brahma*. Lord Shiva, who grants salvation, exists in the heart of all beings as mere witness and is, therefore, called *hridayam* or the one that exists within.

19. Pranagnihotra Upanishad

The hymn of *Prana* that is beyond all empirical knowledge yet is also the essence of all *Upanishads*, dealing with sacrifice in the body, by which a man becomes free from life without having any knowledge of sacrifices like *Agnihotra* or Philosophy like *Sankhya,* is explained in this *Upanishad.*

It starts with the explanation of the procedure to be followed while the external form of sacrifice is being performed. It includes the utterance of the three verses which are the requests to God to deliver man from calamities and to protect from evil spirits, to give food that is clean and rich in energy, requesting the sacred water to purify everything and keeping the cooked rice on the ground as per procedure.

Then prayers and offerings are made and the ritual offerings are consecrated into the fire. After this, one performs the sacrifice in his body. In this sacrifice —

- **Self** is the sacrificer.
- **Intellect** is the sacrificer's wife.
- The **Vedas** are the officiating priests.
- The **ego** is the *Adhvaryu* priest.
- The **mind** is the invoking priest.
- ***Prana*** is the assistant of the chief priest.
- ***Apana*** (lower abdomen) is the assistant of *Adhvaryu* priest.
- ***Vayana*** (distribution of energy to all parts of the body) is the first chanter of the mantras.

- ***Udana*** (throat and mouth) is the *sama* singer.
- ***Samana*** (the central regions of the body and organs of digestion) are the assistant *hotri* priests.
- The **body** is the altar.
- The **nose** is the interior of the altar.
- The **crest** is the wooden container of the *ghee*.
- The **two ears** are the two *ghee* offerings.
- **Eyes** are the two parts of the *ghee*.
- **The neck** is the libation.
- The **five *tanmatras*** (sound, touch, taste, smell and sight) are the assistants of the *Brahma* priest.
- The **elements** are the attendants.
- ***Gunas*** are the supplementary offerings.
- The **tongue** is the final sacrifice.
- The **teeth** and the **lips** are the middle libation.
- The **palate** is the recitation of hymns.
- **Memory** is the *samyorvaka* formula.
- The **compassion**, **forebearance**, **non-violence** are the *ajya* oblations.
- ***AUM*** is the sacrificial post.
- **Desire** is the cord.
- **Mind** is the chariot.
- **Lust** is the sacrificial animal.
- The **hair** is the *durva* grass.
- The **sense organs** are the sacrificial vessels.
- **Organs of action** are the oblations.
- **Non-violence** is the *ishtis*.
- **Renunciation** is the sacrificial fee.
- The **post-sacrificial bath** that follows is the death.

This *Upanishad* concludes by pointing out that in this body all divinities exist and the one who dies in the city of Benaras or the Brahmin who reads this secret doctrine contained in this *Upanishad*, attains liberation in one's life.

20. Rudra-Hridaya Upanishad

This *Upanishad* talks about the knowledge of the pure state of the Supreme Absolute.

Sri Sukha after prostrating before Lord Shiva in his heart, wearing the sacred *Rudraksha* and *Bhasma*, asked his father, Veda Vyasa about the real God of Gods in whom all the existence resides. He further asked Vyasa whether anyone can please all the *devas* by worshipping that single God.

Vyasa replied, "All *devas* are in Rudra, as they all are his own different manifestations. On the right side of Rudra is Sun, the four-headed Brahma and the three fires. Uma, Vishnu and Soma, the moon are on his left side. Hence worshipping Shiva is worshipping Vishnu as well. While Rudra is the generator of the seed, Vishnu is the embryo of the seed. Shiva is also Brahma, and Brahma is Agni. Rudra is Brahma as well as Vishnu. Everything in this Universe is filled up with Shiva who is the masculine aspect, and Uma who forms the feminine aspect. *Vyakta* and *Avyakta* are Uma and Rudra respectively. The combination of Uma and Rudra is Vishnu. Vishnu, therefore, is the *Paramatman*, the eternal *Atman* of the Universe. The entire creation of *Svarga*, *Martya* and *Patala lokas* is a big tree and Vishnu is on the top of this tree. Brahma is the stem or action and the root or cause is Shiva. For the benefit of the world, Rudra has taken these three forms. Rudra is *Dharma*, Vishnu is world, and Brahma is the knowledge. By singing '*Rudra, Rudra,*' one gets rid of all sins. Uma is Saraswati and Lakshmi. While Rudra is Sun, Uma is shadow, night, *swaha*, *shastra*, creeper, flower etc. A devotee should worship Rudra with these mantras."

Then Vyasa asked his son Sukha to meditate upon the eternal *Parabrahma* which is beyond the reach of the senses, that is pure existence, knowledge, and bliss. This cannot be understood by speech or by mind. Everything is that, and there is nothing more to know beyond that.

The two *Vidyas* are *Para Vidya* and *Apara Vidya*.

Para Vidya is *Moksha Shastra*. It deals with the philosophy of the Absolute Truth that is not understandable, without qualities, impersonal, formless, eternal, omnipresent, imperishable and known by the wise sages only.

Apara Vidya is the study of the four Vedas. It does not discuss the nature of *Atman*.

Absolute Shiva created this world by means of severe penance through *Jnana Marga.* This world is nothing but *Maya*. It is super-imposed on the Lord just as a rope on a serpent. In reality, there is no creation at all. Everything is Absolute. One who knows this, gets liberated. Only through *Jnana* one can realise this *Sansara.*

Ajnana or ignorance must be removed and one should take refuge in Lord Sadashiva. This alone is the real wisdom. *Pranava* the bow, *Atman* the arrow, and *Paramatman* the target, are one and the same ash Sadashiva.

There are no Sun, Moon, Stars, Wind or *devatas* over there. Only, the Lord exists. The *Jiva* and the *Paramatman* both residing in the body are like two birds. While the *Jiva* eats the fruits of *Karma*, the *Paramatman* is not touched by anything. The *Paramatman* is the witness or the inner *sakshi*. He assumes the form of *Jiva* through his *Maya* just as air inside a pot seems to be different from the air outside it. But everything is only Shiva, *Advaita*, and the one Absolute without any difference.

When one understands that All is One, the *Omkara*, the Absolute, then there is no room for sorrow or *Maya*. Then it is very easy to attain the *Paramananda*. One should think that the Supreme Lord is the basis of all Universe, the *sat-chit-ananda*, then the *Atman* becomes one with *AUM* or the Absolute. The one who knows this Truth is the real *Muni.* He becomes the *Parabrahma* himself and attains everlasting peace.

21. Saraswati Rahasya Upanishad

The holy sages requested Asvalayana to tell them about how the knowledge that is won illumines the content of the word '*Tat*'. For this, Asvalayana said that he won the supreme perfection by worshipping Saraswati by reciting ten holy verses based on Saraswati and the *Rig Veda* verses.

Then the sages asked him to tell them about that meditation by which Goddess Saraswati is pleased.

Then, Asvalayana told them about those ten verses. He said that the one who worships Goddess Saraswati with faith and devotion, is blessed with conviction within a period of six months. He becomes spontaneous in prose and poetry.

Saraswati herself stated that even Brahma won eternal knowledge, the Brahmanhood through her. By equilibrium of the three qualities of *Sattva*, *Rajas*, and *Tamas,* she becomes *Prakriti* in which *Chit* shines as a reflection in a mirror. *Prakriti* itself shines through the reflection of '*Chit*'. There are two forces for *Maya*. One is projection and the other is concealment. The first projects the world, both Subtle and Gross. The second covers the gulf between the creation and *Brahman*. The person whose *Maya* is low, this gulf between creation and *Brahman* disappears.

She further said that one should always practise concentration. There are two types of concentrations – concentration with aspects and concentration without aspects.

Concentration with aspect is again of two types – Concentration that is conforming to word and secondly to the object of desire. One should meditate on consciousness as a mere spectator of these aspects.

Concentration without aspects includes meditating continuously abandoning objects and words for deep self experience. There, the ignorance of body disappears and the Supreme Self is realised. All the doubts vanish and all actions go.

22. Sarrerika Upanishad

The body is a combination of the five elements of Nature. They are —

- **Earth** which is hard
- **Water** that is liquid
- **Fire** that is hot
- **Air** that moves
- **Space** that is porous

For the five organs of senses the objects are —

- Sense of **hearing** – space
- Sense of **touch** – air
- Sense of **sight** – fire
- Sense of **taste** – water
- Sense of **smell** – earth

For the organs of action, the objects are **tongue** for speech, **hands** for catching, **feet** for walking, **arms** for holding, and **genitals** for pleasure.

The four inner senses are mind, intellect, egoism, and self-conscious mind. They are for volition, doubt, determination, affection and decision. At the tip of the neck is **mind**, on the face is the **intellect**, in heart is the **egoism**, and at navel is the **self-conscious mind**.

Our body has attributes of all the five elements namely earth, water, fire, air and ether. They are found in the following way —

- The parts of **earth** in the body are the bone, skin, nerves, hair and flesh.
- Parts of **water** in the body are in urine, phlegm, blood and semen.
- **Fire** is in hunger, thirst, laziness, delusion and sex.
- The parts of **air** are in circulation, and movement of the eye.
- Parts of the **ether** are lust, anger, greed, delusion and fear.

Further, the attributes of earth are in sound, touch, form, taste and smell. The attributes of water are in sound, touch, form and taste. The attributes of fire are in sound, touch, and form. The attributes of air are in sound and touch, and finally, the attributes of ether are in sound alone.

The qualities of *Sattva* are non-violence, truth, non-stealing, non-possession, calmness, cleanliness, service, contentment, honesty, faith, non-injury, and happiness. It is the highest quality.

The qualities of *Rajas* are feeling of doing, enjoyer, speaker, and it belongs to the middle order with the knowledge of rituals.

The *Tamasic* qualities are sleep, laziness, delusion, attachment, sex, theft, and so on. This quality is the lowest level.

The **waking** state rests on five organs of senses, of action, and four inner senses.

The **dreaming** state rests on four inner senses.

The **dreamless** sleep rests on mind as the instrument.

In the fourth state that is beyond these three states, the soul alone is active. The **empirical** self is the knower that rests between awareness of objects and indifference towards them.

The five organs of sense and action with the five *Pranas* are called as *Panch Pranas* or vital airs (*Prana, Udana, Samana, Vayana and Apana*).

The mind and intellect form the *Linga Shareera.*

The mind, intellect, self-conscious principle and so on form the eight *Prakritis*. The sixteen others are ear, skin, eyes, tongue, nose, arms, genitals, hands, feet, vocal organ, sound, touch, form, taste, and smell.

The twenty-three others are the *Tattvas* or aspects of reality, relating to *Prakriti*. The twenty-fourth is *Avyakta*, the chief *Tattva* and the last or the twenty-fifth *Tattva* is the *Purusha* or Self.

23. Sarva Sara Upanishad

This *Upanishad* explains what are different states like bondage, liberation, *Avidya* or ignorance etc.

The **bondage** of the soul is the Self looking upon things other than itself and thinking as itself. This results in bondage of the soul.

Moksha or **liberation** is the cessation of false idea found in bondage.

Avidya or **nescience** is that which causes egoism.

Vidya or **knowledge** is that by which egoism is eliminated.

Jagrat or **wakeful** state is when the Self perceives gross objects with its senses.

Swapna or **dream** state is when there is desire even in the absence of sound.

Sushupti or **dreamless** state of *Atman* is when all the organs cease from activity and there is non-differentiation.

Turiya or the **transcendental** state, that is beyond the three earlier states is when the essence of consciousness that is manifesting itself as the three earlier states is also the witness of the states, but in itself is devoid of any state and remains in oneness.

The *Annamaya kosha* is the aggregate of all the six sheaths composed of food.

The *Pranamaya kosha* is when all the fourteen kinds of *Vayus* or air, starting with *Prana* are in this sheath.

Manonmaya kosha is when the *Atman* is united with *Annamaya kosha* and *Pranamaya kosha*, through the organs they perform.

Vijnanamaya kosha is when the soul shines united with the three sheaths stated above, with the awareness of the difference and non-difference.

Ananda maya kosha is when these four sheaths stated above, remain in knowledge of *Brahman*.

When the soul dwells in the body as the seat of the idea of pleasure and pain, it is *Karta* or agent.

When the soul makes a link to the present body based on its past good and bad deeds, still without receiving a body, it is *Jiva* or the individual soul.

The *Linga Shareera* or the subtle body is that which is imperishable due to the proximity of the Self and the consciousness. Within that is the *Kshetrajna* or knower of the *Kshetra* or body.

The *Atman* manifests itself as *Antaryamin*, the internal ruler. When the *Atman* shines forth without any limitations, as a unified mass of consciousness that is independent and pure intelligence, it is called *Tvam* that is found as the inner self. That which is *Satya* or truth, *Jnana* or knowledge, *Ananta* or infinite and *Ananda* or Bliss is *Brahman*. This reality cannot be described. It is eternal; it is the essence of intelligence, without beginning or end and is known as *Jnana*.

Ananta is found in all phenomena of creations as bliss or *Ananda*. It is that *Paramatman*, Supreme self or *Parabrahma*. It is all pervading, self-luminous, pure existence, knowledge, ever joyful, witness, pure consciousness and so on.

24. Skanda Upanishad

In this *Upanishad*, Skanda tells that due to an iota of compassion of God, he became a mass of knowledge. The one who realises that Consciousness is different from matter becomes a mass of knowledge. He is Shiva, Hari, Supreme God and *Brahman*.

Jiva is Shiva and vice-versa. The bound one is *Jiva*. *Jiva* released from *Karma* becomes the eternal Shiva.

Then Skanda bows to Shiva who is Vishnu and to Vishnu who is Shiva. The body is a temple. The Deity Shiva is the *Jiva*. After worshipping God with flowers, the flowers must be thrown away and one should worship God by identifying oneself with God.

Perception of non-difference is knowledge. Removing mental impurity is bath. Control of senses is cleanliness. One should take alms for sustenance and live without duality. Such a person will attain liberation.

The *Upanishad* ends with Skanda's prayers to the Supreme sacred seat of power.

25. Sukha-Rahasya Upanishad

The sages asked Brahma to tell them the *Rahasya Upanishad* and Lord Brahma narrated the following story.

"Once Vyasa told Lord Shiva that the time has come to educate his son Sukha. Lord Shiva told sage Vyasa that if he imparted the knowledge of the *Brahman* to Sukha, he would depart after getting detachment. Vyasa then told Shiva that his son Sukha may become omniscient and get four kinds of *moksha* during his *Upanayanam* or the sacred thread ceremony, when the knowledge of *Brahman* is imparted. Shiva then imparted the knowledge of *Pranava* to Sukha. Sukha after learning about the Supreme *Brahman AUM*, desired to know the inherent meaning of '*that thou art*'. Shiva was pleased at his request and imparted the *Rahasya Upanishad* that has six parts, by knowledge of which one gets liberated directly."

This *Upanishad* is stated to be the crown of all *Upanishads*. There is no need for holy rites, pilgrimages, mantras and so on for a wise man who meditates upon *Brahman*. One will be blessed with 100 years of life if one meditates on the meanings of the major *Upanishads*. The same is obtained by the wise person who utters this *Upanishad* once. Then Shiva imparted that knowledge and the secret of meditation to Sukha.

The four major teachings of Lord Shiva are —

- *Consciousness is Brahman*
- *I am Brahman*
- *That thou art*
- *This self is Brahman*

Within the body, 'Being' remains witness to the intellect and is called 'I'. This Being is *Brahman*. It is the single one without anyone alike, without name and form, and is always called 'That'and 'Thou.'

One is in a state of dream of 'I' and 'Mine' because of the absence of knowledge. The knowledge should be obtained from a Guru or teacher and then it should be thought of and meditated upon. This gives full knowledge. The knowledge of *Brahman* leads one to *Brahman*.

Lord Shiva then told Sukha that this knowledge imparted by Shiva, at the request of Vyasa, will make Sukha a *Jivan Mukta*.

Sukha who got the knowledge from Shiva got up and bowed to Shiva. He gave up all possessions and went away.

Seeing this, Vyasa went after his son and he was overjoyed to hear that the whole world was hailing Sukha.

This *Upanishad* ends with a statement that whosoever learns this knowledge through the Guru's grace gets released from all sins and attains liberation.

26. Shvetashvatara Upanishad

The name of this *Upanishad* is after the sage who taught this *Upanishad*. It belongs to a later period. There are six chapters in it with 113 verses. Almost all basic teachings and concepts of *Bhagavad Gita* are found here.

It deals with the unity of all souls and the world and the principle of one God namely, Rudra.

It identifies the Supreme *Brahman* with Rudra who is the material and efficient cause of the world and its protector and guide. The emphasis here is not on *Brahman*, the Absolute or Impersonal God but on personal *Ishwara* who is omnipotent and omniscient and who is manifested as Brahma or Rudra or Lord Shiva who is the Superior Being. He is the Universal Soul who created this Universe, rules the world, protects and withdraws the world at the time of delusion.

Pashu is the individual soul and *Pasha* is the bond that chains the individual soul to the world that is only illusion. *Pashupati* is Lord Shiva who maintains and controls the Universe and who frees his devotees from *Pasha* or bondage. It teaches the unity of the souls and the world in the one Supreme Reality.

Devotion to God is emphasised here and states that by knowing God one is released from all fetters. Through *karma* (action), *gunas* (qualities) emerge are to be transcended. By discipline and meditation, mind and thoughts are controlled and this results in the realisation of the soul.

Breathing techniques are also mentioned in this *Upanishad.* Once the students of *Vedanta* were discussing among themselves about the existence of *Brahma.* Later, through meditation they realised that the self-luminous power exists in every being. He is the source of everything but is also incomprehensible. We think of him as the Universe, the one having innumerable aspects. The *Jiva* is blessed by Him and then attains immortality. This is the **Supreme** *Brahman.*

Knowing this truth, the knower of Vedas gets liberation. It is the Lord who supports everything in the Universe. The one, who is ignorant of this truth, gets attached to material pleasures. Once he comes to know him, all the shackles are removed. With this realisation of the Self, becomes infinite, universal, and free from the sense of doership.

God is imperishable and immortal. By meditating on him, by becoming one with him, all illusions of the mind vanish. All bondages are removed with the knowledge of God. Through the realisation of this truth, deaths and births cease. Through meditation, by going beyond the consciousness of the body, one reaches the third state namely, the Universal Lordship. He then becomes *Brahman*, the one without a second form. This is the ultimate truth. There is nothing to know beyond this.

Through the power of meditation, one realises that the *enjoyer, enjoyed* and the *power that brings enjoyment* are all three aspects of *Brahman*. By meditating on *Pranava*, through introspection, the *Atman*, which hitherto existed in latent state, is perceived.

Through practice of yoga, the wise ones cross over all fearful currents by means of the raft of *Brahman*.

Meditation should be practised in caves or in any other pure place where there is even ground and where the atmosphere is peaceful and pleasing to the mind, and where there is no dust, wind, fire, dampness or disturbing noises. Several forms like snow, smoke, sun and wind appear to distract one in the beginning stages of yoga.

The first signs of entering yoga are – lightness of body, clear mind, clear complexion, beautiful voice, agreeable odour, and least excretions.

Later, when the truth of *Atman* is seen, one realises oneness. When the *Atman* in the body is understood as the self-luminous entity one gets freed from all sins.

This divinity that is all-pervading is the first-born or *Hiranyagarbha*. He is inside all of us as the indwelling self, who is present everywhere. He pervades the entire Universe. Through his own *Maya*, he appears as the Divine Lord. He creates, protects, and controls all forces working in all the worlds. Those who realise this truth become immortal.

Higher than the personal God is the infinite Supreme *Brahman* who is concealed inside the bodies of all and at the same time envelops the entire Universe. The one who knows this truth becomes immortal.

Supreme *Brahman* shines like Sun. The only way to escape from the cycle of births and deaths is to realise him. He is the greatest, highest, minutest, formless, biggest and is free from misery. The one who knows this becomes immortal.

Supreme *Brahman* is all-pervading, omnipresent, benevolent, and dwells in the hearts of all beings. He is that imperishable internal light that controls everything and guides the intellect of all beings and enables them to attain Salvation. He assumes the form of the size of a thumb. The one who knows this becomes immortal.

He spreads over the entire Universe. He is the friend and ruler of all. He is the Lord of all the worlds. Without any sense organs, he can see, hear and use all the senses. He knows everything but there is none who know him. He is the foremost, greatest, infinite being. He is subtler than the subtlest and greater than the greatest. With divine grace, one realises this truth. He is fire, sun, air, moon, stars, firmament, water, man, woman, youth, old age, birds and animals, clouds, seasons, oceans, and everything. He is *Prajapati* and *Brahman*. He is without beginning and end and beyond Time and Space. All the worlds are born from him.

The *Upanishad* goes on to tell about the story of the two beautiful birds, one sitting on the tree and enjoying the fruits, whereas the other merely watching and sitting. The bird that enjoys the fruit is the individual soul that gets entangled and forgets his divine nature and becomes miserable. When he sees the other, and realises that the other is the Lord of all, the mere witness beyond all *gunas*, who is pure consciousness with all greatness, he is relieved of his misery.

Prakriti or Nature is *Maya* and the great Lord is the Lord of *Maya*. One attains infinite peace by realising that self-effulgent Lord, who appears in myriad forms. In the wheel of creation, the hub and the circumference are *Brahman* and the middle part is the manifestation of *Prakriti* with its diverse nature. All beings revolve around this vast *Brahma-chakra*. The individual soul takes birth as per its good and bad deeds. Since one enjoys and assumes responsibility for his actions without seeing the invisible hand of God, he becomes bound to the world. The *Jiva* or soul moves with the illusion that the Self that is hidden inside is different from it. This illusion goes on until the realisation comes and one attains immortality. The soul is caught helplessly by *Prakriti* until the divine grace of God frees the one from the bondage. Then one becomes free from the cycle of birth and death and merges with the Lord, the Creator.

God, the Superior Soul that is hidden in the heart can be understood and ignorance or *maya* can be overcome only through the heart that is full of devotion and the mind that is full of *jnana* through meditation.

This *Upanishad*, then describes the glory of the Lord and prays to the Lord for good thoughts.

This *Upanishad* ends with the statement that this highest mysticism should be taught only to a worthy disciple, who has the supreme devotion to God and an equal degree of devotion towards his spiritual teacher.

27. Taittiriya Upanishad

This *Upanishad* is a part of *Taittiriya Aranyaka* and begins with a prayer to Varuna, Aryaman, Indra, Brihaspati, Vishnu and *Brahman* for blessings, grace and protection. It lays down the rules of *Brahmacharya* or student life, its importance, about Vedic chanting and meditation on *Pranava*.

This *Upanishad* also mentions the different *koshas* or sheaths of man. They are —

- *Annamaya Kosha*, the sheath of food
- *Pranamaya Kosha,* the sheath of vital breath
- *Manonmaya Kosha,* the sheath of mind
- *Vijnanamaya Kosha,* the sheath of understanding
- *Anandamaya Kosha,* the sheath of bliss in which the Self dwells

The five features of the Self namely, *Prana, Vyana, Apana, Udana, Samana* are also explained here.

1. About the **Universe** it says, the earth is the first form, then comes heaven, in between is Space, and air is the connecting element.
2. Regarding **Light** it says, first the air came then the Sun. Water formed in the middle. Lightning is the connecting element.
3. Regarding **Knowledge** it says, teacher is first, then comes the taught. Learning forms the middle. The connecting element is instruction.
4. Regarding **People** it says, mother is the first, father the second, and progeny in the middle. The connecting element is procreation.
5. Regarding **Individual** it says, the lower jaw is the first form, the second is the upper jaw, speech is in the middle. The connecting element is tongue.

Further this *Upanishad* says that those who understand this get associated with progeny, cattle, food, and *Brahman*. It is divided into three parts, namely, the *Shikshavalli*, *Brahmanandavalli*, and *Bhriguvalli*.

The *Shikshavalli* deals with the science of phonetics and pronunciation, meditation, knowledge and progeny. *Shiksha* is the first of the six Vedangas of the Vedas. Then a prayer is uttered on *AUM* for intelligence, protection, knowledge, prosperity, good disciples, fame, purification of sins, and finally realising *Brahman*. Things that are to be practised like learning, teaching of righteousness, truth, austerity, control of outer senses and inner organs and good social conduct are emphasised. Finally, it gives instructions to the disciples about performance of duties, offerings to be made with modesty. This section ends with a prayer to God.

The *Brahmanandavalli* section states that the knower of *Brahman* attains the highest. Then it goes on to say all about the creations of *Brahman*, about the self which is made of food, the inner-self which is made of air, constituted by mind, knowledge and bliss. It says that in the beginning there was only the unmanifested *Brahman*. From *Brahman* emerged the manifested. One becomes blissful by coming into contact with that source of joy. He controls and protects everything in the Universe. The enlightened man who realises this *Brahman* has no fear. He is not affected by anything.

In the *Bhriguvalli,* we find Bhrigu approaching his father Varuna wanting to know about *Brahman*. Varuna asks his son to crave for that knowledge. Bhrigu, therefore, practised meditation. He then realised food as *Brahman*. Then he approached his father again for the knowledge. Again he was asked to meditate. This went on till Bhrigu realised vital force as *Brahman*, then mind, knowledge, and finally bliss as *Brahman*. The highest goal for one is to realise *Brahman* because that is truth and knowledge.

This *Upanishad* ends by saying that he who knows this becomes well-established in *Brahman*.

28. Tejo-Bindu Upanishad

There are six chapters in this *Upanishad*.

The **first** chapter begins with the statement that the supreme meditation should be upon *Tejo-bindu* or the seed or source of spiritual light, that is nothing but *Atma* of the entire Universe which is located in the heart of a being and which is of the size of an atom. It is very subtle, in the form of *soma*. This seat is above the reach of speech and mind. It is *Brahman* and the highest seat of Vishnu. It is beyond mind, difficult to perceive, changeless, unknowable, above Space and is in the heart. It is above all states of feelings and cravings. The parts of yoga are —

- *Yama* or control of organs of senses and actions
- *Niyama* or religious observance
- *Tyaga* or renunciation of the objects of Universe

- *Mauna* or silence
- *Asana* or posture in which one sits with ease without fatigue for meditation
- *Mulabandha* where the mind is bound, seeing all bodies equal
- *Pranayama* or control and regulation of breath
- *Pratyahara* or subjugation of senses
- *Dharana* where one indulges in good thoughts
- *Atmadhyana* and *Samadhi*

After realising that all parts of yoga are pointing to the same *Brahman*, one should get absorbed in that. One should perceive the whole world as *Brahman*. *Samadhi* is that state when from the state of changelessness the yogi moves on to the state where he forgets even that state due to the cognition of the nature of *Brahman*. This kind of bliss should be practised by a wise man until all his cognition unites with *Atman*. Then he becomes a *Siddha*. The state that he attains then is inexpressible. When *Samadhi* is practised one has to overcome obstacles like absence of right inquiry, laziness, inclination to enjoyment, absent-mindedness, distraction, impatience and sweat.

It is through worldly thoughts that one gets entangled in it. Through thoughts of *Brahman*, one gets fullness and becomes blessed. Such people always remain in *Brahman* while the others go through births and deaths repeatedly.

In the **second** chapter, we find Kumara requesting Lord Shiva to explain the nature of *Chinmatra*. It is existence, self-action, mantra, spiritual wisdom, water, earth, Vedas, *Brahman*, *Chinmaya*, the non-dual essence, the world, past, present, future, substance, time and so on. In fact, everything is *Chinmatra*. The one who perceives the 'I' to be pervading everywhere is liberated with this spiritual wisdom.

In the **third** chapter again, we find Kumara asking Shiva, his father, to tell him about the realisation of *Atman*. To this Shiva says, "I am *Parabrahma*, the Supreme bliss, Divine wisdom, the sole supreme, unconditioned, permanent and *Sattva*. There is no 'I' in me. I am beyond the *Turiya* state; I am pure consciousness, real and pure. The mantra *Aham Brahmasmi* or **'I am *Brahman*'** removes all ignorance and gives spiritual wisdom and bliss."

In the **fourth** chapter, Kumara asks Lord Shiva to explain to him about the nature of a *Jivan Mukta* and Shiva replied, "One who always stays in *Atman* is a *Jivan Mukta*. He is beyond the three bodies. He is pure consciousness and *Brahman* and is bliss. He knows that he is *Brahman*. He is *Chinmatra* undifferentiated, pure consciousness with no desire for objects, devoid of all thoughts of existence of anything other than *Brahman*. *Videha Mukta* is one who has become Brahma, whose *Atman* has attained quiescence, who is bliss and is a *mauni*. He does not even think 'I am *Atman*' like a *Jivan Mukta*. He has abandoned all thought of even 'I am *Brahman*' and he is filled with bliss."

In the **fifth** chapter, we find Sage Nidegha requesting the great Sage Ribhu to explain to him the difference between *Atman* and Non-*Atman* and Ribhu replies to him, "*Atman* is full of the nature of bliss, of spiritual sound, without enjoyment, and contemplates nothing whatsoever. There is no word as Non-*Atman*. All is *Brahman*. Whatever exists or is seen in the world is unreal."

In chapter **six,** the reply of Ribhu continues. He says that everything is *Sattva* and consciousness and pervades everything. Only *Brahman* is there, nothing else. It is only bliss or *Sachidananda*. Everything is of the nature of *Sattva*. There is nothing different from *Brahman*. All the rest seen, heard and spoken of are *Asattva* or unreal. They are the result of *Maya*. This great science of Shiva should be taught for a year and a half to the superior souls, whose minds are purified with devotion to Guru.

By studying this *Upanishad* once, a person can become one with *Brahman*.

29. Varaha Upanishad

Sage Ribhu performed long penance and at the end Lord appeared before him in the form of a boar. The Lord told Ribhu to ask for a boon. Ribhu with great devotion requested the Lord to impart to him the knowledge of *Brahman* that is the Lord's nature. The Lord replied, "The organs of sense are five namely, eyes, ears, nose, tongue and skin, similarly the organs of actions are five and the vital airs are five. The *tattvas* are twenty-four, the elements are five. The bodies are three, namely, gross, subtle and causal, and the states of consciousness are also three, namely, waking, dreaming and dreamless sleep."

The total *tattvas* are thirty-six coupled with *Jiva* —

The **six changes** of *tattvas* are existence, birth, growth, transformation, decay, and destruction.

The **six infirmities** are, hunger, thirst, grief, delusion, old age, and death.

The **six sheaths** are skin, blood, flesh, fat, marrow and bones.

The **six foes** are passion, anger, avarice, delusion, pride, and malice.

The **three** *gunas* are *sattva, rajas* and *tamas.*

The **three** *karmas* are *prarabdha, sanchita* and *agamin.*

The **five** *actions* are talking, lifting, walking, excreting and enjoying.

Then comes thought, certainty, egoism, compassion, memory and complacency as part of *Jiva*.

He further adds, "Those who worship me in the form of a boar, who is the aggregate of these *tattvas* are released from ignorance and its effects, and become *Jivan Muktas*."

In the **second** chapter, we find Ribhu asking the Lord to impact him in to the supreme *Brahma Vidya* and the Lord replied, "By performing one's duty one becomes detached. Then the virtues must be obtained by practising. The sense organs must be subdued and the concept of 'mine' should be given up. One should identify oneself with the Lord. One should know that *Atman*. That man, who sees the *Atman* that is beyond all castes and orders of life, becomes *Brahman*. Such a person becomes immortal. He is not afraid of anything. He knows that everything is *Brahman*, that is consciousness, all-pervading, full, bliss and indestructible. After this realisation, there will be no more experiences in this world. He has neither bondage nor emancipation. Whosoever meditates on *Atman* for at least forty-five minutes is released from all bondage."

The *Paramahamsa*, though living in the world, is not in the world. He is indifferent towards everything except the Lord.

Upavasa means union of *Jivatma* and *Paramatma* and not the religious observances and torturing the body with fasts. Just by beating the hole where a snake resides, you cannot kill the snake that is still inside the hole. A man attains indirect wisdom when he knows theoretically that there is *Brahman*. He is said to attain direct cognition when he realises that he himself is *Brahman*. When a yogi realises that his *Atman* is the absolute, he becomes a *Jivan Mukta*.

The word for bondage is 'mine'. The word for *Moksha* is 'not mine'. All thoughts of 'mine' should be given up and one should rest content in *Atman*.

Sankalpa results in existence of the Universe. This should be abandoned and the mind should be fixed on that which is changeless or *nirvikalpa*, and one should meditate upon the Lord residing in the heart.

Whatever is *Chit* or Consciousness is only *Chinmatra*. This Universe is *Chinmatra. Karma* arising from ignorance does not affect the person who has no desires, who has given up his self. Such a person, although living in the world, is not affected by anything.

The *Jiva* and *Ishwara* have all evolved out of the Universal consciousness. The one, who sees everything as *Chit* is *Vijnani*. He is akin to Shiva, Hari and Brahma. The mundane existence that results in sorrow is only an illusion of the mind. So one should contemplate on *Brahman* alone. How long the body lasts has no concern for those who are well versed with the knowledge that *Chit* alone is body. The wise ones, therefore, do not identify themselves with their gross or subtle bodies. If this identification of oneself with *Brahman* is realised, then all affinities for objects cease to exist.

When *Atman* and *Manas* become identified, *Samadhi* results. The person who desires all wealth of yoga should practise concentration with a subdued mind on the spiritual sound *AUM* alone.

In the **third** chapter, the knowledge of *Brahman* is given again. Everything that is seen and heard is *Brahman* and is the nature of *Sat* through the annihilation of *Asat*. To an exalted yogi, the Universe shines as Absolute Consciousness. One should practise in silence and say, "I am *Parabrahma*". This is the truth, absolute and undivided consciousness and nothing else.

Brahman is neither body nor organs of senses. It is *Sat-Chit-Ananda* Lord Vishnu. The root of mundane existence is *Chit*. It must be cleaned with repeated effort. Only the one who has no *Atmajnana* longs for *siddhi* that is attained by mantras, medicines, religious activities etc. But these things cannot help one to attain the essence of *Paramatman.*

In this *Upanishad*, we also find Nidagha asking Ribhu to enlighten him about the characteristics of *Jivan Mukta* and Ribhu explains the seven stages of development of wisdom.

- The **first** stage is *Shubhechha* or good desire. It indicates the desire to become wise.
- The **second** stage is *Vicharana* or enquiry.
- The **third** is *Tanumanasi* or pertaining to the mind in which the hankering after the objects gets thinned due to the earlier two stages.
- The **fourth** is *Sattvapatti* or the attainment of *Sattva* in which after the earlier stages, the purified *Chit* rests on *Atman.*
- The **sixth** stage is *Padartha Bhavana* or analysis of objects, when after the earlier five stages, one does actions only when impelled by others.
- The **seventh** and the final stage is *Turiya*. After exceedingly long practice in the earlier six stages one gets fixed on the contemplation of *Atman* alone. This chapter goes on to explain about *Pranava*, and about the nature of waking, dreaming, dreamless sleep and *Turiya* state.

The one who functions in the first three stages mentioned above is called *Mumukshu*. One who is in the fourth stage is the *Brahmavit.* The one in the fifth stage is *Brahma Vidvara*. The person who is in the sixth stage is called *Brahma Vidvarya* and finally the one who is in the seventh stage is the *Brahma Vidvarishta.*

The first three stages are attained amidst differences and non-differences because for the one who is in the waking state Universe exists.

In the fourth stage, one sees the Universe as a dream, as the mind gets firmly fixed on the non-dual *Brahman*, having no duality. For such a one, only *Sattva* remains.

In the fifth stage, one is always in non-state. He is free from all types of differences.

In the sixth stage, one gets freed from all affinities. He is like one sleeping when one is very tired.

In the seventh stage, one remains in *Brahman*, that is consciousness where there is neither Self nor non-Self. He becomes the reality himself. One has to discard all distinctions of seer, sight, and seen with their affinities and meditate upon *Atman.* Such a person always remains calm and composed. For him, the waking state is unknown. He is free from all affinities. His heart is pure and above all emotions. He is not attached to anything. He is not afraid of people and people are not afraid of him. He rests in *Chinmatra* and is free from all changes of *Chit*. Everything is Shiva.

Further on, this chapter gives the names of sages and about the two paths explained by Sukha and Vamadeva for attaining *Brahman*.

While **Sukha's path** offers instantaneous salvation, Vamadeva's path is for gradual salvation. Those who follow Sukha's path become *Sadyo-Muktas* and they are emancipated immediately after their body wears away.

Sage Vamadeva's path leads to repeated births and deaths and finally one gets emancipation by means of yoga, *sankhya* and *karmas*.

In *Varaha Upanishad*, Nidagha asks Lord Ribhu to enlighten him about the rules in the practice of yoga and Ribhu replies, "The body is composed of five spheres or elements — the *Prithvi* or earth that is solid, *Apas* or water that is liquid, *Tejas* or fire that is bright, *Vayu* or wind that has motion and *Akasha* or ether that pervades everywhere."

- One breathes 21,600 times every day and night due to *Vayu.* Folds in body arise if there is diminution in *Prithvi* sphere.
- If there is decrease in *Apas*, greyness of hair appears.
- If there is decrease in *Tejas*, there is loss of hunger and lustre.
- If there is decrease in *Vayu*, there is continuous tremor.
- If there is decrease in *Akasha*, one dies and the *Prana* flies up in the air due to decrease in these elements.

One should practise *Mantra Yoga, Laya Yoga* and *Hatha Yoga.* In each form of yoga, there are eight steps. They are *Yama, Niyama,*

Asana, Pranayama, Pratyahara, Dharana, Dhyana and *Samadhi.* Then this *Upanishad* explains about all these steps. The wheel of nerves has twelve spokes. *Kundalini* is located here. Then this *Upanishad* tells about the various *nadis*. In these spokes of wheel, the twelve *nadis* carry the twelve *Vayus* from left to right to different parts of the body. The *nadis* are like clothes of different colours.

The *Upanishad* ends with a statement that whosoever recites this *Upanishad* becomes *Jivan Mukta*.

30. Yoga Kundalini Upanishad

The **first** chapter of this *Upanishad* starts with the mention of *Chit*, *Prana* and *Vasanas*. A person should control *prana*. *Vayu* is controlled through moderate food, postures and *Shaktichala* that is taking up of *Kundalini shakti* from the navel upwards to the middle of the eyebrows. The two things that are necessary for this practice are *Saraswati chalana* and restraint of *Prana*. Then by practice, *Kundalini* becomes erect. By rousing the *nadi* upwards *Kundalini* is roused. Then this chapter explains the actual practice of yoga by means of *Saraswati chalana* and restraint of *Prana*, the posture, and the evils that are destroyed by the practice of yoga.

The **second** chapter tells that the knower of *Khechari* is freed from old age, diseases and death, but this science is very difficult to master. When the ascetic masters the science of the psychical powers, he gets *Siddhi*. One who gets this knowledge should practise it carefully.

Khechari Shakti is *Kundalini Shakti*. This chapter tells about the practice of this science.

The **third** chapter explains the *Melana mantra*, the six *chakras* and the practice of yoga.

31. Yoga Shikha Upanishad

In the **first** chapter of this *Upanishad*, we find Lord Brahma asking Lord Shiva to explain to him as to how all living beings surrounded by illusion attain salvation.

Lord Shiva replied, "The one who aspires salvation, should learn *jnana* and yoga together. Through victory over *prana*, mind is won. Only yoga can give victory over *prana*.

Yoga Shikha means the head of all yogas. It is the greatest of all *jnanas*. After sitting in a proper posture, the sight should be concentrated on the tip of the nose. After controlling hands and legs, the letter *AUM* should be meditated upon with a concentrated mind. If one continuously meditates on *Parameshwara*, he will appear before that person. The four steps of the great *mahayogas* are namely, *Mantra Yoga, Laya Yoga, Hatha Yoga* and *Raja Yoga.*"

Then this chapter goes on to explain about the *chakras* in the body.

In the **second** chapter, it is said that the world functions due to Maha Maya, Maha Lakshmi, Maha Devi and Maha Saraswati and it explains these powers. Then this chapter explains about *nada* or the spiritual sound.

The **third** chapter explains about the great *nada* and the use of *Pashyanti*, the *nada* coming out of *Para Shakti* and reaching this knowledge.

In the **fourth** chapter, it is said that there is no cause for any differentiation, if the divine power that is single is seen. We see everything as world. But world is not different from *Brahman*. It is ignorance that makes a man believe that the body is attached to the soul.

In the **fifth** chapter, it is said that the one who worships his Guru or teacher as his God, gets all the *jnana*.

The **sixth** chapter is about mind. When the mind is firm, there is salvation. When mind is destroyed, the world also gets destroyed. When a man realises that there is no mind, he sees the *Parabrahma*. But it is very difficult. One can cross the sea of birth by the power of constant practice of yoga with the help of a teacher.

32. Yoga Tattva Upanishad

This *Upanishad* explains the knowledge of yoga for the benefit of yogis who are freed from all sins by hearing and studying this knowledge. The Supreme *Purush* is Vishnu and he is the lamp on the path of truth.

Brahma, the Creator, once after paying respects to Lord Vishnu requested him to explain the truth of yoga and the Lord replied, "*Maya* makes all souls immerse in happiness and sorrow. *Kaivalya* gives them emancipation with the destruction of *Maya*. This self-shining state cannot be described even by the *devas* or *shastras*. The seat of *Paramatman* which is free from decay, becomes *Jiva* or Self due to the result of its past virtues and sins. A bubble rose in *Paramatman* and in this bubble *Ahamkara* arose. In that, the body made of five elements came up. The *Jiva* that is freed from all qualities and attributes like passion and anger is considered to be alone."

Jnana coupled with yoga gives *Moksha*. *Jnana* is an important means for salvation. It emerges when the real nature of *Kaivalya* as the supreme seat which is stainless, partless, and of the nature of *Sachidananda* without birth and death is understood.

In *Mantra Yoga*, one practises mantras along with proper intonations. Then one obtains wisdom along with *Siddhis*.

Laya Yoga is with absorption of *Chit*. In this yoga, one has to contemplate upon Lord as a whole all the time.

Hatha Yoga is of eight paths namely, *Yama, Niyama, Asana, Pranayama, Pratyahara, Dharana* and *Dhyana,* that is contemplation on Lord Vishnu in the middle of the eyebrows, and *samadhi,* which is the state of equality.

This *Upanishad* then explains each of the paths in detail.

In *Yama,* the chief factor is moderate eating.

Non-injury is the most important in *Niyama*.

Asanas are the important postures namely, *siddha*, *padma*, *simha* and *bhadra*. One comes across obstacles like laziness and idle talk during the initial stages of practising yoga. By means of virtues, a wise man should overcome them. Then one should sit in *Padmasana* or in Lotus Posture on an even, smooth ground without any disturbance. Then he should salute his deity by keeping his body erect and his hands folded.

Next he should practise *Pranayama*. With continuous practice of *Pranayama* for about three months, the *nadis* get purified. When *nadis* get purified, one experiences external signs like lightness of body, glow on the face, leanness of body and calmness etc.

According to *Pratyahara*, a person who practises yoga has to take only light and mild vegetarian food.

Dharana and *dhyana* states help the yogi reach the state of meditation. After some time, *Kevala Kumbhaka* or cessation of breath without inhaling or exhaling comes. With practice, the yogi shall be able to move on earth and later leap from the ground like a frog. He will be able to perform extraordinary feats. However, he should not disclose any of his powers to others. Both excretion and sleep get decreased for such a yogi. With greater practice of yoga, he will attain *Bhuchara Siddhi*, through which he will be able to bring all creatures of the earth under his control. Wild animals will die if he will touch them. His looks will become very beautiful. However, he should maintain *Brahmacharya* or celibacy. For destroying all his past sins, he should repeat the *Pranava Mantra AUM* sitting in a lonely place.

After that, the second state called the *Ghata* state is obtained by constant practice of suppression of breath. *Ghata* state is that where there is perfect union of *Prana* and *Apana*, *Manas* and *Buddhi*, *Jivatma* and *Paramatma*. At this stage, he should consider every thing that he sees, smells, tastes, touches and hears as *Atman*. Then he obtains wonderful powers like clairvoyance, ability to become invisible, ability to transport himself instantaneously, and so on. Even then, he should not exercise his powers before anybody and should never enjoy gains. He should live in the world like a recluse to hide his powers. By constant practice of yoga, he then attains *Paricharya* state. The breath along with *Agni* pierces the *Kundalini* and enters the *Sushumna*. Then when one performs *Dharana* for two hours, he attains mastery. He gets freed from all sins. For such a person, there is no fear from water, his body is not burnt by fire even if he enters it, there is no fear from wind for him, and he obtains powers levitating in the sky. His body becomes strong. Such a person has no death.

When *Dharana* is practised to perfection, he attains *Samadhi*, the state where the *Jivatma* unites with the *Paramatma*.Through his own will, he is able to take any form. He is able to live as long as he likes. The *Upanishad* then explains the various types of yogic practices.

Shakhas of Shukla Yajur Veda

In the *Shukla Yajur Veda*, there were originally 17 branches or *shakhas*, but only two are available now. They are —

1. *Vajasaneyi Madhyandina*
2. *Vajasaneyi Kanva*

Both these branches are broadly known as *Vajasaneyi Samhitas*.

The *Madhyandina shakha* is prevalent all over North India.

The *Kanva shakha* is found in Maharashtra, Tamil Nadu, Andhra Pradesh and in Orissa with a slightly different text. This *shakha* was once prevalent in Nepal.

The *Vajasaneyi Samhita* consists of 40 chapters or *adhyayas*, *328 anuvakas* or sections and 1975 mantras. In this *Samhita*, each chapter does not have a separate title and the *Brahmana* passages are not mixed as in the *Krishna Yajur Veda*.

Brahmanas of Shukla Yajur Veda

Two *Brahmanas* of *Shukla Yajur Veda* are available. They are —

Shatapatha Brahmana

Shatapatha Brahmana means *Brahmana* of hundred paths. It contains a hundred discourses dealing with information relating to ceremonies and the philosophy of sacrifices. It is one of the oldest prose texts in Sanskrit. It belongs roughly to the period 800 BC to 2000 BC. The mythological section in this deals with the myths of Creation and the deluge of Manu. It also gives elaborate explanations about the preparation of altars, ceremonial objects, ritual recitations, and *soma* sacrifices along with the symbolic attributes of each and every aspect of the Vedic sacrifices.

Madhyandina Shatapatha Brahmana of the *Vajasaneyi Madhyandina shakha* and *Kanva Shatapatha Brahmana* of *Kanva shakha* are surviving *shakhas* of *Shukla Yajur Veda*. The *Madhyandina Satapatha Brahmana* is divided into 14 *Kands* and contains 100 *Adhyayas*, 68 *Prapathikas*, 436 *Brahmanas* and 7179 *Kandikas*. There are two major parts here. The first 9 books are the textual commentaries of the 18 books of the corresponding *Samhita* portion of the *Yajur Veda*. The last 5 books have supplementary as well as additional material. It also includes the *Brihad Aranyaka Upanishad.*

Kanva Brahmana

The *Kanva Brahmana* is divided into 17 *Kands*, 104 *Adhyayas*, 435 *Brahmanas* and 6806 *Kandikas. The Kanva Brahmana* too consists of 100 discourses that provide information on ceremonies and the philosophy of sacrifices. After *Rig Veda,* this text is considered the most important work.

Aranyakas and Upanishads of Shukla Yajur Veda

Aranyaka

The *Aranyaka* of *Shukla Yajur Veda* is *Brihad Aranyaka.* It forms the 17th book of *Kanva Shatapatha Brahmana* and the 14th book of the *Madhyandina Shatapatha Brahmana.* It has 8 sections. The 1st and the 2nd *Prapathikas* that are in *Madhyandina* version deal with the *Pravargya* rites and the last six *Prapathikas* form the *Brihad Aranyaka Upanishad.*

Upanishads

There are 19 *Upanishads* that belong to the *Shukla Yajur Veda.* They are —

1. Adhyatma Upanishad

This *Upanishad* discusses the inner self of all beings that is present in every thing and which is sinless, heaven born, luminous, and is the soul of Lord Narayana. It talks about the removal of the ego by devotion to *Brahman*, identification of Self with the subject and the witness of intellect and its operations. It also discusses the rejection of the identification with the world, body and *shastras*, destruction of mind by removing the superimposition of the feeling of 'I', disappearance of the mind with the knowledge of the self by meditating and by dissolving the Self in the Supreme Self. It also highlights the way to become the Absolute by removing the subtle body, attaining the essence by liberating one from the grip of egoism and by dissolution of impulses by perceiving everything as Spirit.

The *Upanishad* further talks about concentration and detachment with everlasting peace, attaining liberation with the knowledge that 'I am Brahman' or *Aham Brahmasmi.* This is the moment when there are no more *karmas* except the past ones which are like the arrows already released from the bow.

2. Advaya-Taraka Upanishad

This *Upanishad* speaks about illusion that results in the differentiation of the living being from God.

It talks about understanding and examining the illusion, with the knowledge of negation or *Neti*, *Neti* (not this, not this) realising the *Advaya Brahman* that does not possess two forms.

This *Upanishad* also speaks about yoga for attaining salvation by getting rid of all sins and mastery of yoga for becoming a yogi.

The different types of yoga, understanding the *Turiya* state or the *Purushartha* with the help and blessings of a great teacher are also discussed here.

3. Bhikshuka Upanishad

This *Upanishad* deals with the four kinds of mendicant monks namely, *Kutichaka, Bahudaka, Hamsa* and *Paramahamsa* who seek liberation.

Kutichaka ascetics are the hut-dwelling ascetics who live on eight mouthfuls of food and follow the path of yoga.

The *Bahudaka* ascetics live in holy places of sacred waters and take eight mouthfuls of food from alms from the houses of Brahmin sages and follow the path of yoga.

The *Hamsa* ascetics are those who stay only for one night for shelter in a village, five nights in a town, and seven nights or more in holy places. They live on cow's urine and other products from cows and follow the path of yoga.

Lastly, the *Paramahamsa* ascetics are those who live under the shades of trees, deserted houses or in cemetery. They may or may not wear anything. They are wandering monks and seek shelter only for the night in a deserted house, temple, caves, bank of a river, anthill, potter's hut, place where there is the ritual or *yajna* fire and near water. They seek alms from anyone just for sustaining the life breath. They are beyond all formalities and they see only *Atman* in one and all and identify themselves with *Brahman*.

4. Brihad Aranyaka Upanishad

This *Upanishad*, which is one of the oldest and the longest *Upanishad* dates back to around sixth century. It is considered by some as the most important of all *Upanishads*. '*Brihad Aranyaka Upanishad*' means 'The Great Forest Book'. This *Upanishad* is in the *Aranyaka* of *Shukla Yajur Veda*. This Upanishad consists of six chapters in three *Kands* or parts.

1. The *Madhu Kand* analyses the relationship between the individual and the Universal Self and their basic identity.
2. The *Muni Kand* or *Yajnavalkya Kand* consists of a dialogue between Yajnavalkya and his wife Maitreyi about philosophical justification of the teachings of *Khila Kand*.
3. The *Khila Kand* is about various rituals of worship and meditation and the three stages of religious life namely, *Shravana* or hearing the instructions in the teachings, *Manana* or reflection of what is taught, and *Upapati* and *Nididhyasana* or contemplative meditation. It forms a part of *Shatapatha Brahmana*.

The main message of this *Upanishad* is that, one should meditate with the awareness that one's soul is one with all things. Whosoever knows this is *Brahman*. The soul is real and immortal. It is incomprehensible, indestructible, unattached, and unaltered. Also, it is consciousness. When one removes the desires in one's heart and controls the senses and mind, he would reach God or *Brahman* and that is liberation.

The three cardinal virtues namely, *Damana* or self-restraint, *Dana* or alms-giving and *Daya* or compassion are mentioned in this *Upanishad*.

This *Upanishad* also explains the process of Creation. In the beginning, only *Hiranyagarbha* existed. He, the *Viraj*, created everything later including the mind, thoughts and other things.

The *Upanishad* then tells about the sacrifice of *devas* to surpass *asuras*, about Creation, Self, meditation and rites, about *Prajapati* and Gods and the origin of the four castes.

There is a conversation between Sage Gargya and Ajatashatru about the gross and subtle forms of *Brahman* and the conversation between Yajnavalkya and Maitreyi about immortality, and the Self which is the ruler of everything.

5. Hamsa Upanishad

This *Upanishad* is about Gautama asking Sanat Kumara for the knowledge of *Brahma Vidya.*

This *Upanishad* has the nature of *Hamsa*, since it explains the nature of *Hamsa* and *Paramahamsa* for the benefit of *Brahmacharis*.

It explains about the contemplation on *chakras* and ultimately becoming formless through the destruction of *manas*. At this point, virtues and sins get burnt away and the one who meditates shines as *Sadashiva* of the nature of *Shakti*, that pervades everywhere and becomes eternal.

6. Ishavasya Upanishad

This *Upanishad*, also called *Isha Upanishad*, is very short. It derives its name from the opening word of the text *Ishavasya* or *Isha*. It is the end of the *Vajrasaneyi Samhita* of *Shukla Yajur Veda* and it is the last chapter of the *Samhita*. Its main purpose is to teach the essential unity of God and the world. It states that *Ishwara* pervades the entire world. We must dedicate everything to him and attain the *Paramatman*. It stresses the relation between the Absolute and the world and points out that a person's material and spiritual goals need not be contradictory to each other. It asks one not to covet the wealth of others and live a long life by performing *karma*.

One should see God's glory in all that lives and moves. One should know that nothing belongs to him and everything belongs to God. Once, this realisation comes, all things bring pleasure because then one begins to consider himself as an instrument of God. It is by renunciation and absence of possessiveness that the soul is saved. Action does not bind the doer.

Brahman is that which moves and yet moves not. It is far, yet near. It is within all and also without all. He who perceives all beings in the Self does not entertain any hatred on account of that perception. God never moves but is swifter than thought. He is stationary and the senses and mind cannot perceive Him. Those who see God within themselves and in others lose all fear and sorrows.

God is light and everything comes from Him. He is pure, has no body, and is transcendental. He is eternal. He is all-pervasive and controls all. He is independent of the Universe but the whole Universe depends upon Him. He is below, above and everywhere.

When a man realises that all beings are but the Self, and when he sees all beings in one soul then there can be no delusion. This *Upanishad* concludes with a prayer to *Surya*, *Agni* and the Creator to help the *Atman* understand and follow the proper paths of knowledge and action.

The last three verses, especially the ones that are chanted during cremation, say that since the whole world belongs to the Lord there is nothing that we can claim to be our own. Hence, we should lead our life without claiming any ownership of any deed that we have done or the things, which God gave us for use.

7. Jabala Upanishad

Yajnavalkya clearing the doubts of Brihaspati forms the subject matter of this *Upanishad.*

Brihaspati asks Yajnavalkya about Kurukshetra, the famous holy place that destroys sins and protects the good, where Gods perform sacrifices and which is the abode of *Brahman* that is present in all beings.

Yajnavalkya provides answers for this question and also for the question put by Sage Atri to him as to how one without the sacred thread can be called a Brahmin.

Yajnavalkya says that the conviction that 'I am the Self' forms the sacred thread. Liberation in the case of Kshatriyas, in the case of those who are entitled to renunciation and in the case of *Paramahamsa* is also explained in this *Upanishad.*

8. Mandala Brahmana Upanishad

There are five *Brahmanas* in this *Upanishad.*

The **first** *Brahmana* is about Yajnavalkya seeking the knowledge of *Atma Tattva* from Lord Narayana and the Lord describing the eight-fold path of yoga along with *jnana.* They are *Yama, Niyama, Asana, Pranayama, Pratyahara, Dhyana, Dharana* and *Samadhi.* It also talks about the body having five stains namely, passion, anger, breathing out, fear and sleep. It also highlights the way for removal of all these, adhering to the subtle path and overcoming *gunas*, seeking *Taraka* which is in the middle of the two eyebrows, *kundalini* that shines like crores of lightning and is subtle where *tamas* gets destroyed. This *Upanishad* describes one becoming *akasha*, *parakasha*, *mahakasha*, *tattvakasha* and *suryakasha*. It also talks about the two-fold yoga, namely the *Purva* and *Uttara*.

In the **second** *Brahmana*, Yajnavalkya requests Purusha to describe the *Antar Lakshya* and *Purusha* gives the answer. He describes the light in the *Purva* and *Uttara* stages, hearing the sound of *Pranava* or *AUM*, in which *manas* gets absorbed, attaining the state of *Unmani*, which is the state beyond *manas* and becoming *Amanaska* or one without *manas.* It says that the real meaning of worship is by *dhyana.* It also discusses about *Avahana*, *Asana*, *Padyu*, *Snana Sandal*, attaining the state of *chitta*, about *Naivedya*, *Pradakshina*, *Namaskara*, *Shruti* and *visarjana* or the completion of worship. The state of being *Kaivalya Jyoti,* becoming *Brahmavit*, the state of *Samadhi*, becoming *Jeevan Mukta*, the five *avasthas* or stages namely, *jagrat, svapna, sushupta, turiya* and *turiyatitha* are also described in it.

In the **third** *Brahmana*, Sage Yajnavalkya asks Purusha to explain again the nature of *Amanaska* or the one without the *manas* and Purusha replies to him.

This *Brahmana* contains a detailed explanation of the great secret of *Amanaska*, the attainment of the *Unmani* state that is the state of 'I am *Brahman*'.

In the **fourth** *Brahmana*, Yajnavalkya asks Purusha to teach him about the nature of the five-fold divisions of *Akasha.* Lord Narayana explains the divisions as *Akasha, Parakasha, Mahakasha, Suryakasha* and *Paramakasha.* He says that a true yogi is the one who has the realisation of nine *chakras*, six *adharas*, three *lakshyas*, and five *akashas*.

The **fifth** *Brahmana* is about *manas* that is in bondage with worldly things and the *manas* that has no bondage which is suitable for salvation. It also describes the nature of one who is *amanaska* and who becomes a *Paramahamsa* or an *Avadhutha* and describes his greatness.

9. Mantrika Upanishad

This *Upanishad* tells about the nature of sages beholding the Absolute and who are beyond the three *gunas*. It says that the Lord's *maya* brings beings into existence. However, *maya* is experienced by the ignorant only, and not by the sages. Lord alone enjoys the *maya* through contemplation and action.

It also tells about the understanding of the Lord in different manners by different people, about how the great seers conceive the Lord as everything, one and all-pervading, and about the nature of *Brahman* or Lord.

10. Muktika Upanishad

This *Upanishad* describes the scene where Sri Rama, along with his wife Sita is sitting in the state of *samadhi* and his brothers are meditating. The great *Bhakta*, Hanuman, asks Sri Rama to explain his true nature. He also wants to know how one can be released from bondage without strain. Sri Rama states that *Vedanta* is his breath and explains about the four Vedas, each having *Upanishads* and states that even by reading one verse from the *Upanishads* with devotion one gets united with the Supreme, Sri Rama.

Then Hanuman raises doubts about different kinds of liberation spoken by sages. Rama explains the four kinds of liberations, namely, *Salokya, Saroopya, Samipya* and *Kaivalya* out of which the real type of liberation is *Kaivalya*.

Sri Rama further tells Hanuman about —

- The greatness of uttering *Taraka* mantra
- Getting *Sarupya* that will wash off all sins

- How one who worships Sri Rama attains all the four kinds of liberation
- The need for reading and assimilating *Mandukya Upanishad* for obtaining *Kaivalya* type of liberation
- How the one who is unable to understand that *Upanishad* gets the knowledge from ten *Upanishads*
- How if even then one is unable to obtain the required knowledge should study thirty-two *Upanishads*
- The need for one to obtain knowledge from all the 108 *Upanishads* in order to obtain *Moksha*
- How the knowledge of these lead to the destruction of identification of the Self or *Atman* with the body, senses, and mind

He also describes the greatness of the *Upanishads* and the people to whom these should be taught.

Further on, Anjaneya requests Sri Rama to explain to him about the *Shanti mantras* of the different Vedas. Sri Rama then gives the list of 10 *Upanishads* of *Rig Veda* which contain the *Shanti mantra*, the 19 *Upanishads* of *Shukla Yajur Veda*, 32 *Upanishads* of *Krishna Yajur* Veda, 16 *Upanishads* of *Sama Veda* and 31 *Upanishads* of *Atharva Veda*.

Then Hanuman asks Sri Rama about *Jeevan mukti.*

Sri Rama explains about it on the basis of the 10 *Upanishads* and about two kinds of human efforts which are for and against *shastras*.

Then Sri Rama asks Hanuman to practise the destruction of mental impressions and teaches him the importance of giving up *Vasanas* or cravings to become detached. He also teaches him about the destruction of mind, giving up the state of *Jeevan mukta* and entering into the *Videha mukti* stage.

11. Niralamba Upanishad

This *Upanishad* contains questions and answers that are to be known for dissolving the misfortunes of ignorant humans.

It explains who is the *Brahman,* the *Prakriti*, Vishnu, Rudra, Indra, Yama, Sun, Moon, Gods, demons, and evil spirits.

It also talks about men, women, animals, deed, non-deed, knowledge, ignorance, pleasure, pain, heaven, hell, bondage, liberation, a disciple, sage, austerity, and the supreme abode.

It defines that which is sought after, that to be rejected, and the one who renounces and so on.

12. Paingala Upanishad

This *Upanishad* discusses meditation and its effects. Paingala approached his teacher Yajnavalkya and after serving him as a disciple for 12 years, he requested his Guru, the teacher, to enlighten him about the supreme mystery of aloneness. Yajnavalkya explained him *Brahman* which is without a witness or consciousness. He also highlighted the appearance of *Mahat* reflecting the consciousness of *Hiranyagarbha*, the emergence of ego reflecting the consciousness of *Virat*, the emergence of the five elements composed of the three *gunas*, emergence of unlimited crores of microcosm from the elements, *Prana* and organs of action emerging from the *Rajas*, the emergence of inner organ and guardians of sense organs from the *Sattva*, God entering into the macrocosm, and the individual bodies deluded by *maya* becoming *Jiva*.

Again Paingala asked Yajnavalkya as to how the omnipotent Lord of all the worlds becomes *Jiva*. For this question, Yajnavalkya replied by explaining about the five states namely, wakefulness, dream, dreamless sleep, swoon and death, and rebirth as per the results of past deeds, seeking liberation at the end of many lives and about bondage.

Paingala put another request to Yajnavalkya to explain to him about the major text or *Mahavakyas*, namely, '*Thou art that, thou that art, thou Brahman art*' and 'I am *Brahman*' which are to be meditated upon, *Tat* and *Tvam* that is *Brahman* which is non-different from the Self, about meditation and concentration, liberation in life by meditating on the illumining Self that is of the size of a thumb located in the centre like a smokeless flame, immutable and immortal.

Finally Paingala wanted to know from Yajnavalkya about, how a knower or *jnani* acts. Yajnavalkya replied that the one seeking liberation takes twenty-one generations across the sea of *Samsara* (world), while the knower of *Brahman* does the same for 101 generations. Then he compared the Self to the rider of the chariot. He compared the body to the chariot, the intellect to the charioteer, the mind to the reins, the senses to the horses, and heart to the multi-storeyed mansions.

Regarding the behaviour of the liberated soul who has the knowledge of 'I am that', he states that there are no duties or Vedas for such a soul. Standing on one foot, doing penance for 1000 years is less than one-sixteenth of the yoga of meditation. So meditate on truth alone.

Purification, mutterings, sacrifices, and pilgrimages have meaning only till truth is realised.

The *Upanishad* ends with a statement about the greatness of studying *Upanishads* every day.

13. Paramahamsa Upanishad

In this *Upanishad* Narada asks Lord Brahma about the path and duties of *Paramahamsa* yogis and Brahma enlightens Narada about this.

Lord Brahma says that the path of a *Paramahamsa* is resting in the ever-pure *Brahman*. He is the one who has realised the eternal *Brahman*. He always lives with the consciousness and *jnana* that 'I, myself, am Brahma', and 'I am *Brahman*' and he is the one who reaches the end of his desires.

14. Satyayaniya Upanishad

This *Upanishad* asserts that the mind attached to objects of the senses is the cause of all bondage, whereas the mind that is detached from the objects of senses leads to liberation. Hence for liberation, the mind has to be detached from the objects of senses and is to be focused on *Brahman* because, 'As the mind, so one becomes'. Only one who knows and realises that he is *Brahman* reaches that Supreme abode.

This *Upanishad* also tells about the nature of *Paramahamsa*, about the four kinds of ascetics namely, *Kutichaka, Bahudaka, Hamsa* and *Paramahamsa*. It also talks about the nature of these ascetics, the practice of yoga and about the realisation that one is the *Atman* undifferentiated from the Universal Self.

There is realisation of *Brahman* leading to everlasting bliss, the consequences of abandoning asceticism, renunciation of one person in a family leading to blessings for hundred generations of his family before and after him, and the need for supreme faith in God and Guru.

15. Subala Upanishad

This *Upanishad* is in the form of dialogue between Sage Subala and Brahma about the Universe and the Absolute. It provides ten lessons.

The **first** lesson has two sections. These deal with the subsistence and dissolution of the Universe.

The **second** lesson has the third, fourth and the fifth sections. These teach about the Universal *Atman* or *Brahman*, achieving this by means of truth, charity, austerity, celibacy, and detachment by observing self-control, compassion and by means of other good qualities. It says that the lotus in the midst of the heart blooms in many ways. The Supreme Being living there assigns places to the organs like ear, eyes etc.

The **third** lesson that is in the sixth section is about *Purusha*, the Lord Narayana. Sages look at this as the eye spread in the sky and enhancing the glory of the sky.

The **fourth** lesson in the seventh section is about the nature of the inner controller, the immortal being inside the body, the Lord Narayana. This is the doctrine of *Nirvana.*

The Self in the body is explained in the **fifth** lesson that is in the eighth, ninth and the tenth sections. The wise behold this Self that is immortal, fearless, painless and seedless into which all things are resolved. One who knows the seedless *Brahman* becomes seedless. He is not affected by anything. The Self can be achieved only by remaining calm, restrained, withdrawn, and tolerant and with concentration. In the tenth section, we find the questions put by Raikva and the answers to those questions. All the worlds are in *Brahman* like gems in a string, the knowledge of which is *Nirvana* or liberation stated in the Vedas.

The **sixth** lesson in the eleventh section is regarding the upward path about which Raikva asked.

The **seventh** lesson is in the twelfth and the thirteenth sections are about *Samadhi.* This lesson explains about the food which is proper to eat, and the nature of sages.

The **eighth** lesson in the fourteenth section explains about the food and also becoming one with the supreme deity, beyond which there is neither existence nor non-existence.

The **ninth** lesson in the fifteenth section relates to the question put by Raikva about that, which is burnt by the mass of knowledge, the spirit, the Vedic knowledge of liberation.

Imparting *Brahma Vidya* is discussed in the **tenth** lesson. It discusses matters like, to whom the lessons of the doctrine of liberation, as explained in the *Subala Upanishad*, should be taught.

16. Tara-Sara Upanishad

This *Upanishad* contains three chapters.

In the **first** chapter, we find the question put by Bhardwaja to Yajnavalkya as to where one should go for understanding Kurukshetra considered as the place of sacrifice of the *devas*, the spiritual seat of all beings, and the place of study of the Vedas and the reply of Yajnavalkya.

Kurukshetra, also known as *Avimuhter*, is the place where Rudra initiates one into the *Taraka Brahman* when the *Prana* goes out. Bhardwaja again wanted to know as to what is *Taraka*, that which helps in crossing mundane existence.

Yajnavalkya replies stating that *Taraka* is *Aum Namo Narayana.*

- *Aum* is the nature of *Brahman*
- *Namo* is the nature of *Prakriti*
- *Narayana* is the nature of *Para Brahman*

Through this *Taraka* or *Ashtakshara* or the eight letter mantra, Brahma or '*AUM*', Vishnu or '*NA*', Maheshwara or '*MA*', '*NA*' or *Ishwara*, '*RA*' or *Virat* of the Universe, '*YA*' or the *Purusha*, '*NA*' or God, '*YA*' or *Paramatman* are produced.

The **second** chapter is about the worshipping of '*AUM*'. It is supposed to have eight subtle syllables. This is *Taraka*. This chapter also provides the explanation of '*AUM*' that represents the past, present and the future and other than these.

The eight subtle syllables are: '**A**' is the first letter, '**U**' is the second letter, '**M**' is the third letter, **Bindu (.)** is the fourth letter, **Nada** is the fifth letter, **Kaala** is the sixth letter, **Kaalatitha** is the seventh letter and beyond all these is forming the eighth.

The **third** chapter is about the question put by Bhardwaja to Yajnavalkya about the mantra through which *Paramatman* is pleased and shows his *Atman* to persons. This chapter also has the reply of Yajnavalkya stating that the one who has mastered the eightfold mantra '*AUM*' reaps its benefits and finally attains the state of Lord Narayana himself.

17. Trisikhi Brahmana Upanishad

Trisikhi Brahmin asked the Sun God as to what are body, soul, and God.

The Sun God replied, "Lord Shiva is all these in different forms. He gives light to *Brahman* or *Sattva*. This again gives rise to *Mahat*. From *Mahat* emerges egoism. Egoism results in five *Tanmantras*. These five *Tanmantras* give rise to the five elements or the *Panch mahabhootas*. These constitute the twelve aspects of early concepts of physical existence and the concepts of Godliness."

This *Upanishad* then talks about the origin of the earth, the seat of Gods, egoism and actions in the heart of the body which is like a lotus flower with stalk, about the *Atma* or soul that is shining and located on the tip of the head, churning of mind resulting in painful thoughts, performance of duties resulting in becoming slave to duties.

It also discusses how by forsaking, peace is attained, how wisdom is attained by sending soul power to head by practising yoga.

Then the *Upanishad* talks about becoming a yogi by means of wisdom and through the practice of yoga, about controlling sensory organs by pure knowledge of *Atma* and obtaining the real state of *Samadhi* which is the realisation of the unity of the *Jeevatma* with the *Paramatma* and about the nature of such a man who has realised the truth.

18. Turiyatita Avadhuta Upanishad

Lord Brahma once approached Lord Narayana and asked him about the path of *Avadhuta* after the *Turiyatita* stage.

Lord Narayana told him about the *Avadhuta* who is an embodiment of dispassion and a visible form of wisdom and personification of the Vedas and the various stages of such a soul. He described these stages starting from the hut-dwelling ascetic, then to the stage of a mendicant monk, then to the stage of a *Hamsa* ascetic and then becoming *Paramahamsa*, about the nature of a *Paramahamsa* who is completely absorbed in non-duality of *Atman* and who finally becoms one with the *Brahman* or '*AUM*' or *Pranava*.

19. Yajnavalkya Upanishad

King Janaka once requested Yajnavalkya to tell him about renunciation.

Yajnavalkya explained to him about the four stages of life namely, *Brahmacharya*, *Grihasthashrama*, *Vanaprastha* and *Sanyasa*. He also explained to him about the performance of the sacrifices like *Prajapatya*, *Agneyi*, and *Traidhataviya* for becoming a *sanyasi*.

Then Sage Atri asked Yajnavalkya to tell him about how is the one without sacred thread is a Brahmin.

To this Yajnavalkya replied, "The conviction that 'I am the self-effulgent *Atman*' becomes the sacred thread of such a person."

Then Yajnavalkya went on to explain the path of a mendicant *sanyasi* or monk. He also talked about the well-known *Paramahamsas* of yore and the nature of *Paramahamsas*. He told him about the conviction of such a person that Consciousness is all-pervading and everything and everybody is nothing but Consciousness which is the highest stage.

7
Atharva Veda

Atharva Veda Samhita

Atharva Veda is the last of the four Vedas. It is referred to as the Veda of the wise and old. It is a collection of hymns of diverse nature. This Veda is associated with the name of the ancient poet Atharvan, meaning 'the wise old one'. This Veda is also associated with the name of another seer called Angirasa and therefore this Veda is also referred to as the *Atharvangirasa Veda.* This Veda is dual in nature, dealing with sorcery on the one hand and *Shanthi pushti* rites on the other which are associated with these two sages. Atharvan also means a fair priest in Vedic Sanskrit.

It is believed that this Veda was composed by two clans of fire priests known as Bhrigus who were also called Atharvans and Angirasas, although it also included the compositions of clans like, Kaushikas, Vashishthas and Kashyapas. Hence, it is also called *Bhrigvangirasa Veda.*

Atharva also means that which is stationary, unwavering and unchanging referring to the neutrality of personality. This Veda is sometimes referred to as *Brahma Veda* as it is chanted by a set of priests called *Brahma* and probably also because it has many hymns dealing with spirituality. Another name for this Veda is *Kshatra Veda* as it has several hymns relating to war, rites of coronation and so on. This Veda is believed to have been composed in a later period. This Veda has simpler language than that found in the other Vedas. It is much longer than *Sama Veda* and *Yajur Veda* and one-sixth of this Veda is from *Rig Veda*. The Samhita portion of this Veda is different from the other three Vedas as it deals more with the things and the corresponding sacrifices to achieve them. This Veda was for a long time not accepted as authoritative Veda because of its contents. But later it was elevated to the position of Vedas. This Veda was supposed to have been written around 1500 BC.

Hymns of Atharva Veda

The *Shaunakiya Atharva Veda* has 4 *Prapathikas* divided into 20 *Kands* or chapters, subdivided into 730 *Suktas* or hymns and they are further subdivided into 5987 mantras and a small section of prose. The hymns in the 20th *Kand* are mostly from *Rig Veda*. The Pippalada has approximately 7950 mantras.

We find a fusion of prose and poetry in this Veda. About one-seventh of this Veda is common to *Rig Veda*. Some verses are common to the other two Vedas as well. It is said that Vyasa taught this Veda to his disciple Sumanta. This Veda is meant for the Atharva Vedic priest called Brahma for correcting the mispronunciations and wrong performances that might have accidentally committed by the other three categories of priests during the performance of sacrifices.

This Veda has 2 parts —

(i) Atharva

(ii) Angirasa

The *Atharva* is for softer use and the *Angirasa* has some harsh usages.

The hymns of this Veda contain lot of knowledge about the physical and material world and spirituality. There are charms against enemies, demons, wizards, harmful and poisonous animals like snakes, sickness of man and cattle, and also against those who oppress Brahmins. There are also hymns for positive effects like obtaining and ensuring love, happy family life, health, longevity, protection during journeys, luck in gambling and things like that. However, the major part of this Veda is concerned with diseases and their cure, rituals for long life, rituals for fulfilling one's desires, building and construction, trade and commerce, statecraft, penance and so on. Simultaneously in this Veda, one can also find high philosophical ideas that are very close to the *Upanishads*. The verses are referred to as *Siddha* mantras. The verses here are for various special purposes. They include even the practical sciences. The verses glorify the curative powers of the various medicinal plants and herbs and also water. Many verses also discuss diseases like cough and jaundice believed to have been caused by male and female demons. References are found about the sweet-smelling herbs and magic amulets for curing diseases. There are also verses relating to sins and their atonement, errors in performing rituals, their expiatory acts, and also topics relating to politics and philosophy.

Hymns called *Bheshajani*, for successful childbirth, romance, virility, and fecundity are also found in this Veda. A few beautiful, philosophic and poetical passages are contained here. A hymn about Mother Earth or *Prithvi* glorifying this planet with all its creatures is one such poem. This hymn expresses the oneness of human life and nature. The rituals connected with *Shantika*, *Paushtika*, and *Abhicharika Vidya* that include cure of diseases, acquiring wealth etc are also explained here.

The bewitching or the negative spells called *abhichara* for causing harm and even diseases to enemies were mostly aimed at serpents and demons.

It also elaborates on yoga, the human physiology, different ailments, social structure, spirituality, natural beauty and national religion. There are also facts relating to astronomical and medical sciences as well as spiritual meditation. *Ayurveda* is considered as the *Upa Veda* of the *Atharva Veda*.

The *Atharva Veda* is perhaps the first Indian text explaining diseases and medicines. There are hymns identifying the cause of diseases in the form of agents like the *Gatudhanya*, the *Kimldi*, the *Krimi* and the drugs to kill these agents and cure the diseases. For example, the hymn 1.2 describes leprosy and recommends herbs for treating this disease. Brain as an important and critical organ of the body is also mentioned in this Veda.

The *Atharva Veda* includes almost everything in practical life like, success in love and the realisation of other worldly ambitions.

There are mantras to drive away misfortunes and disasters and for destroying the enemies. There are references to deities not mentioned in the other Vedas. The gods found in the other Vedas are invoked with love. But some of the fiery spirits addressed to in this Veda are approached with fear and favours are asked from them to ward off the evil sprits.

Some of the deities mentioned in the hymns are, *Rohita, Phatrh, Vidhata, Parameshthi, Varuna, Kala*, and *Kama*. There are also mantras addressed to fiery spirits. There are references of military practices and the associated Kshatriya rites. A variety of devices such as an arrow with a duct for *apaskamba* (poison), castor bean poison, poisoned nets, hook traps, use of disease spreading bugs, and smoke screens are explained here.

Mantras are found for specific rituals like marriage, funeral and so on. The hymns also stress the importance of discipline, knowledge, water having medicinal properties as the elixir of life, healthy and strong body, marriage, agriculture, domestic ceremonies, funeral ritual, coronation, unity that leads to prosperity, service to the nation, sweet and soft speech, abstinence from violence, kindness, politeness, performing good actions, keeping away all that pollutes the mind, fearlessness, yoga, benevolence and so on.

Things that result in bad effects namely evil deeds, sensual attachment, hatred, and anger are also mentioned in the hymns. One can find hymns relating to magic, spells and sorcery in this Veda. There are hymns mentioning rituals for destroying enemies as well. There are also hymns relating to human physiology, social structure, spirituality, appreciation of natural beauty and national religion. It is said that the science of magic or *mantrikam* has its root in this Veda.

Agni is worshipped for personality and for overcoming all evils and sins. There are hymns describing atoms as forming the stone, the stones joining to form the rocks, and the rocks held together to form the earth. This Veda has a separate *Gayatri mantra*.

Skambha, that is considered as a common thread running through all manifest and un-manifest existence is described in this Veda as Indra representing all existence. Further the hymn describes *Skambha* as the heat spreading in the entire Universe as waves of water, its units being the Gods.

Unlike in the case of other Vedas, people who want to learn this Veda are required to go through a second *Upanayanam* for learning it. All the hymns whether they are invocations, out of love or out of fear, clearly indicate that our ancestors were aware of the power of mind very well.

Shakhas of Atharva Veda

It is said that there were nearly 9 original *shakhas* in this Veda. They are *Paippalada*, *Stauda*, *Mauda*, *Shaunakiya*, *Jajala*, *Jalada*, *Brahmavada*, *Devadarshana* and *Charanavidya*.

In addition, a few more ancient *Atharva Veda* schools are mentioned in certain *Puranas* and they are, *Sumantu, Kabhanda, Kumuda, Lalkyana, Babhravya, Munjakeshi, Shaulkayani, Nahlatrahalpa, Linkalpa* and *Sahitavedi*.

However, of all the above, only two recensions are available now. They are —

- *Paippalada Shakha*
- *Shaunakiya Shakha*

The *Paippalada* followers are found in Orissa, Bihar, and West Bengal. It is said to have thrived once upon a time in Coastal Andhra Pradesh.

The *Shaunakiya Atharva Veda* followers are found in Gujarat, Karnataka, Rajasthan, Coastal Andhra Pradesh, Uttar Pradesh, and Himachal Pradesh.

The *Staudayana Atharva Veda* followers are not found now. But it is said that it was followed in central and eastern Uttar Pradesh.

At present no followers are seen for *Shaulkayani* and *Munjakeshi* recensions either.

The *Charanavidya* and *Jajala* are also said to have existed in Gujarat, Central India and Rajasthan once but they are not seen now.

The *Mauda Shakha* was followed once upon a time in Kashmir. Now it is not available.

Content of Atharva Veda

The *Atharva Veda* is divided into 10 books.

- The **first** book is in two parts. Both the parts relate to charms to cure diseases and possessions by demons of diseases.
- The **second** book is about prayers for long life and health.
- The **third** book again has two parts. They tell us about the imprecations against demons, sorcerers and enemies.
- The **fourth** book is about charms pertaining to women.
- The **fifth** book deals with charms pertaining to royalty.
- The **sixth** book contains charms to secure harmony, influence in the assembly, and so on.
- The **seventh** book explains charms to secure prosperity in house, field, cattle, business, gambling, etc.
- The **eighth** book relates to charms in expiation of sins committed.
- The two parts of the **ninth** book consists of prayers and imprecation for Brahmins.
- The **tenth** book that forms the final book of this Veda contains the cosmogenic and theosophic hymns.

Brahmanas of Atharva Veda

The only surviving *Brahmana* of the *Atharva Veda* is *Gopatha Brahmana*. There are two parts of this *Brahmana* —

- *Purvardha*
- *Uttarardha*

The *Purvardha* or the first half of the *Brahmana* glorifies the *Atharvan* and the related priests. The *Purvardha* contains a number of lectures.

The second half, which is called *Uttarardha* contains legends related to the other *Atharvan* priests. The *Uttarardha* consists of critical appreciation of the rituals. It is largely based on the material gathered from the other three Vedas. It is believed that this text originally had 100 *Prapathikas*.

Aranyakas and Upanishads of Atharva Veda

Aranyaka

This Veda has no *Aranyaka* texts.

Upanishads

According to *Muktikopanishad*, there are 93 *Upanishads* associated with this Veda. *Upanishads* numbering about 31 are now in existence.

The 31 *Upanishads* associated with this Veda are —

1. Annapurna Upanishad

The great Yogi Nidagha prostrated before Ribhu, and requested him to impart the knowledge of Self to him and wanted to know how Ribhu attained the state of Brahma, and Ribhu replied, "The divine Annapurna is the illustrious *Maha Lakshmi.* She is the eternal bliss, desire, fulfilment and everything."

He then went on, "My father instructed me the 27 syllables given by a host of female ascetics in praise of her and I prayed to her with those syllables." They were —

ऐं, ह्रीं, सौं, क्लीं, ॐ नमो भगवती अन्नपूर्णे
ममाभिलाषी तव अन्नं देहि स्वाहा।

Aim̐, Hrīm', Saum', Klīm', Aum' namo bhagvati annapūrṇe mamābhilāṣi tav annaṁ dehi swāhā

(Salutation, O Divine Annapuna, vouchsafe the food I desire.)

Ribhu said, "I have been chanting this always. After many days, the Divine Annapurna appeared before me. Pleased with my prayer, she told me to ask for a boon. I asked her for the knowledge of Self. She agreed and blessed me and disappeared. Then, the knowledge dawned on me. There are fivefold delusions in this world."

Due to the **first** delusion, *Jiva* is believed to be separate from God.

Due to the **second,** the attribute of agency dwelling in the Self, which is not real, appears to be real.

The **third** is *Jiva* possessing attachment.

The **fourth** is that the God is considered as a changing one.

Due to the **fifth** delusion, world is taken to be real.

"But there was a flash in my mind about the cessation of this fivefold ignorance. Instantaneously, my mind got assimilated to *Brahman*. So in this way you too can obtain knowledge."

After hearing this with all humility, Nidagha requested Ribhu to impart to him the knowledge of *Brahman*. In response, Ribhu asked Nidagha to believe in *Aham Brahmasmi* (I am *Brahman)* ever manifest and pure. He said, "In this way after quietening and purifying the mind, one obtains *Nirvana*. Everything that you see is like a mirage. On the other hand, what is not seen is beyond the range of the sixth sense and you have to realise that. When devoid of all desires of objects, when *chitta* or consciousness subsides, there comes the knowledge. The liberated self experiences the state beyond the fourth state. This happens only to the wise and not to the ignorant ones. Through right knowledge, this state can be obtained. The inner cool of that person who perceives the world and the objects as not related to self is what is called concentration."

"In the state of contemplation, there is steadiness of mind that is empty of latent impulses. The mind's imagination of being the doer is the cause for all sorrows. A person who becomes non-attached to everything is always inwardly withdrawn wherever he is. When the inner cool is won, the world is also cool. To attain this state, one must enquire, '*Who am I? How is everything brought about? How do death and birth happen?*' Then you will get the greater benefit of investigation. When all objects and the world are renounced, then only the supreme Self, the transcendental light will shine. Only then the Self can be won. Hence renounce everything, knowing that everything is only the vibration of consciousness and is not permanent. Only when the mind and ego subsides, one can realise this truth. When the mind is killed with the mind, then Supreme bliss is obtained. The attached mind, even with long austerities is bound." Then Nidagha asked about bondage and liberation and Ribhu replied, "The exclusive attachment of the body is the binding. One should know that everything is Self only. This has to be developed by practice and this is the fourth state. In this state, a person is in everlasting bliss. The dwindling of the mind in which all desires dry up is called liberation. A *Jivan Mukta* lives unattached in the pure being, the Self. He does not bother about the past, present or future. He is steadfast, blissful, polished, simple, sweet, and never indulges in self-pity. He is the one who has realised that '*all the world is Self alone'*. At that stage only *Brahman* remains. Plurality exists in imagination only."

Then Nidagha asked about liberation without body.

Ribhu said that in the region of Sumeru, Sage Mandavya became liberated in life with the teachings of Kaundinya. After becoming a *Jivan Mukta,* this sage decided to withdraw all his sense-organs and he started meditating. He attained the knowledge of a new-born infant – the unqualified state of consciousness or the state of pure Being. Then he became the unuttered, motionless, the illuminator of lights. When all desires dry up, Self is won. This *Upanishad* then gives the story of two birds corresponding to the *Jivatma* and *Paramatma*. When the mind ceases to ponder, mindlessness arises and it yields supreme tranquillity. The wise know that liberation is non-attachment. When one beholds all beings in one's Self, one becomes *Brahman*. This *Upanishad* ends with the statement that whosoever studies this Upanishad with the blessings of his teacher become a *Jivan Mukta* and he himself becomes *Brahman*.

2. Atharvasikha Upanishad

Sage Pippalada, Angira, and Sanath Kumar approached the great

Sage Atharva and requested him to explain the chief aspect of meditation, the holy syllable on which to meditate, who can meditate, and who is the God of meditation.

To this, Sage Atharva replied, "The mantra *AUM* has to meditated upon."

The **first** letter of this mantra '**A**', indicates the *Rig Veda*, earth, Brahma, the eight *Vasus*, *Gayatri mantra*, and *Garhapathya* or household fire. It is the creative aspect.

The **second** letter '**U**', denotes the *Yajur Veda*, ether, Rudra, the eleven *Rudras*, *Trishgup mantra*, and *Dakshinagni* or the fire of the south, that is, the funeral pyre. It is the destructive aspect.

The **third** syllable '**M**', indicates the *Sama Veda*, heavens, Vishnu, the twelve *Adityas*, *Jagatichanda mantra*, and *Ahavagni*, the sacred fire of Vedic sacrifices. This is the maintaining aspect.

The **fourth** half-hidden syllable is the *Atharva Veda, Samvartaka* or the fire of exchange, *Gunas* of *devas*. It is *Purushottam* and self-shining *Brahman*. The fourth hidden syllable and the hidden sound when pronounced for the first time, takes one to the *Sahasrara Nadi* via *Sushumna Nadi*.

Thus *AUM* is *Pranava Mantra*. It is the mantra of meditation. Because of this meditation, Vishnu won over everyone and Brahma obtained the position of Creator. It is advised that the five Gods, Brahma, Vishnu, Rudra, Ishwara, and *Shiva* are to be worshipped in the form of *Pranava*. Even if one meditates on these for one second, he gets more benefits than performing a hundred fire sacrifices. One should learn and understand this for attaining salvation.

3. Atharvasiras Upanishad

The *devas* prayed to Rudra as everything imperishable and eternal. Later he explained about the various names of Lord Rudra, their meaning and his greatness.

4. Atma Upanishad

The spirit manifests itself in three ways – the Self, the inner Self, and the Supreme Self. The organs are born and die. They constitute **Self**.

The **inner Self** is indicated by the elements and mental feelings like desire and pleasure. The **Supreme Self** is imperishable. One has to meditate upon Him with yogic steps like, breath control, withdrawal from sense organs, fixing up of mind, contemplation, and concentration. He is to be understood as the minutest of the minutest. He cannot be known but can be won. He is neither born nor perishes. He is beyond *Gunas*. He is spectator, pure, whole, subtle and invisible. The knower of *Brahman* delights in himself without the senses of '**I**' and '**Mine**'. Though living in body, he is without body. He is not affected by good or bad. The one, who stays as the pure unqualified Self, is himself the manifest Shiva. The knower of *Brahman* finally becomes one himself. For such a one, there is no rebirth as bondage or liberation both are set by *Maya* and do not pertain to the Self.

5. Bhasma Jabala Upanishad

Once Bhusunda, a descendent of Jabali, went to Kailash and prayed to Lord Shiva. He requested him to impart to him the essential knowledge of all Vedas and the process of using *Bhasma* or the sacred ash. He wanted to know what *Bhasma* was made of, where it should be applied, what mantras were to be recited at the time of its application, which persons were fit for the recitation of mantras.

To this, Lord Shiva explained the method of making *Bhasma*, how it had to be preserved, how it should be purified, how the devotee had to apply it from his head to toe and how to perform the morning prayer with *Bhasma*.

He also explained the need to apply *Bhasma* and worship Lord Shiva daily, about wearing Rudraksha beads, performing *Sandhya*, the sanctity of the place Benaras, and the greatness of praying to Lord Shiva.

6. Bhavana Upanishad

This *Upanishad* explains about the holy teacher who is *Para Shakti*. It talks of the power of the body, the four *Purusharthas* namely, *Dharma, Artha, Kama,* and *Moksha,* the body, the resolutions, the energy and the six seasons which form the six tastes.

It further describes the knowledge that is the material for worship, destiny and sentiments like love etc, the nine abodes, the sixteen powers like the elements, sensory organs, organs of evacuation and generation, feet, hands, speech, lust and so on.

It then explains the fourteen powers, the five vital and minor breaths, the digestive fire as well as the ten aspects of fire, qualities of cold and heat, and the three *Gunas*. It further explains the sounds, mind, attachment and aversion.

This *Upanishad* tells that the unmanifest are the divinities. Absolute awareness is *Kameshwara*. The supreme divinity, *Lalita* is the blissful self. The act of oblation is the merger in the Self of all distinctions of an individual and his existence.

This is the meditation on the inner wheel. The one who thus meditates becomes Shiva-Yogi.

7. Brihad Jabala Upanishad

This *Upanishad* is divided into 8 *Brahmanas*.

In the **first** *Brahmana*, we find Bhusunda approaching Lord Kalagni Rudra and requesting him to tell him about the greatness of applying *Bhasma*, the sacred ash and wearing Rudraksha beads.

Kalagni Rudra said that this has already been told by Sage Pippalada and there is nothing more to tell. So Bhusunda requested the Lord to tell him about the route to salvation as told by the great Jabala. Then this *Upanishad* tells as to how *Bhasma* came from the dung of the golden cow **Nanda**, black cow **Bhadra**, red cow **Surabhi**, white cow **Susheela** and multi-coloured cow **Sumana**.

The different names of the holy ash are —

- *Vibhuthi* because it gives wealth
- *Bhasitam* because it destroys all sins
- *Bhasmam* because it makes materials glitter
- *Ksara* because it protects one from dangers
- *Raksha* because it protects one from the fear of ghosts, devils, demons, and diseases like epilepsy

In the **second** *Brahmana*, we find Bhusunda asking Kalagni Rudra to tell him about the *Bhasma Abhishekam* or bathing in the ash. The ash of the fire that burns the world pervades the whole world. In this, strength of fire ash becomes an integral part. Those who understand this strength of ash do the sacred ash bathing, by uttering the mantras, for burning all sins committed and for attaining salvation.

In the **third** *Brahmana*, the fourfold method of preparing *Bhasma* is explained. These methods are called *Anukalpam, Upakalpam, Upopakalpam* and *Akalpam*. Applying the *Bhasma* prepared by any one of these methods leads to salvation.

In the **fourth** *Brahmana*, we find Bhusunda requesting Lord Kalagni Rudra to tell him the significance of wearing *Bhasma* in three lines on the forehead. The Lord tells him that one has to apply it on forehead, chest, stomach, neck, middle of the body, wrists, back of the body, top of the body and on the head with the appropriate mantras. When one applies *Bhasma* on the forehead, one should meditate on Lord Shiva and similarly while applying on other parts of the body, he should continue chanting of mantras for removing the sins committed in the previous births.

In the **fifth** *Brahmana*, it is said that dishonoring the three lines of *Bhasma* is same as dishonoring Lord Shiva and those who apply it with devotion wear the Lord himself. Forehead without *Bhasma* is a deserted forehead and life without worshipping Lord Shiva is a deserted life. The holy ash that is born out of fire burns off all the sins of people who apply *Bhasma.*

In the **sixth** *Brahmana*, the greatness of *Bhasma* is stated again. The holy ash or *Bhasma* grants all sorts of wealth and washes off even sins like *Brahmahatya*, that is killing of a noble man or the knower of *Brahman.*

The **seventh** *Brahmana* is about King Videha approaching

Sage Yajnavalkya and requesting him to explain to him the way of applying the holy ash and Yajnavalkya explaining the method of *Bhasma Jyoti* to him.

Kalagni Rudra once told Sanath Kumar about the origin of Rudraksha and stated that the one who touches or wears Rudraksha beads gets the same result as of giving a thousand cows in charity.

In the **eighth** *Brahmana*, the greatness of *Brihad Jabala Upanishad* is told. It is said that the one who reads this *Upanishad* daily would be blessed by all Gods, would attain the world where there is eternal happiness without any sorrow, which is full of peace and purity and that is praised by Gods like Brahma.

This *Upanishad* ends with the words '*Aum Satya*' (Truth is supreme).

8. Dattatreya Upanishad

Once Brahma asked Lord Narayana about the efficacy of the *Taraka* mantra. The Lord replied, "The one who meditates upon Lord Narayana who is *Datta*, the great Lord, will not be caught in *maya* in the course of worldly existence."

After meditating thus, Brahma said that after negating everything only *Brahman* remained.

Then this *Upanishad* explains about the one, six, eight, twelve and sixteen-syllable mantras of Dattatreya, the *moola mantra* of Dattatreya and so on.

This *Upanishad* ends with a statement that the one who knows all about this knowledge and practice becomes holy and attains the fruits that he gets by chanting *Gayatri mantra*, *Maha Rudra mantra* and the *Pranava mantra* innumerable time. All his sins are destroyed.

9. Devi Upanishad

All the Gods one asked the Goddess as to who she was and where she came from.

She told them that she was essentially *Brahman*, from whom the world consisting of *Prakriti* and *Purusha* emerged. She was the void, bliss and non-bliss, knowledge and ignorance, the world and no world, Vedas and no Vedas, born and unborn, below, above and around.

She further said that she was the one who moved with all Gods, the states of consciousness, wealth-giver and protector of all. She also said that the one who knows her essence attains the abode of God.

Hearing this, all the Gods bowed to her and prayed to her seeking protection in all possible ways.

This *Upanishad* then goes on to explain the greatness of worshipping the goddess. It also states that by reading this *Upanishad* both in the morning and in the evening, one is able to destroy all sins. If one reads it in the midnight, it results in perfection of speech.

Its reading before the new image of the goddess brings the presence of the deity. Its recitation at the time of consecration of an image of goddess makes it the centre of energy.

By reciting it on Tuesdays before the deity, one overcomes death.

10. Ganapati Upanishad

This *Upanishad* starts with the worship of Lord Ganapati as the creator, maintainer, destroyer, *Brahman*, the essence asking for the protection of one and all everywhere.

It says that the one who meditates on Lord Ganapati knowing that he is the Supreme, becomes a yogi above all yogis.

The one who studies this text of *Upanishad*, moves towards *Brahman* and is always blissful, not bound by obstacles.

The one who recites this *Upanishad* both in the morning and evening is liberated from all sins and attains *Dharma, Artha, Kama* and *Moksha*.

This *Upanishad* ends by telling the great results of worship of Lord Ganapati with prayers.

11. Garuda Upanishad

Lord Brahma gave the knowledge of *Brahman* to Narada, Narada to Brhatsena, Brhatsena to Indra, Indra to Bhardwaja and Bhardwaja to his pupils.

The mantra of worship is then given in this *Upanishad*. This *Upanishad* states that snakes do not bite the one who hears this great knowledge during the new moon night. Snakes do not bite a person during his lifetime if he recites and follows this great knowledge given in this *Upanishad* on the new moon nights.

If one teaches this knowledge to eight Brahmins, he is able to remove the snake poison from any one by merely touching it with grass or with a piece of wood or with ashes.

One who teaches this knowledge to a hundred Brahmins releases the poison by a mere glance.

One who teaches this great knowledge to a thousand Brahmins is able to remove snake poison by means of his thought alone.

12. Gopala Tapaniya Upanishad

There are two chapters in this *Upanishad*.

In the **first** chapter, the questions put by some sages to Lord Brahma and Lord Brahma's replies are given.

The sages wanted to know as to who the supreme personality of Godhead was, whom death fears, what was that by knowing which everything was known, and who created this world.

Lord Brahma replied, "The supreme personality of Godhead is *Krishna* or *Govinda* or *Gopijanavallabha*. Death fears him. By knowing him everything is known. By chanting the word '*Swaha*', he created the world."

Then the sages wanted to know the details about Krishna.

Brahma said, "*Krishna* means the one who delivers one from the sin. *Govinda* means the one who is famous on earth, in the Vedas, and among Surabhi cows. *Gopijanavallabha* is the one who enchanted the Gopis. *Swaha* is the potency of the Supreme power. Together all these refer to Supreme Power. The one who worships on this supreme power gets liberated."

Then Brahma described Krishna, "A person who chants the mantra about Krishna even once quickly attains the association with the Supreme Personality of Godhead."

Then Brahma explained about the worship of Govinda and the mantras. Those who desire liberation worship him. Govinda grants the transcendental knowledge.

Then Brahma told the sages about the five-word mantra '*AUM*' and Govinda, its importance, the nature of this mantra, the eighteen-syllable mantra given by Govinda to Brahma for the activity of Creation, and the greatness of this mantra.

The **second** chapter is about the replies of Lord Krishna to Gopis for their questions as to which Brahmin should they give the charity.

Lord Krishna replied that the charity should go to Sage Durvasa.

Then the Gopis asked Krishna how to cross Yamuna waters and reach Krishna who blesses everyone.

Krishna asked them to utter the word '*Krishna*' and the Yamuna would give way to them.

The Gopis did as was told by the Lord. They went to Sage Durvasa. Accepting their charity, the sage explained to them about the real Krishna and about Creation.

He said, "The Supreme personality of Godhead is Lord Krishna, who is Gopala. The all-pervading Lord Gopala is *AUM*."

The *Upanishad* then tells about how the Lord gave the most pious prayers and the ability of creation to Brahma thus making him great Creator.

13. Hayagriva Upanishad

There are two chapters in this *Upanishad*.

In the **first** chapter, we find Narada approaching Lord Brahma and requesting him to impart the knowledge of *Brahman* to him and the reply of Lord Brahma. He said the one who masters the mantras of Hayagriva, would know all the scriptures including *Shruti*, *Smriti*, *Ithihas* and *Puranas* and would be blessed with prosperity. Then he gave those Hayagriva mantras and prayers consisting of 29 letters.

In the **second** chapter, the single-lettered *Hayagriva* mantra of knowledge of *Brahman* which gives one mastery over words, wealth, and eight occult powers is given. After chanting the *Hayagriva* mantras, one should chant the specific Vedic mantras.

This *Upanishad* says that the one who reads this *Hayagriva Upanishad* on *ekadasi* day (the eleventh day) is blessed by *Hayagriva*. He becomes a great man and attains salvation.

14. Krishna Upanishad

When the sages living in the forest approached Lord Rama, they wanted to embrace him. For that Sri Rama told them that they could do so as Gopis when he would be born as Krishna in his next incarnation.

This *Upanishad* tells about the incarnation of Lord Rama as Lord Krishna and how mercy, the Mother Earth, humility, control of senses, truth, and broken curd pots were born as Rohini, Satyabhama, Sudama, Sage Uddhava, Sage Akrura and the ocean of milk respectively.

Sage Kashyapa was the mortar and Goddess Atri became the rope with which Lord Krishna was tied.

Kali became his Mace and the bow became Saranga, the illusion of God.

The harvest season became the meals in the house and the lotus that the Lord held became the seed of the world.

In this manner, the Vaikuntha of the Heaven was brought down to earth.

The *Upanishad* says that the one who understands this is freed from bondage and attain salvation.

15. Mahavakya Upanishad

Based on his inner experience, Lord Brahma explained the knowledge contained in this *Upanishad*. By uttering Ajapa *Gayatri mantra* namely, '*Hamsa Soham*' the knowledge that 'This Sun is *Brahman*' is obtained.

Paramatma sets in after controlling *Prana* and *Apana* by *Pranayama* and by long and continuous practice of *Pooraka* and

Rechaka and after concentrating the mind on Brahma. This experience is merging with *Brahman*.

This *Upanishad* says that whoever reads this *Upanishad* gets the same effect as reading all Vedas and attains Lord Maha Vishnu.

16. Mandukya Upanishad

This *Upanishad* is named after the Sage Mandukya and has twelve verses. It discusses the principle of *AUM* and its metaphysical importance with the four states of waking, dreaming, dreamless sleep and beyond. It says that the Supreme Self is manifested in the Universe in its gross, subtle and causal aspects. The four states of consciousness namely, waking, dreaming, sleeping and transcendental consciousness are aspects of Godhead but the last stage is all-inclusive and ultimately the real state. These are associated with the three elements of the sacred chant '*AUM*', and the silence in the fourth *ardhmatra.*

Thus *AUM* is identified with *Brahman*. Adi Shankara's teacher Guru Gaudapada wrote the first systematic exposition of *Advaita Vedanta* based on this *Upanishad. Manduka* means frog. The frog leaps. Similarly one has to leap from waking, dreaming, sleeping stages to transcendental consciousness. Through intense meditation on *AUM*, that is *Akshara Upasana*, one will surely reach the fourth state.

This *Upanishad* contains only twelve mantras that are packed with meaning and show the oneness of individual Self and the *Brahman* through the four *padas* of *Pranava*. It is considered to be the subtlest and most profound of all *Upanishads* that leads to the path of enlightenment.

The explanation of the letter *AUM* that is past, present and future, and transcends the following states are also stated in this *Upanishad.*

- The first letter '**A**' or the waking state is *Vaishvanara*. In this, one enjoys all gross objects.
- The one, who knows the second letter '**U**', or the state of dream is *Taijasa.* is inwardly conscious and enjoys the subtle objects. He becomes equal to all and only those who know *Brahman* are born in his family.

- *Prajna* is the third letter '**M**', or the state of dreamless sleep, in which everything is absorbed and there are no desires or dreams. One gets unified with consciousness and full bliss.
- The fourth part of half matra is transcendental stage. It is beyond all thought, duality and beyond knowing. It is auspicious and non-dual.

He who knows all these stages enters the Self. The Universal soul has two aspects namely, *Vaishvanara* and *Virat*. The microscopic aspect is known as *Vaishvanara* and the macroscopic aspect is called *Virat.*

17. Mundaka Upanishad

The name of this *Upanishad*, is derived from the word '*Mund*' or to tonsure. It means the one who understands this *Upanishad* is liberated from any kind of ignorance. It points out that those who perform *Karma* or actions with attachment are subjected to rebirths. When one becomes detached, he becomes immortal.

This *Upanishad* has three chapters and each chapter has two sections. It teaches the distinction between the higher knowledge about Supreme *Brahman* and the lower knowledge of the material world. It says that it is by the higher wisdom and not by sacrifices or worship that one can realise *Brahman.*

This *Upanishad* mainly deals with the importance of knowing the Supreme *Brahman* through which one will be able to realise the Self.

Brahma who was the first among Gods imparted the knowledge of *Brahman* to his eldest son Atharva. Atharva imparted that knowledge to Angira. He passed it on to Satyavaha, who in turn taught this knowledge to Angiras. Once Sage Shaunaka approached Angiras and requested him to teach him that thing, by knowing which, everything becomes known. Angiras said that there are two kinds of knowledge, higher and lower according to Vedas.

The **lower** knowledge is knowledge of the Vedas and *Smritis* like *Vedangas* namely, phonetics, ritual, grammar, definition, metrics and astrology and so on.

The **higher** knowledge is the knowledge of the imperishable. The formless *Brahman* that is higher than the imperishable and is the source and the goal of all beings may be found in the secret of the heart. By higher knowledge, the wise realise *Brahman* that cannot be perceived or grasped. It is without source or origin, eternal and all-pervasive.

From that imperishable, the Universe emerged. From that Universe, food came. From food, *Prana* or *Hiranyagarbha* was born. Then came the mind, the five elements, the worlds, and immortality.

The Vedic sacrifices lead to perishable results. Those who perform Vedic sacrifice undergo old age and death again and again. These ignorant people do not understand that the higher knowledge leads one to liberation. It is by higher wisdom and not by Vedic sacrifices, which this *Upanishad* considers as unsafe boat, that one can cross the empirical world and reach the *Brahman*.

The *sanyasi* and the householder who performs his duties in a detached manner and meditates, reaches the *Purusha* who is immortal and imperishable. One should resort to renunciation and should go to a teacher to obtain the knowledge of *Brahman*.

The wise men, by meditating on the Self, realise this bliss of immortality. Once the *Brahman* is realised all the knots in the heart get loosened, and all doubts vanish. One no longer engages himself in *Karma*. He goes beyond all good and evil, and sees only oneness in all beings.

From the imperishable, different beings are born and they ultimately merge into it. The *Purusha* is transcendental, formless, birthless, without vital force and mind, pure, imperishable and the superior most. From him, the mind and vital force, senses, space, and the elements emerged.

For the indwelling Self in all, Heaven is the head, Sun and Moon are the two eyes, the Directions from the two ears, Vedas are speech, Air is vital force, and the whole Universe is the heart. From his two feet, the earth and fire emerged.

He is the source of everything. From him, all Gods, all other beings, and the qualities emerged. The sense organs, oceans, mountains and all are only *Purusha* consisting of *Karma* and knowledge. It is subtler than the subtlest and immortal. The one who knows this Supreme, immortal *Brahman* residing in the heart destroys the knot of ignorance. It should be penetrated through meditation with mind absorbed in its thought. *AUM* is the bow, *Atman* is the arrow, and *Brahman* is the target. One should become one with it. Only the Self and nothing else is to be realised. This is the true God. This knowledge is the bridge to immortality. The Self should be meditated upon with *AUM*. The Self is conditioned by the mind and carries the vital forces and the body. Through this knowledge, the wise realise Self.

The one who realises the glory of the soul gets liberated. It is inside the cavity of the heart of each being. The Self cannot be seen or grasped. It can only be realised through meditation. It is not attained by study or intellect or by hearing.

The ascetic who is devoid of all desires, renounces everything, transcends death, reaches the divine and becomes immortal. The one who realises this *Brahman* becomes *Brahman* himself. As rivers ultimately flow or merge into the ocean, similarly the liberated soul merges itself with *Brahman,* that is God.

This *Upanishad* says that this knowledge should be imparted only to those who are engaged in the practice of discipline and are devoted to *Brahman*.

18. Narada Parivrajaka Upanishad

This *Upanishad* has nine chapters. Once Narada, the celestial sage came to the sacred Naimisha forest where sages always perform *yajna*. There Shaunaka and the other sages greeted him and welcomed him after paying due respects. Although, they were well-instructed in spirituality, still they requested Narada to teach them the means of liberation from worldly bondage.

Narada replied, "The one born in a good family, when completes twelve years of life as *Brahmachari* and knowledge, then spending the 25 years as a householder and performing the duties of a *Grihastha,* spending another 25 years as a forest-dweller, performing his duties as a *Vanaprasthi* and after becoming free from all desires of thought, word and deed and latent desires becomes *Sanyasi* such a person becomes peaceful, self-controlled, liberated."

This is the **first** *Upadesha* (teaching) of this *Upanishad.*

Then the venerable sages requested Narada to tell them about the mode of renunciation. For this, the celestial sage Narada said that it was better to know this truth from Brahma, his grandfather.

After completing the *yajna* which they were performing, the sages along with Narada went to *Satyaloka* that is also known as *Brahmaloka*. There Narada requested Lord Brahma to impart that knowledge.

Brahma, after hearing the request from Narada remained steady in deep meditation for a short time. He then told Narada that he would give that knowledge that was imparted to him by the Supreme Being or *Virata Purusha* in the form of *Purusha Sukta* hymn and the secret doctrine of the *Upanishads*.

Brahma, after repeating what Narada had told the sages about the means of liberation said that when one becomes free from all desires, he becomes mature enough to embrace renunciation.

This is the content of the *Upadesha* of the **second** chapter of this *Upanishad*.

Then, Narada asked Brahma as to who was entitled to renounce worldly life and what was the mode of their life.

Brahma replied, "There are some who do not deserve to embrace *Sanyasa*. These include the eunuch, deformed and blind persons, one who is guilty of crime, and the one who has fallen from right conduct. A wise man renounces the world after completing the required procedure as per the Scriptures. Only when there is desirelessness, one should embrace *Sanyasa*. Even in the stage of *Brahmacharya*, one can take *Sanyasa*, provided he has all his sense organs under his control. Such a person must live on alms, remove his tuft of hair along with the sacred thread, and possess an even mind in which the knowledge 'I am *Brahman*' is engraved. Such a person becomes an embodiment of peace, quiescence, purity, truth, contentment, straightforwardness. Such a person loves all in thought, word and deed. After discharging his duties with the ten virtues or right conduct namely, contentment, forgiveness, self-control, non-stealing, purity, control of senses, humility, scriptural learning, truth and temper and after studying *Upanishads* in the prescribed manner, one may renounce worldly life. For such a person, the body experiences no pleasure or pain even when he is alive. He becomes the *Paramahamsa*. He wears only a pair of loincloth, the patched garment. After giving up everything, he wanders alone. He abandons all faults like passion, anger, pride, greed, and delusion. He attains liberation when he is freed from pride, egotism, wickedness, cruelty, and when he possesses knowledge of the Self. In solitude, he meditates upon *Brahman* in thought, word and deed. He neither welcomes death nor rejoices life."

This *Upanishad* then tells about the marks of such a *Sanyasi* who gets liberated.

Again Narada asked Brahma as to how the being without a sacred thread could be a Brahmin and Brahma replied, "For a *Sanyasi*, the thread of indestructible, transcendental *Brahman*, the wisdom only has meaning, and not the external thread that he wears. He will maintain silence and the conduct of such a person will be incomprehensible to ordinary men."

Then Brahma spoke about different kinds of ascetics and their nature, about meditating on the Superior *Brahman* and the ultimate liberation and cleared all the doubts lurking in the mind of Narada.

19. Nrisimha Tapaniya Upanishad

It comprises two *Upanishads*. They are —

1. *Nrisimha Poorva Tapaniya Upanishad*
2. *Nrisimha Uttara Tapaniya Upanishad*

Nrisimha Poorva Tapaniya Upanishad

It consists of five *Upanishads*.

The **first** *Upanishad* starts with a description of Lord Narasimha who is partly human and partly lion. He is *Parabrahma*, he is *Neela Lohita* as his neck is black and the top of it is red, he is *Shankara*, doing good to all. He is also *Pashupati* holding the bow '*Pinaka*'. He is the Lord of Vedas, the Lord of Brahma and is praised by *Yajur Veda*. Those who know this would attain immortality.

In the **second** *Upanishad*, the *Narasimha Mantra* that is the supreme of all mantras is explained. By uttering this mantra, the *devas* won over death, sins and family life.

In the **third** *Upanishad*, we find *devas* requesting Brahma to teach them the power of this king of mantras, the *Narasimha Mantra*, and its roots. This is followed by Brahma's reply along with the explanation given by the sages.

The **fourth** Upanishad explains the parts of this *Narasimha Mantra* as imparted by Brahma to *devas* as per their requests. *Pranava, Savitri, Yajur Lakshmi* and *Narasimha Gayatri* are the four parts of *Narasimha Mantra* and the one who knows this attains salvation.

The *Pranava Mantra* is nothing but *AUM.*

The *Savitri Mantra* is *Astakshara* or eight-letter mantra that increases one's stature and wealth.

The *Yajur Lakshmi Mantra* has 24 letters. The one who knows this mantra enjoys great wealth and fame.

Vedas and the *devas* will live forever with the one who knows the *Narasimha Gayatri Mantra*.

Brahma then told the *devas* about that mantra by chanting of which God will reveal his form.

In the **fifth** *Upanishad* we see Brahma explaining to the sages about the *Maha Chakra* or the *Sudarshana Chakra*, which according to the great sages would fulfil all wishes and is also the gateway to salvation. Brahma also told them that the one who chants the *Narasimha Mantra* daily without any desire would be able to control fire, wind, sun, moon, water, *devas*, plants and poison.

Nrisimha Uttara Tapaniya Upanishad

There are nine chapters in this *Upanishad.*

In the **first** chapter, we find the *devas* approaching Lord Brahma and requesting him to teach them about the soul that is more minute than the atom and also about the letter *AUM.*

AUM, as described by Brahma, is past, present and future. Both *AUM* and the soul are *Brahman*. With *Brahman* and soul joining together and with the realisation that the imperishable *Brahman* is *AUM* and finally becoming one with that, one should go beyond that.

The soul that is gross and enjoys pleasures has four branches or stages as given below —

- The first branch is when it is awake and when it enjoys gross feelings with its seven organs and nineteen faces with its ten senses, five *Pranas*, namely, mind, brain, sensibility and ego.

- In the second part, that is, in the dream state its feelings are very minute and it enjoys the minute sense with seven organs and nineteen faces.
- In the third part, that is, in the state of dreamless sleep, one is the personification of knowledge.
- The above three stages are mere illusion. Soul is the only real form. In the fourth part of *Turiya* state, which is beyond the three earlier stages, there is only consciousness. It is beyond understanding and imagination. It can only be perceived with the firm belief that there is only soul. It is that aspect of God that is beyond all knowledge.

In the **second** chapter, a description of the four branches of *Brahman*, which form the essence of happiness and also about the four letters of *AUM*, is given. The one who uses the *Narasimha Mantra* would understand the *Turiya*.

In the **third** chapter, deep meditation on *Pranava* or *AUM* and the merging of everything in *AUM* in *Turiya* is explained.

In the **fourth** chapter, the meditation upon the soul as *Omkara* and *Parabrahma* with the *Turiya Pranava* sound is explained.

In the **fifth** chapter, it is stated that the one who meditates as stated earlier in this *Upanishad* exists as *Brahman* and attains *Brahman.* He who worships the soul in letter *AUM* attains *Brahman* in the form of Narasimha and understand *Parabrahma* and shines as *Parabrahma Narasimha.*

In the **sixth** chapter, the worship of Nrisimha by *devas* to get rid of the *asura* (evil) qualities in them and its four effects on them are explained.

In the **seventh** chapter, the meditation on *AUM* is explained.

In the **eighth** chapter, the soul that is *AUM* or *Narasimha* is explained.

In the **ninth** chapter, we find Prajapati explaining about *AUM*, that is the soul. *Atma* or soul is mere witness. It is lion, a form beyond thought. It appears different due to ignorance. The sensory organs are not able to perceive it and hence it is not known even when it is apparently known.

Prajapati, therefore, told the *devas* to see *Atma* as 'I am it and it is me'.

The *devas* did as they were told by Prajapati and all their illusions disappeared.

20. Parabrahma Upanishad

Shaunaka approached Sage Pippalada of Angiras family and requested him to tell him as to how the *Brahman*, the *Hiranyagarbha,* created all beings.

Sage Pippalada replied, "The *Brahman* that is beyond all *gunas*, that is partless, pure, indestructible is the Creator. As non-doer of actions one realises his oneness with *Brahman*. But as the doer of actions, with attachment, he reaps the fruit. He is not dragged to ignorance if he performs actions with detachment. Just as a hawk after flying in the sky, and after getting tired, goes to its nest, similarly, the Self also after remaining in the waking and dreaming state due to *avidya* (ignorance) rests in dreamless sleep, that is knowledge and bliss.

In the fourth state of *Turiya,* the Self rests. *Pranava* is the Self. Then this *Upanishad* explains about *Brahman*. The ascetic discards the worldly tuft and sacred thread, and wears the threefold thread consisting of *Pranava*, *Hamsa* and *Nada,* which remain in his consciousness. The ascetic has to discard the external world, tuft and thread and hold on to the tuft and sacred thread in the form of the sacred syllable *Pranava* and *Brahman.* This helps him equip himself for liberation.

21. Paramahamsa Parivrajaka Upanishad

Lord Brahma approached his father Lord Vishnu and requested him to tell him as to who was entitled to renunciation, who was the *Paramahamsa* and what were his characteristic features.

Lord Narayana replied, "The wise one who has undertaken *Sanyasa*, after successfully completing his duties as a *Brahmachari*, *Grihasta* and *Vanaprasthi* as per the Vedic scriptures is entitled to renunciation."

Then Lord Narayana explained the features of a *Paramahamsa* monk. Thereafter Lord Brahma asked Lord Vishnu about *Brahma*

Pranava and the Lord explained the sixteen parts of *Brahma Pranava*, which are the quadruples in the four states of waking, dreaming, dreamless sleep and *Turiya,* and about *AUM*.

The four parts of waking or *Jagrat* state pertain to the letter '**A**', the four parts in the state of dream or the state of *Swapna* pertains to the letter '**U**', the four parts of *Sushupti* or dreamless sleep state pertain to the letter '**M**', and the four parts of *Turiya* state that is beyond all the three earlier states pertain to the *Ardh matra*.

This is *Brahma Pranava* worshipped by ascetics. By this, *Brahman* is realised and this is liberation in the disembodied state or *Videha mukti*.

Then Brahma asked as to how one can discard all worldly activities by just discarding the sacred thread and tuft. To this Lord Narayana replied, "The one who has the knowledge of the non-dual *Atman* has the real sacred thread. His deep absorption in meditation is his light. He is the one who is an illumined being, a sage, the noblest and the most superior. Such *Paramahamsas* are very rare to be found in this world. He alone is the *Purusha* or the glorified one. He is always satisfied and is free from cold, heat, happiness, hunger, misery, sorrow, thirst, delusion, old age and death. He is free from the six properties of the body, like birth, existence, change, growth, decay and death. He is above all rules and duties of the world. He bows to none, does not worship any God, is free from blame or praise, and does not resort to mantras or rituals. He is firmly established in consciousness and Supreme Bliss. He always meditates upon the *Brahma Pranava*. Such a one is *Paramahamsa*."

22. Pashupata Brahmana Upanishad

This *Upanishad* starts by stating the greatness of Lord Shiva, Pashupati and the Lord of all beings.

Lord Shiva is the witness for everything. He controls the mind. The soul also acts because of him only. The sensory organs act because of him.

This *Upanishad* says that by having discipline in food habits, mental discipline develops, which eventually leads to wisdom that solves all problems. The one who sees *Brahman* in everything sees *Brahman* in himself.

23. Prashna Upanishad

This *Upanishad* is in the form of questions. It is supposed to belong to a later period, probably after the time of Buddha.

Prashna means question. This *Upanishad* has six sections dealing with six questions put to the sage by his disciples who were keen on knowing things like nature of the ultimate cause, the power of *AUM* and the relation of the Supreme to the world. The six questions put are —

1. What is the origin of the various beings?
2. Who are the deities that sustain them?
3. How does life imbibe the body?
4. What is the truth about wakefulness, dream and dreamless sleep?
5. What purpose is served by being devoted to *AUM*?
6. What is the relationship between the Supreme God-head and the individual Self?

Sages like Sukesha, Satyakama, Kausalya and Kabandi approached Sage Pippalada for knowing the Supreme *Brahman* and requested him to teach them that knowledge.

Pippalada asked them to live for a year with full control of senses, with *Brahmacharya* and with faith and then approach him for that knowledge.

The sages after living for a year in such a manner approached Pippalada again and asked him the six questions.

1. **Kabandi** asked Pippalada as to the source from which all beings are born.

Pippalada replied, "The Lord of all creatures, created a couple first. Then food and *Prana* emerged for producing beings. The Sun is *Prana* and the Moon is food. The former while rising absorbs all living beings into its rays. The Sun which is the life of all beings, exists in a hundred forms. By searching for the Self through the control of senses, *Brahmacharya*, faith and meditation, one conquers the Sun."

2. Then the **sage born in Bhrigu's** family asked Pippalada about the number of deities who sustain a being and who among them is the chief.

Pippalada answered, "The deities that support and illumine the beings are space, air, fire, water, earth, speech, mind, sight, and hearing. But the life breath or *Prana* is Supreme. It is *Prana* that sustains beings, and not the elements or sensory organs. The sensory organs and elements obey the *Prana* in the same way as the bees obey the queen bee. The *Prana* is subtle as well as gross. It is the nectar. It is Indra, Rudra, preserver, and Sun. In fact, it is everything."

3. Then **Kausalya** asked Sage Pippalada, from where the *Prana* was born, how it entered this body, how it resided there, how it departed from the body and how it supported the external things.

Pippalada answered his questions, "*Prana* is born from the Self, the soul or *Atman*. He enters the body, due to the actions of the mind. *Prana* engages the other organs as a king employs all the others under him. *Prana* resides in the eyes and ears and places, *Apana* in the two lower parts of the body. In the middle, *Samana* distributes the food all over the body. The Self, the subtle body is in the heart. There are 101 chief nerves in the body. Each of these nerves has 100 divisions. Each one of these divisions is divided into 72,000 sub-branches or *nadis*. Among these *nadis*, *Vyana* moves. *Udana* moves upward due to virtues, moves downwards due to sins and to the human world due to virtues and sins. The external *Prana* is Sun. The air that is within is *Samana*. The air outside is *Vyana*. *Udana* is luminous. One enters into *Prana* in rebirth as per whatever he thought at the time of death. *Prana* with *Udana* and soul leads to the world of his desire. One who knows all about *Prana* achieves immortality."

4. Then the **grandson of Surya** asked Pippalada about the organs that go to sleep, which keep one awake, the deity who experiences dream, into whom happiness occurs and into whom everything merges.

Pippalada replied, "Just as the sunrays get unified during sunset and disperse during sunrise everything gets unified in mind during sleep. *Prana* alone keeps awake in the body. In the dream state, the mind experiences greatness. In the dreamless state, everything gets merged into the Self just as the birds return to their nests on the tree after flying for long. The one who realises this attains the Self. He becomes omniscient."

5. Then **Sage Satyakama** asked Pippalada as to which is the world that is won by the one who meditates upon *AUM* till death.

The great Sage Pippalada answered his question, "*Brahman* is *AUM*. The one who meditates upon *AUM*, as consisting of one letter, becomes enlightened and is born on earth as human being and becomes great with self-control, countenance and faith. The one who meditates on *AUM*, with the help of the second letter, identifies himself with the mind. He is lifted to the world of moon and becomes great. Anyone who meditates on the supreme *Purusha* with *AUM*, with the three letters becomes unified with the sun. He is freed from sin and is lifted up to the world of Brahma. If the three letters are closely joined together then such an enlightened man remains undisturbed. The enlightened man reaches supreme reality that is beyond old age and death through *AUM*."

6. Then **Sage Sukesha** asked Pippalada as to where *Purusha* exists.

Pippalada replied, "*Purusha* exists inside the body and all the sixteen limbs of *Purusha* originate from him. The sixteen parts or limbs are life, faith, space, air, light, water, earth, senses, mind, food, virility, discipline, mantra, action, world and individuality and all these parts are like spokes of a wheel with the Spirit at its hub. He created *Prana*. From *Prana* came faith, space, air and food. From food came vigour and self-control. Just as the rivers get merged into the sea ultimately, similarly the sixteen parts disappear on reaching the Ultimate and become *Purusha*. The one who realises this becomes immortal. Beyond this *Purusha*, the Supreme *Brahman*, there is nothing."

24. Rama Rahasya Upanishad

This *Upanishad* is not available.

25. Rama Tapaniya Upanishad

This *Upanishad* is in two parts —

1. *Rama Poorva Tapaniya Upanishad*
2. *Rama Uttara Tapaniya Upanishad*

Rama Poorva Tapaniya Upanishad

This *Upanishad* starts with a description of the greatness of *Rama Tattva* that is immeasurable and eternally joyful and indicates *Parabrahma*.

The entire world exists in the seed *Rama* as the Banyan tree exists in the seed.

Then this *Upanishad* tells about Sri Rama.

The *devas* approached Sri Rama and requested him to give his protection and grace to them. All those who meditate upon him attain salvation.

Rama Uttara Tapaniya Upanishad

Lord Shiva chanted *Rama Mantra* in Varanasi. Sri Rama told Shankara that whosoever worships him gets rid of all the sins including *Brahma Hatya*. Those who learn the six letter mantra of '*Rama Raya Namaha*' from Brahma or from Lord Shiva or from their disciples attain salvation. One who is about to die gets salvation if Lord Shiva utters this mantra in his ears. Brahma Maha Vishnu, who is none other than Narayana and *Parameshwara,* in his mind worshipped him with 47 mantras. The one who worships the Lord with this mantra sees the Lord in person and attains immortality.

26. Shandilya Upanishad

There are three chapters in this *Upanishad.*

In the **first** chapter, we find Shandilya requesting Atharvan to impart to him the knowledge of eight *angas* or parts of yoga that is the means for attaining *Atman.*

Atharvan replied, "The eight *Angas* of yoga are *Yama, Niyama, Asana, Pranayama, Pratyahara, Dharana, Dhyana* and *Samadhi.*"

Anga-1

Yama is of ten kinds. The ten kinds of yama or forbearance are —

1. *Ahimsa* or not causing pain to anyone by thought, word or deed
2. *Satya* or speaking truth that conduces the well-being of all through thought, word and deed

3. *Asatya* or not coveting others' property by thought, word or deed
4. *Brahmacharya* or following celibacy
5. *Daya* or kindness to all
6. *Arjava* or maintaining equanimity in thought, word or deed
7. *Kshama* or patience to all praise blame, pleasant or unpleasant
8. *Dhriti* or firmness of mind during misery, challenges of life
9. *Mithahara* or moderation in food by taking simple light food, and leaving one-fourth of the stomach empty
10. *Shaucha* or cleanliness both external or cleanliness of body and internal or cleanliness of mind through *Adhyatma Vidya* or the knowledge of Self

Anga-2

Niyama or religious observances are also ten. They are —

1. *Tapas* or observance of penance
2. *Santosha* or being happy with whatever one has
3. *Astikya* or the belief in merits and demerits of actions as per the Vedic teachings
4. *Dana* or charity of any kind to deserving persons
5. *Ishvara pujana* or worship of Gods with a pure mind
6. *Siddhanta Shravana* or enquiry into the significance of Vedanta
7. *Hrih* or the feeling of shame on account of undesirable acts that are contrary to the rules of society and Vedas
8. *Mathi* or faith in the paths prescribed by the Vedas
9. *Japa* or chanting of mantras that is learnt from the teacher

   It is of two kinds, namely, the spoken *japa* and mental *japa*. The spoken *japa* is either loud or low. The loud utterance of mantras gives the effect as stated in the Vedas and the low utterance of mantras give more reward than the loud utterance. The mental *japa* is contemplation of the mantra by the mind. It gives a reward that is even more than the low spoken mantra.

10. *Vrata* or the regular observance of disciplines as prescribed in the Vedas

Anga-3

The *asanas* or the sitting postures are eight in number. In each posture, the yogi sits with ease and keeps his body erect. These eight *asanas* are —

1. *Swastika Asana*
2. *Padma Asana*
3. *Siddha Asaba*
4. *Mukta Asana*
5. *Goumukha Asana*
6. *Vira Asana*
7. *Bhadra Asana*
8. *Mayura Asana*

These *asanas* are explained in detail in this *Upanishad.* With these postures all ailments and poisons in the body are destroyed. One may use any posture according to one's liking and ability. The one who gets mastery over postures conquers the three worlds and his *nadis* also get purified.

Then Shandilya wanted to know how the *nadis* were purified, how many *nadis* were there in the body, what vital airs were there in them, what were their seats and what were their functions. Atharvan explained about *Prana* in humans, animals and in birds. He described the *Chakra* with twelve spokes, the *Jiva* riding upon *Prana* that is in the middle of the *Chakra*, the coiled up *Kundalini Shakti*, the fourteen principal *nadis*, the most important, invisible and subtle *Sushumna nadi* which leads the path towards salvation, the *Ida* and *Pingala nadis*, and the ten kinds of *Vayus* that move in all *nadis*.

Anga-4

There are three kinds of *Pranayamas*. After obtaining the knowledge of *nadis* one should purify them through *Pranayama*. The place to be selected for the performance of *Pranayama*, and the practice of three kinds of *Pranayama* are then explained. The external signs during the early stages of practice, and how a regular and constant practice of *Pranayama* leads to regaining of youth, elimination of diseases in the body, purification of brain, and disappearnce of hunger, thirst, sleep, idleness are then explained.

This *Upanishad* then goes on to explain about the two kinds of *Kumbhaka* or restraint of breathing namely, *Sahita* and *Kevala*. As a result of the knowledge of *Kevala,* the *Kundalini* arises and the yogi becomes lean, serene-faced, clear-eyed, hears the spiritual sounds and becomes free from all diseases. Then the various *Mudras* are explained. Finally, the yogi would be able to give up all cognition of objects and with the mind absorbed, *Kaivalya* is attained. Another way to repress the mind is through *jnana.*

Anga-5, 6

This *Upanishad* describes about the five kinds of *Pratyahara* or the drawing away of the sense organs from attachment, three kinds of *Dharana.*

Anga-7

There are two kinds of *Dhyana.* They are —

1. *Saguna*
2. *Nirguna*

They are explained in the *Upanishad.*

Anga-8

There is only one kind of *Samadhi,* which is the unification of *Jivatma* with *Paramatma* without the distinction of knower, known and knowledge. It is extreme bliss and pure consciousness.

In the **second** chapter, we find Shandilya asking Atharvan to teach him the science of *Brahman.*

Atharvan replies, "*Brahman* is *Satya, Vijnana* and *Ananta* in which the entire world is interwoven and from which all originated and into which all get merged. When that *Brahman* is known, everything is known. He is without form and qualities, and can be defined by *jnana,* yoga and wisdom. He is omniscient, the Lord of all and the inner soul of all beings. He creates, supports and destroys everything. He is nothing but *Atman.*"

The **third** chapter is about Atharvan clearing the doubts of Shandilya as to how the dissolution of the Universe arose from *Brahman* that is *AUM,* and how it existed and absorbed in it. Atharvan explained in great detail about the three forms or aspects that arose from *Brahman,* namely, the *Nishkala* or partless, *Sakala* or with parts and *Sakala- Nishkala,* that is with and without parts. He also explained how *Brahman* created the beings. Then Shandilya asked Atharvan about '*Sattva*' that is essence of bliss and consciousness and how he is called *Parabrahma* and *Atman*.

He is called *Atman* because he gets and takes back everything, and is everything.

He is known as *Maheshwara* because by the sound of the words and by his own power, the great Lord governs everything.

He is also called *Dattatreya* because the Lord, pleased with the hard penance of Atri, offered Himself to be born as the son of Atri and his wife Anasuya.

He, who contemplates upon the Supreme that is only Him, becomes the knower of *Brahman* and is freed from all sins and attains liberation.

27. Sarabha Upanishad

Maheshwara, is the Lord of all Lords, father of the world, who created Brahma and gave the Vedas to him, father of Vishnu and the other *devas,* the one who destroyed the world at the time of deluge, took the fearful form of Sarabha, which is a combination of eagle, lion and man and killed Narasimha who was destroying the world, and he who was wearing the hide became *Veera Bhadra*.

He tore away the fifth head of Brahma. He kicked *Kala*, the God of death and drank the poison *Halahala*. He gave the holy *Chakra* to Lord Vishnu. He can grant salvation directly.

Anyone who reads this *Upanishad*, that is also called 'the great knowledge of Pippalada' or makes others read it has no more births and deaths and attains liberation and becomes similar to *Brahman*.

28. Sita Upanishad

The Gods wanted to know from Prajapati as to who Sita was and what her form was. Prajapati replied, "Sita is *Prakriti*. Her essence is *Maya*. Her form is unmanifest. She is faultless and is decked with ornaments. She is the Vedic speech. She sprang up from the tip of the plough. She sustains the Universe and all beings. She is everything and assumes the form of everything. She illumines all the worlds. She revolves as the wheel of time, and the wheel of the Universe. By mere closing and opening of her eyes, she brings about creation and protection. She is the power of yoga. She rests on the right side of the Lord's chest as *Srivatsa*. She is surrounded by all Gods. All divinities pay obeisance to her. She is vested with miraculous powers. She is extolled by the scriptures and all Gods adore her."

29. Surya Upanishad

This *Upanishad* tells the glory of golden Narayana with the blessed Sun or *Savitar* who inspires the thoughts of human beings. The Sun or *Surya* is the Self of the world. All beings are born from him. He is the manifest *Brahman*, namely, Rudra, Vishnu, *Rig Veda* and so on. Everything is born from *Aditya* or the sun and is protected by him.

He, who worships *Surya* every day facing him, is a *Brahmin*. *Surya* relieves the worshipper from the fear of great diseases, poverty and sin.

A person, who worships *Surya* on mid-day facing him, released from the five great sins.

He, who recites the *Savitar Vidya* or knowledge at dawn, becomes very fortunate. The one who recites this during morning, mid-day and evening gets the benefits of a 100 *yajnas* and also conquers death.

30. Tripad Vibhuthi Maha Narayana Upanishad

This *Upanishad* explains the principles behind the *Tripat Narayana* philosophy, which if understood and grasped, can weed out all illusions pertaining to the world.

Lord Narayana through his desire created all living beings, and the vital air (*Prana*), the mind and all sense organs, earth, and sky were created.

From Narayana emerged Brahma, the deity of all creations.

- Indra is the ruler of all *devas*, Prajapati, who is the Lord of the people, twelve *Adityas*, eleven *Rudras*, eight *Vasus*, Vedas etc. All these forces emerge from Narayana and merge into him as per one of the *Upanishads* of *Rig Veda.*
- Narayana is omnipresent and omnipotent. All deities are various forms of Narayana. He is also all-pervading Space,

Time and Direction. Everything that exists and does not exist is Narayana. The one who understands this becomes one with Lord Narayana and becomes Narayana himself. That is what one of the *Upanishads* of *Yajur Veda* states.

- The one who chants the *Ashtaksharam* or the eight-syllable mantra '*Aum Namo Narayana'* lives long and finally attains liberation or *Moksha.* This is what is said in one of the *Upanishads* in *Sama Veda.*
- That blissful Supreme Being or *Brahman* resides within everyone. It is *AUM* or *Pranava*. The one who chants *AUM* gets rid of all bondages of this world. The one who chants '*Aum Namo Narayana*' attains Vaikuntha, Lord Narayana's abode. A pure blessed heart filled with spiritual knowledge is Vaikuntha. From there, a flash of lightning rises. That represents the various forms of Narayana. He is within all beings and controls all their activities. He is *AUM*, the Supreme Being. This is what is stated in one of the *Upanishads* in *Atharva Veda.*

The one who chants this mantra in the morning is able to destroy all his sins committed during the previous night.

The one who chants this mantra in the evening becomes able to destroy all sins committed during the day.

The one who chants this mantra during mid-day, looking at the Sun is able to destroy all major and minor sins as described in the Vedas and finally becomes one with the Supreme Being 'Narayana'.

31. Tripura Tapini Upanishad

Lord Sadashiva assumes the guise of Prajapati, Vishnu, Rudra and becomes Tripura. The earth, heavens, the atmosphere and the ether are the result of his power.

This *Upanishad* starts with a prayer to Tripura, the Goddess of the three cities. She is the supreme knowledge. Everything in the Universe is born out of Shiva and Shakti. That sole deity evolves as the visible world. The one who masters this knowledge pervades everything.

This *Upanishad* then explains the *Tripura Mantra*. Whosoever chants this *Tripura Mantra* attains everything and all enjoyments and reaches the Supreme *Brahman.*

Then this *Upanishad* tells about the incantations of Agastya, Shanmukha and so on. Sadashiva asked the Gods to know that there is nothing other than *Brahman* and everything ultimately merges into *Brahman*.

Then He described Trikuta, the Great Bhargavi, and the power of Spirit and asked them to meditate on her after clarifying the incantation of Tripureshi. Then the Lord explained to the Gods about the gateway to liberation – the Sri Chakra and asked to worship the seat of the syllable *AUM*, in that and worship her with mantras of Maha Lakshmi. Then she would manifest herself and the worshippers see *Brahman* and achieve immortality.

Then the Lord explained the mystic marks and expounded the heart of Gayatri pertaining to Tripura. Then the Gods asked him to tell them about *Mrityunjaya Mantra* as revealed through the hymn on *Trayambaka*. Then the Lord explained about the mantras pertaining to Shiva, Vishnu, Surya and Ganesha by which Bhagavati reveals herself.

The supreme abode of Vishnu is the sky. He is the *Vasudeva* or the dweller in all. The twelve-syllabled mantra of Vasudeva is '*Aum Namo Bhagavate Vasudevaya*'. He, who knows this, crosses over all hardships, lives a long life, achieves mastery over beings and enjoys possession of cattle and wealth. Meditation on *AUM* denotes inward bliss, the *Brahman*.

- In the morning, **Gayatri** is worshipped.
- At mid-day, **Savitri** is worshipped.
- At dusk, **Saraswati** is worshipped.

The Ajapa, '*Hamsa*' is to be uttered without break. The Lord told the Gods that whosoever utters these mantras and worships the Goddess attains immortality.

Then the Gods wanted to know about the Supreme Self. The Supreme Self is nothing but the Consciousness. That must be recognised. The enlightened knower is *Brahman*. The cause of bondage or clinging to objects is due to mind. When the mind is withdrawn from objects, there is release and then the mind ceases to exist. That is the Supreme state. One should control the mind until it reaches the heart. This is the knowledge and meditation. Yogis dissolve themselves with Self or *Brahman* and get liberated.

In all states of waking, dreaming and sleeping, the Self is only one. For the one who goes beyond these states, there is no rebirth. The Self that is one, is seen as many. Differences are perceived only as long as one is under illusion. When the darkness of illusion disappears, one sees the unity.

The lower *Brahman* is the world and the other one is Supreme *Brahman*. Through studies the lower *Brahman* is realised. After that, one should discard everything as one discard the husk to obtain the grain – the higher *Brahman*.

8

The Other Related Texts

Vedangas

Vedangas are considered to be the affiliates to the Vedas. They form *Sutras* or proverbs. These are explanatory limbs (*Anga)* or parts of the Vedas.

These were first mentioned in the *Mundaka Upanishad*. It was only later that they became independent disciplines. *Vedangas* help in understanding the secret meanings contained in the Vedas. There are six *Vedangas* or aspects of Vedic knowledge. There are two groups of *Vedangas*.

- The **first** group is connected with the texts of Vedas, namely, *Shiksha*, *Vyakarana*, and *Chhandas*.
- The **second** group is connected with the meaning of the Vedas, namely, *Nirukta*, *Jyotisha*, and *Kalpa*.

Shiksha is considered as the **nose** of the Vedas, the *Nirukta* form the **ears**, the *Vyakarana* is the **mouth**, the *Chhanda Shastra* is the **feet**, and *Kalpa* forms the **arms** of the Vedas.

1. Shiksha

It mainly deals with the science of Vedic phonetics or pronunciation common to all the Vedas and phonology of Sanskrit mantras. It is the science of proper articulation and pronunciation of Vedic hymns that are considered to be very important. It consists of the knowledge of letters, and use of organs of pronunciation and phonetics. It points out that the defective pronunciation of Vedic mantras is considered to bring harmful effects and should be corrected.

The oldest phonetics textbooks are the ***Pratisakhyas*** that explain the pronunciation, and intonation of Sanskrit language and the Sanskrit rules of *Sandhi* according to different *shakhas* or schools.

The four *Pratisakhyas* that are preserved even now are —

1. *Rig Veda Pratisakhyas* of the *Shakala Shakha*
2. *Shukla Yajur Veda Pratisakhyas*
3. *Taittiriya Krishna Yajur Veda Pratisakhyas*
4. *Atharva Veda Pratisakhyas* of *Shaunakiya Shakha*

These are like manuals and explain how to recite the Vedic hymns.

2. Vyakarana

It is the linguistic analysis of Sanskrit grammar. Ancient books on Vedic grammar are all extinct now. It is believed that once upon a time there was a *Mahesh* grammar and an *Ayendra* grammar, both of which no longer exist. Only Sage Panini's grammar written around the 5th century BC is available now. It contains eight chapters. Hence, it is called *Ashtadhyayi.*

It is believed that once Lord Shiva played his hand drum (*damaru*) towards the end of his divine dance (*tandava*). It brought out 14 distinct sounds. Sage Panini could grasp these sounds due to the divine grace of the Lord. He then composed Sanskrit grammar based on those sounds. Panini's grammar has 4000 *Sutras*. There are several parts in it. But the core of Panini's grammar is *Ashtadhyayi* containing the rules. The parts are —

1. *Shiva Sutras* relating to **phonology**
2. *Ashtadhyayi* about **morphology**
3. *Dhatupada* that is a **dictionary of the verbal roots**
4. *Ganapatha* explaining the **primitive nominal stems**

At the end of *Ashtadhyayi*, *Unadi sutras*, which describe the formation of words of the Veda *Samhitas*, are given. These are supposed to be used along with *Nighantu,* the special detailed dictionary of the words contained in the *Samhitas* of the Vedas and *Nirukt*, a detailed dictionary of Vedic words.

3. The Chhandas

Chhanda Shastra is the oldest work about Vedic meters existing today. Vedic verses have mainly five varieties of meters. The number of *padas* in a verse, and the number of syllables in a *pada* divide the meters. The different types of meters are —

- *Jagati* having 4 *padas* of 12 syllables
- *Trishtubh* having 4 *padas* of 11 syllables
- *Viraj* consisting of 4 *padas* of 10 syllables
- *Anushtubh* with 4 *padas* of 8 syllables
- *Gayatri* with 3 *padas* of 8 syllables

The *Chhanda Shastra* is given in a treatise of *Pingalacharya.* It consists of the *Prosody*, or metre of the Vedic mantras. It has eight chapters.

4. The Nirukta

Etymology is dealt with in *Nirukta.* It contains glossary of difficult and rare words found in the Vedas. The philosophy of the Vedic mantras and the difficult Vedic words are explained here.

The *Nirukta* of Sage Yaska is divided into three parts —

- *Naighantuka* that is the collection of **synonymns**
- *Naigama* that deals with collection of words peculiar to the **Vedas**
- *Daivatha*, which are words related to **duties and sacrifices**

Nirukta is the basis for the later lexicons and dictionaries.

5. Jyotisha

It deals with astronomy and astrology. It studies the heavenly bodies. It gives the rules to calculate the positions of planets and stars based on Lunar signs as Moon is nearer to the earth than the Sun and therefore exerts greater influence on man and earth.

Jyotisha is associated with Sage Garga. The original author of *Jyotisha* is believed to be the Sun God. Later, Sages like Garga elaborated this science. It tells about the period and seasons when various Vedic rituals are to be performed, like Full moon day, New moon day and so on. There are three parts in Vedic astrology. They are —

1. *Siddhanta* or **Astronomy** with its application to astrology
2. *Samhita* or **Mundane Astrology** containing predictions, *Vaastu Shastra*, and omens
3. *Hora* or **Predictive Astrology** containing several branches

There are many branches of *Hora Jyotisha*. They touch almost all aspects of life. They are —

- *Jatak Shastra* – Predictions based on the horoscope of individuals
- *Muhurta* – Astrology for selecting the most beneficial time for getting the maximum return
- *Swar Shastra* – Prediction based on name and sounds
- *Prashna* – Predictions on the basis of time
- *Ank Jyotisha* – Numerology or astrology, based on numbers
- *Nadi Jyotisha* – Ancient treatise on palm leaves dealing with detailed individual predictions
- *Tajik Shastra* or *Varsha Phal* – Annual horoscope based on Sun
- *Jaimini Sutras* – Timing of events as per Jaimini
- *Nasht Jatakam* – Tracing or rewriting the lost horoscope
- *Stree Jatak* – Female astrology

The other related branches of *Jyotisha* are —

- *Griha Samudrika* or **Astro palmistry**
- *Hasta Rekha* or *Samudrika Shastra* or **Palmistry**
- *Padatal Shastra* based on the **lines and signs of the sole**
- *Shakun Shastra* that are **predictions based on omens**
- *Swapna Vidya* that deals with the **interpretation of dreams**

- *Kapal Vidya* in which a person's character and capabilities are judged by examining the **shape of his skull**
- *Akriti Vidya*, that is judging a person on the basis of **structure and moles** on the body

6. Kalpa

Kalpa means ritual. It tells about the methodology of different rituals for sacrifice and ceremonies to be followed while performing the rituals. It also tells about the duties of a child, student, householder, king, *Sanyasi* etc.

Kalpas are manuals. They teach ritual, philosophy and grammar. There are four types of *Kalpa Sutras* —

i) The *Shrauta Sutras* or **collective sacrifice** based upon *Shruti*, explaining the ritual of Vedic sacrifices. The *Shrauta Sutras* of the *Yajur Veda* have *Shulva Sutras* that are rules of the cord, measurement and construction of different kinds of altars that are required for the Vedic sacrifices. Along with the *Sutras* there are also treatises called *Parishishta* on various subjects related to scriptures and Vedic religion.

ii) The *Sulba* or **Vedic rituals** dealing with the measurements of the area, the fireplace, the altars etc, for performing any Vedic sacrifice.

iii) The *Grihya Sutras* or **family rituals** dealing with domestic rules for marriage, birth, naming ceremonies, *Upanayanam*, last rites etc.

iv) The *Dharma Sutras* or **occupational duties** dealing with the ethics, customs and laws. This became the chief source of law books later.

It is said that *Shiksha* and *Chhandas* are intended for the correct recitation of the Vedas, the *Vyakaran* and *Nirukta* are meant for understanding the Vedas, and finally the *Jyotisha* and *Kalpa* are for the proper employment of the Vedas at Sacrifice.

Upa Vedas

The *Upa Vedas* are called secondary Vedas. They amplify and apply the Vedic knowledge. There are four *Upa Vedas*. Each one is an appendage to the Vedas. They are—

1. Artha Veda

It relates to statecraft and is the science of sociology, political administration and economics. This is related to the *Rig Veda*. This *Upa Veda* deals with acquisition of material wealth by rightful means.

Neeti Shastra, *Shilpa Shastra*, and the sixty-four *Kalas* and other metaphysical subjects have also been dealt with in this *Upa Veda*.

2. Dhanur Veda

This is the science of defence and war and the method of making the weapons for war purposes. It also lays down the rules for warfare. It is related to *Yajur Veda*.

Precisely it is the science of archery and the use of related weapons. This *shastra* allows the use of weapons for the destruction of evil only. It contains both offensive and defensive techniques of warfare.

It explains in detail about missiles like *Chakra*, the sword and propelled forms of weapons, like *Brahmastra*, *Vaishnavastra*, *Pasupatastra*, *Agneyastra*, etc including the deities involved, the description of the weapons, and mock warfare, etc. It is believed that Sage Vishwamitra or Sage Bhrigu had written this *Upa Veda*.

3. Gandharva Veda

It is the science of music, both vocal and, instrumental, and also dance. It is related to *Sama Veda*.

It is a treatise on music, dance and theatre. It is associated with Bharata. It is said that Brahma composed it by taking the elements from all the four Vedas. He later passed it on to Sage Narada, who in turn, passed it on to Sage Bharata. Bharata combined the aspect of *Shiva Tandavam* with this knowledge and composed the *Natya Shastra*, which forms the basis of Indian classical dance.

The ultimate objective of this *shastra* is to worship God by concentrating the mind on these arts.

4. Ayurveda

It is the science of life and health or medical science. It is considered to be a supplement of *Atharva Veda*.

It is said, that the treatises in *Ayurveda* were composed by Brahma, Ashwinikumars, Dhanvantari, Indra, and *rishis* like Bhardwaja, Atri, Agnivesha, etc.

Later, Charaka wrote *Charaka Samhita* and Sushruta and Vagbhata followed it. This science deals with the maintenance of good health. It tells about medicines prepared from herbs, roots, and fruits. It also contains references to surgery and injections. Broadly, eight types of treatments are dealt with in *Ayurveda*. Besides, pharmacology, the science of sex written by Vatsyayana and the science of rejuvenation written by Sushruta are also found here.

The *Artha Veda*, *Dhanur Veda* and *Gandharva Veda* texts are almost extinct now.

In *Ayurveda* also, all books are not available although the basic theory can be found. A large number of books on the science of preparation of medicines, using herbs, roots, gems, metals, pearls for treating various kinds of diseases are almost extinct now.

Darshanas

Darshana means sight or vision. *Darshanas* or ways of seeing things are the schools of thought and are systems of philosophical treatises. These belong to the category of orthodox schools of Hindu philosophy and are based on Vedas.

The ancient sages explained the inherent philosophy of Vedas in different ways according to their vision. Accordingly, there are six *Darshanas* or six ways of perceiving ultimate truth and are called *Shad Darshanas*. These contain *sutras* or aphorisms of great *rishis*. These are very difficult to understand. Many commentators called *Bhashyakars* have tried to explain *Darshanas* in great detail. The philosophy of the Vedas are explained in the *Darshanas* in a rationalistic manner. *Darshanas* provide the philosophical explanations of the Vedic hymns. These are actually meant for highly learned scholars who have the intelligence to understand and follow the Vedic teachings.

Some of the *Darshanas* do not admit the existence of God as the creator, controller or Supreme power of the Universe. On this basis, *Darshanas* are divided into three categories. They are —

- The *Astika*, the system that believes in God
- The *Nastika*, the system that does not believe in the existence of God
- The *Dwastika*, the system that believes in fate or destiny

There are six *Darshanas* in all.

1. Nyaya Darshana (Logical School)

Akshapada **Gautama Rishi** founded this system around 300 BC. It emphasises the philosophy of logic and analyses the mental process of knowing and deals with internal analysis. In this, there are five chapters each with 2 sections having 537 *sutras*. This is a science of debate and discussions.

According to this system, atom is the cause of cosmic manifestation and by the use of perception of senses, sight, inference, analogy and verbal testimony, knowledge leading to *moksha* results.

It says that the ultimate purpose of life is salvation or complete freedom from pains and salvation can be obtained by knowing the sixteen categories of knowledge which are means of valid knowledge, objects of valid knowledge, doubt, purpose, example, conclusion, constituents of syllogism, ascertainment, debate, destructive criticism, fallacy or mistaken belief, quibble or evasion of the main point of an argument, refutations, points of the defeat of the opponent, and so on.

In brief, this system says that action leads to results called *adrishta*. God supervises and controls but does not change this.

2. Vaisheshika Darshana (Atomic School)

Sage Kanada had propounded this system of philosophy around 6th century BC. It combined with the *Nyaya* philosophy in the 11th century to become the *Nyaya-Vaisheshika* school. It is a supplement to the *Nyaya* philosophy.

According to this, the cause of cosmic manifestation is nothing but a combination of atoms. It holds that the smallest, indivisible and indestructible unit of the Universe is the atom. All physical things are a combination of the atoms of the earth, water, fire and air and all objects of the Universe to infinite number of atoms. The atom is made active through the divine will of God.

It has twelve chapters containing 373 *sutras*. It analyses *Drava* or money, *Gunas* namely *Sattva*, *Rajas* and *Tamas*, *Karma* and so on. *Moksha* is supposed to be obtained by understanding the atomic nature of the Universe and the difference and separation of matter and soul. According to this system, the source of knowledge is perception and inference. In short, it says that the world is the result of *adrishta*, that is the unseen result of *Karma* or actions.

Adrishta determines everything from birth. When the soul gets united with the body, it is birth, and when the soul gets separated from the body, it is death. But later, Kanada's followers introduced the concept of God as the cause of this world.

3. Sankhya Darshana (Cosmic Principle School)

Kapila Maharshi is said to be the author of this system. This philosophy is considered to be one of the oldest philosophical systems. There is no analytical enquiry here.

Sankhya means numbering. It has six chapters and is based on *Smritis* namely the *Puranas* and *Itihas*. It is based on dualism and postulates two eternal and ultimate realities, namely *Purusha* and *Prakriti*. The *Purusha* is the centre of consciousness and *Prakriti* is the source of all material existence.

According to this philosophy, the material nature and physical events are only the manifestations of *Purusha*, the cosmic spirit. Each living being is a *Purusha* that is unlimited and unrestricted. It says that the world is real and is balanced by intelligence, matter and activity. It says that evolution is only a transformation of principal nature from one form to another, since no matter can either be created or destroyed. Everything in the world arises due to *Prakriti*. The *tatva* or the primordial principle that is eternal. *Prakriti* is composed of three *gunas* namely, *Sattva*, *Rajas* and *Tamas*. Their interaction results in evolution. While bondage belongs to *Prakriti*, *Purusha* is eternally free.

Through yoga and the knowledge of the distinction between *Prakriti* and *Purusha*, one can obtain freedom from all miseries, pains and sufferings. Pain is actually the result of the entanglement of *Purusha*, the cosmic spirit that is essentially free, with *Prakriti* or matter. When *Purusha* is misled about its true identity, it gets confused and identifies itself with the physical body, which results in bondage. When the difference between *Purusha* and *Prakriti* is realised through knowledge, the spirit gets liberated.

Knowledge is obtained by three means. They are —

- *Pratyaksha* or direct sense perception
- *Anumana* or logical inference
- *Shabda* or verbal testimony

According to this system, *Prakriti* evolves itself into 24 *tatvas* or principles. These are —

- *Prakriti* which is behind all creations
- *Mahat*, the principle, which is behind intelligence in all living beings
- *Ahamkara*, the ego sense
- *Manas*, evolving from *Ahamkara*
- *Panch Jnana Indriyas* or the five sense organs
- *Panch Karma Indriyas* or the five organs of action
- *Panch Tanmantras* or the five subtle elements which are the root energies of sound, touch, sight, taste and smell
- *Panch Maha bhootas* or the five elements, namely ether, air, fire, water and earth.

The most important are the three *gunas* – *Sattva*, *Rajas* and *Tamas*. When *Purusha* gets freed from the bondage of these three *gunas*, liberation or *Mukti* can be obtained. It teaches that the goal of life is to get absolute freedom from all miseries.

In the earlier *Sankhya* philosophy, there is no mention of God. The concept of God was incorporated later when this system got associated with the yoga system.

4. Yoga Darshana (Yoga School)

There are different traditions of yoga. Originally *Hiranyagarbha* gave the *Yoga Shastra.* All the different *Yoga Shastras* have the same common feature of one pointed concentration on any chosen object. The chosen object may be any part of the body or breath, mantra or any diagram, idea or deity. The ultimate objective of any type of yoga is to attain *Mukti* or liberation through the full control of body, mind and emotions. *Rig Veda* has the earliest record of yoga. Yoga is supposed to be a supplement to *Sankhya* philosophy. The very first yoga was written by Patanjali around 2nd century BC. The important paths of yoga are —

- *Jnana Yoga* that is the path of realisation of the Self and wisdom through knowledge
- *Bhakti Yoga* or the path of devotion and love of a personal God
- *Karma Yoga* that is the path of selfless action
- *Hatha Yoga* emphasising physical control and postures and regulation of breathing
- *Kundalini Yoga* is associated with *Tantra* dealing with spells, rituals, and symbols. In this, both meditation and rituals are given importance. There are three grades of *Tantra* —
    1. *Tantras* that are suitable to people with *Sattvic* qualities (where goodness dominates)
    2. *Tantras* that are suitable to people possessing *Rajasic* qualities (where *karma* or action dominates)
    3. *Kundalini Yoga* which are suitable to people with *Tamasic* qualities (where animal tendency dominates)

The physiology of the subtle body is the basis of *Kundalini Yoga.* According to this yoga, there are seven major centers of psychic energy in the body. These are called *Chakras* and are located in the spinal column of the physical body. *Kundalini*, the coiled up or the latent energy, is located at the bottom of the spine. Through yoga, *Kundalini* is activated and it ascends with force along the spine through the subtle artery called *Sushumna,* and in the process each *Chakra* located in the spinal column gets opened up. Finally,

Kundalini reaches the topmost *Chakra* located in the brain. At that stage, the yogi attains *Samadhi*.

Raja Yoga of Patanjali

Sage Patanjali is stated to be the founder of this system of Yoga. It is also called as *Ashtanga Yoga* or the yoga of eight limbs. The basic text for this system is the *Yoga Sutras* of Patanjali. It maintains that the universal consciousness is the cause of all cosmic manifestations. It is divided into four parts and contains 194 *sutras*.

It deals with physical, mental and psychological exercises for achieving spiritual insight. It stresses self-discipline and concentration for realising the Absolute truth or God. According to this system, evolution occurs in stages requiring several life times. But this order can be reversed through yoga. It teaches the eight-fold path of controlling the body, mind, and intellect, which includes *yama*, *niyama*, *asana*, *pranayama*, *pratyahara*, *dhyana* and *samadhi*.

5. Purva or Karma Mimamsa (Ritualistic School)

It is supposed to be the earliest of all the six systems or *Darshanas*. The earliest work is that of *Mimamsa Sutra* of *Jaimini* written around the 4th century BC. It is known as *Purva Mimamsa* since it deals with the earlier portions or the *Karma Kand* of the Vedas. It is based on *Karma* or the philosophy of action and reaction. It gives rules to interpret the Vedas. The philosophical justifications of the observance of Vedic rituals are also explained in it.

It contains sixteen chapters and the statements that clarify doubts regarding Vedic rituals and their conduct. It says that cosmic manifestation is the result of *Karma* or activities. It justifies Vedic rituals and affirms that by respecting and observing them, one can achieve liberation. Primarily it enquires the nature of *Dharma*. *Dharma* here refers to duty or virtue. According to this system, the source of knowledge of *Dharma* is verbal cognition or the knowledge of words and their meanings. *Dharma* is following the commandments of the Vedas and the other scriptures related to the Vedas. It says that one who follows the teachings of the Vedas and acts accordingly is sure to go to the heaven.

6. Uttara or Brahma Mimamsa (Vedanta School)

It deals with the later portions of the Vedas namely the *Jnana Kand* or Vedanta or the philosophy that began with the *Upanishads*. **Veda Vyasa** propounded this. It interprets the *Jnana Kand* of the Vedas.

When *Purva Mimamsa* merged with Vedanta, it came to be called as *Uttara Mimamsa*. It has four chapters. It explains the process of identifying *jivatma*, the individual soul with Brahma, the universal soul that is the supreme reality. In this philosophy, the world is considered phenomenal. Vedanta is supposed to be an elaboration of *Sankhya* philosophy and *Poorva Mimamsa*.

Since the *shastras* were very difficult to understand, many commentators or *Bhashyakaras* wrote detailed commentaries on them. Later, many other commentaries were written on the earlier commentaries. There are also explanatory writings for each set of *sutras* of the original texts. They are in the form of *Bhashya, Vriti, Vartika, Vyakarana,* or *Tika* and *Tippani.*

Vedanta Sutra

Veda Vyasa composed *Vedanta Sutra* around 500 BC. It is also believed that **Sage Apantaratama** compiled this. Further it is also said, that while Vyasa was engaged in compiling *Vedanta Sutra*, several other sages like, Aitareya, Asmarathya, Audulomi, Karsnajini, Kasakrtsna, and Jaimini and some other sages were also engaged in doing similar works. It is also said that even before the time of Vyasa, sages like Parashara and Karmandibhikshu had discussed the aphorisms in great detail.

The *Vedanta Sutra* is considered as a supplement to Vedas. It contains the essence of Vedic knowledge found in the *Upanishads* in a concise manner. This was compiled by Vyasa to teach the absolute truth contained in the Vedas through logic and arguments. In *Bhagavad Gita*, Lord Krishna says that the *Brahma Sutra* discusses the ultimate goal of life through logic and argument relating to cause and effect. The *Vedanta Sutra* is therefore known as *Nyaya Prasthana* as well. It expounds that the Absolute Truth found in the *Upanishads* is the supreme reality of Godhead and He is the cause of everything in the Universe.

The *Vedanta Sutra* is also known as *Brahma Sutra, Sareerika Sutra, Vyasa Sutra, Badarayana Sutra, Uttara Mimamsa, Vedanta Darshana,* and *Bhikshu Sutra* (since it deals with renunciation or *Sanyasa*).

Vyasa enquired into the *Jnana Kand* of the Vedas, namely the *Aranyakas* and *Upanishads*, and came to the conclusion that it represents the ultimate purpose of the Vedas. Each *sutra* found here is a discourse. There are four *adhyayas* or chapters in this text. In each *adhyaya,* there are four *padas* or divisions. Altogether, there are sixteen divisions. The subject matter in each division is described in the following ways —

1. *Pratigna* referring to the solemn declaration of the purpose of the treatise that is to enquire about the Absolute Truth
2. *Hetu* referring to the explanations of the reasons
3. *Udaharana* which means giving the examples in terms of facts
4. *Upanaya* through which the theme is gradually brought to understanding
5. *Nigamana* that is supporting the stated facts through quotations from the Vedas

In this manner, logic and arguments concerning cause and effect are employed here for understanding the ultimate goal of life. That is why the *Vedanta Sutra* is also known as *Nyaya Prasthana*.

The four chapters or *adhyayas* are *Samanvaya*, *Avirodha*, *Sadana* and *Phala*.

The **first** chapter, *Samanvaya* says that *Brahman* is the only cause of creation, sustenance and destruction of the world.

Avirodha, the **second** chapter is concerned with the objections by a few schools of thought regarding this argument and internal contradictions and proves that *Brahman* is both material as well as the basis of the world. The first two chapters relate to *Sambandha Jnana* or the knowledge of relationship of the living beings with Supreme being or God.

The **third** chapter namely, *Sadhana*, deals with salvation. This is called *Abhideya Jnana*. It explains how one can act in his relationship with Godhead.

Phala, the **fourth** chapter deals with the results of such action, that is, going back to God and is called *Prayojana Jnana*.

In short, the *Vedanta Sutra* forms the essence of the *Upanishads*. It tries to answer these questions – who or what is the individual self? What is the nature of this world? And, what is the basis for all these?

There are commentaries for the *sutras* and they are known as *Bhashyas*. Based on the commentaries, the six systems of philosophy have emerged. Of these, three are more popular than the rest. They are *Advaita*, *Dwaita*, and *Vishishtadvaita*. The less popular ones are *Dvaitadvaita*, *Shuddhadvaita* and *Achintya Bhedabheda*.

The Six Systems of Philosophy

1. *Advaita* or Non-duality

Shankaracharya's commentary of *Brahma Sutra* is based upon monism or *Advaita*. According to this, there is a relation between *Jivatma* and *Paramatma,* the *Brahman*. According to him, God and all the living beings are one and the same. The world is illusory and not real. The ultimate objective of human beings is to achieve release from *Maya* and attain complete union with the *Nirguna Brahman* that is beyond qualities and attributes.

2. *Dwaita* or Dualism

Madhavacharya also known as *Anandatirtha* propounded this philosophical argument. According to him, there is total and eternal difference between the individual self and *Brahman*. He further identifies *Brahman* with Lord Vishnu and says that *Mukti* or liberation from the repeated cycle of birth and death is possible only by surrendering oneself totally to Lord Vishnu.

3. *Vishishtadvaita* or Specific Non-duality

The founder of this philosophy was Ramanujacharya. It maintains a crucial non-differentiation and fundamental identity between *Jivatma* and *Paramatma*. To him also *Brahman* is none other than Lord Vishnu himself. Liberation or *Mukti* from the non-illusory world consists in obtaining a state of bliss similar to that of the ever-liberated *Brahman*, the Lord Vishnu, possessing all superior qualities.

4. *Dwaitadvaita* or Oneness Doctrine

Nimbarka expounded this doctrine. It tries to reconcile the views of *Advaita* and *Dwaita.*

5. *Shuddhadvaita* or Pure Non-dualism

This was given by Vallabha. This doctrine also holds that *Jeeva*, the individual soul, and *Brahman*, the universal soul, are identical. But *Brahman* is personal deity and is to be worshipped with devotion.

6. *Achintya Bhedabheda* or Inconceivable Oneness and Difference

Vidya Bhushan advocated this doctrine. It tells about the oneness as well as difference. However, it is opposed to the *Advaitic* philosophy.

Agamas

Agama means that which has been handed down from the past to the present. These are theological treatises and practical manuals relating to the worship of the Divine and are the primary authority for any ritual, *yajna* and also temple construction. These scriptures deal with the external worship of a particular aspect of God as *Saguna Brahman*. These contain prayers and rituals.

Agama includes *tantras*, *mantras*, and *yantras* in which the external temple worship is explained which includes rituals, rites, and worship of Gods. They are theological and deal with *Jnana* or knowledge, *Kriya* or rituals, *Yoga* or concentration, *Charya* or methods of worship, and *Bhakti* or devotion. *Agamas* also deal with dogmas, charms and spells, temple and idol making, and domestic, social and public festivals.

Each *Agama* has four parts —

- The **first** part deals with philosophical and spiritual knowledge.
- The **second** part is related to yoga and mental discipline.
- The **third** part covers the rules and regulations for the construction of temples.
- The **fourth** part explains the conduct of religious rituals, sacrifices and festivals.

The *Agama Shastra* books are of five categories. They deal with instructions contained in the Vedas for worshipping according to one's level of consciousness. These are as follows —

1. Energy or Shakti Agamas

Shakti Agamas glorify Mother Goddess Shakti (the creative power of Lord Shiva) and deals with the energy worship. In these *Shakti Agamas*, the Mother Goddess is the supreme. *Ishvara* or God occupies a less important position. Here Shakti is considered as both the cause of ignorance or *Maya* as well as liberation.

There are 77 *Shakti Agamas* and they are called *tantras*. They are supplement to *Shaiva Agamas*. It has given rise to *tantric* form of worship, dealing with the magical and occult practices in addition to mechanical, ritualistic, devotional and spiritual aspects of the *tantric* form of worship. It is in the form of dialogue between Lord Shiva and his consort Shakti.

2. Visible Source or Surya Agamas

Surya Agamas deal with the worship of *Surya* or Sun.

3. Controller or Ganapati Agamas

These deal with the worship of Lord Ganesha.

4. Destoyer Or Shiva Agamas

This deals with the worship of Shiva. Lord Shiva is considered to be the supreme ruler of the Universe, the highest Self. Shakti is considered here the natural principle responsible for bondage. This *Agama* says that the union of Shakti with Shiva leads to freedom from all bondage.

There are 28 principal *Agamas* and the most important one among them is *Kamikam*. There were 207 *Upa Agamas*, some of them belonging to the 2nd Century AD, but only 20 fragmentary texts are available now.

5. Ultimate Source or Vaishnava Agamas

This deals with the worship of Vishnu and his various forms. In this *Agama*, Lord Vishnu is considered as the supreme power of the Universe and the source of liberation. There are four kinds of *Vishnu Agamas*. They are —

1. *Vaikhanasa*
2. *Pancha Ratna*
3. *Pratishtharasa*
4. *Vijnana-Lalita*

The *Pancha Ratna Agama* is further subdivided into seven sub-*Agamas*, namely Brahma, Shaiva, Kaumara, Vashishtha, Kapila, Gautamiya, and Naradiya.

It is believed that the *Vaikhanasa Agama* was compiled under the guidance of Sage Vaikhanasa during the early Vedic period.

Altogether, there are 215 *Vaishnava Agamas*.

Tantra Shastra

For those with lesser levels, Shiva is supposed to have given *Tantra Shastras* that have two aspects, the right aspect and the left aspect.

The **right** aspect deals with the regulation for purification of those who are engaged in meat eating, intoxication, illicit sex activities and so on.

Activities like black magic are dealt with in the **left** aspect.

Dharma Shastras

These are law books. There are hundreds of *Dharma Shastras*. These are texts explaining various religious and social norms during different stages of evolution of society. These are named after the *rishis* who wrote them. *Dharma Shastras* can be categorised into three categories. They are —

- *Achara*, consisting of rules regarding daily rituals and duties of the four classes of people
- *Vyavahara*, consisting of rules pertaining to the procedures to be followed for resolving doubts about *dharma*, rules as per the eighteen titles of Hindu Laws

- *Prayashchita* explaining rules about expiations and penances for violating *Dharmic* rules

The main topics dealt with in the *Dharma Shastras* include, *dharma*, caste system, marriage and other rites, *yajna*, the four stages of life, rules of eating, religious gifts, and renunciation, the duties of a king, legal procedures, the eighteen titles of Hindu Law, categories of sins, expiations and penances, *karma*, ancestral rites and the rites for the dead, pilgrimage vows, festivals, and propitiatory rites. The ritual texts are interpreted by making use of *Poorva Mimamsa* system of philosophy.

There are eighteen *Dharma Shastras* that are considered as important. The most important among them are *Manu Smriti*, *Yajnavalkya* and *Parashara*.

These texts give laws governing Hindu society. Of these, *Manu Smriti* or *Manava Dharma Shastra* is considered to be the oldest.

The *Manu Smriti* is modified from time to time to suit the changing times. This is intended for *Satya Yuga*.

The laws of Yajnavalkya were believed to be meant for *Treta Yuga* and the law of Shankha-Likhita and Parashara for *Dwapara Yuga* and *Kali Yuga* respectively.

The other 15 *Dharma Shastras* are: *Vishnu*, *Daksha*, *Samvarta*, *Vyasa*, *Harita*, *Shatatapa*, *Vashishtha*, *Yama*, *Apasthamba*, *Gautuma*, *Devala*, *Shankha-Likhita*, *Usanana*, *Atri*, and *Shaunaka*.

Manu Smriti

Manu Smriti or *Manu Samhita* or *Manu Shastra* is the most important and the most popular and at the same time the most controversial of all the *Dharma Shastras*.

Manu is considered the grandchild of Brahma, the Creator. It is believed that Brahma gave 1,00,000 codes of laws to Manu. Later, Manu reduced the codes to 4000. Civil laws, social obligations, ceremonies connected with birth, marriage, death, the daily duties, code of conduct to be observed by people belonging to the various *varnas* or castes, the conquest senses, freedom from lust and greed, study of scriptures, honouring the older people, respecting parents, injury to none, the process of creation, education, laws of state, punishments, reincarnation, liberation are some of the major topics dealt with at great length in *Manu Smriti*. It is in the form of a discourse by Sage Manu to the *rishis,* who requested him to impart them this knowledge. According to one view, it was written roughly between the 1st and 6th Century AD. There are 2031 verses in it.

About the subject of education, it tells about the rules to be followed during the first stage of one's life.

The observance of *Brahmacharya* while being a student and while learning the Vedas, the need for practising *Yama* or abstention and *Niyama* or observances along with a disciplined life, the need for good character by following celibacy with controlled passions, desires, steadfastness in devotion to truth, righteousness, performance of good deeds are stated as the most important factors while fulfilling one's duties as a student towards fellow humans and to God.

Manu advocated compulsory education after the fifth or eighth year.

Regarding marriage this *smriti* states that a girl three years after attaining maturity should marry and choose a husband who was her equal. A *Brahmachari* after completing his studies should enter married life by choosing a girl of his own class, who must possess good qualities. He considered it better for men and women to remain unmarried instead of marrying persons with incompatible qualities, temperaments and character.

Eight kinds of marriages are explained here. They are —

1. *Brahma*, when the marriage is as per the mutual consent of the bride and the groom
2. *Deva*, where a daughter is gifted to a priest who conducts the sacrifice
3. *Arsha*, when the marriage is as per the wishes of the groom
4. *Prajapati*, which is a marriage with mutual consent of the families
5. *Asura*, that is marriage performed by bribing the bride and the groom
6. *Gandharva*, couple marrying and entering into sex life without the knowledge of the others
7. *Rakshasa*, a marriage by abducting the bride by using force

8. *Pishacha*, which is performance of marriage when the bride is intoxicated, in sleep or suffers a mental disorder.

Regarding the duties of the four classes of society, the scripture states —

- The duties of a **Brahmin** are studying and teaching of the Vedas, performing or assisting the performance of *yajna*, giving alms, and also receiving gifts.
- The duties of a **Kshatriya** include protecting people with perfect justice, giving away gifts, perform Vedic sacrifices and rituals, and studying Vedas and other scriptures.
- The duties of a **Vaishya** are to own and maintain cattle, giving away gifts, perform Vedic rituals, studying Vedas and other scriptures, lending money on interest, and cultivating land.
- The duties of a **Shudra** are to serve the Brahmins, the Kshatriyas and Vaishyas.

However, a Shudra becomes a Brahmin or a Kshatriya or a Vaishya by virtue of his character, qualifications and accomplishments. Similarly, a Brahmin or a Kshatriya or a Vaishya becomes a Shudra, if he lacks the necessary character, qualifications and accomplishments.

This scripture deals with the status of women in a clear manner. It says that if the wife becomes miserable then it results in the unhappiness of the entire family. In other words, happiness of the family depends on the happiness of women. Those who aspire for prosperity and happiness in life should respect women. Only in the families where women are respected, great people are born. They should not inflict pain on women. The father, brother and the husband should provide good food, clothing and ornaments to their women.The good conduct, good character and loving behaviour of the husband makes the wife happy, which in turn leads to continuous prosperity for the family. Only when the first marriage is not fulfilling, remarriages of widows or widowers is to be allowed. Otherwise the widow or the widower must follow celibacy. However if a widow has to continue the family line then, she may adopt children or a man of her choice or a widower can father her children.

Manu Smriti also points out that the one who does not study the Vedas gets degenerated. It also says things about matters relating to the daily life. For example, it asks people to look down while walking, to filter drinking water, to think well before acting, to keep senses under full control like a charioteer who controls the horses, and prevent the mind and soul from going after the material objects. One should follow true religion for enabling one to distinguish between the good and bad, the right and wrong. A man who is an atheist and condemns the Vedas should be expelled from the society and even from the country.

Kalas

Kalas deal with various *Shastras*. Some of these are —

1. Akshara Laksha

Sage Valmiki authored this *shastra*. In this, 35 kinds of Mathematics are explained including Geometry, Algebra, Trigonometry, Geography, Applied Mathematics, and so on. It is believed that the earlier writings by Sages like Kashyapa, Ganapati, Surya, Brihaspati, Jaimini, Anjaneya formed the basis for this work.

2. Shabda Shastra

Kandika Rishi is supposed to have written this *shastra*. It deals with sounds, echoes of moving and non-moving objects, mechanically reproduced sounds and measurement of the pitch of sounds and velocity of sound.

3. Lakshana Shastra

Sage Shakatayana authored this *shastra*. It is a science that determines sex in animate and inanimate living beings.

Babhrumuni wrote *Kanya Lakshana* in which 32 marks are given for chastity.

Sage Garga wrote *Saguna Shastra* that analysed good and bad effects of the sounds of birds and speech of humans.

4. Shilpa Shastra

Sage Kashyapa wrote this *shastra*. He gave details about 307 varieties of *shilpas*, 11 types of construction of temples, palaces, halls etc. It is said that he based his theory on the earlier works by Vishwakarma, Maya Maruti and Chaya Purusha.

5. Supa Shastra

It is the science of cookery. **Sage Sukesha** composed it. He analysed 108 varieties of preparations and 3032 kinds of dishes.

6. Malinee Shastra

Sage Rishya Shringa composed it. It deals with the science of flower arrangements.

7. Science Of Time

Lord Kartikeya wrote this s*hastra*. It analyses the divisions of time, their classification into auspicious and inauspicious moments and the deities presiding over each of these moments.

8. Samudrika Shastra

It is believed that this s*hastra* was first given by the Lord of the ocean who noticed the auspicious marks on the body of Lord Vishnu reclining on *Adishesha*. It is said that **Sage Narada**, **Lord Kartikeya**, **Varaha** and **Mandavya** developed this s*hastra* further and also included palmistry in it.

9. Dhatu Veda

This is given by **Ashwini Kumaras**. It is the science that deals with the natural and artificial substances, like metals, chemicals, their combination and transmutation.

10. Visha Shastra

Ashwini Kumaras are supposed to have written this science, which deals with poison. It analyses 32 kinds of poison, their properties, preparation, effects and their antidotes.

11. Chitra Karma Shastra

It is the science of Fine Arts and was authored by **Bhima**. It deals with 200 varities of drawings. It also explains the drawing of a figure of a person on the basis of his hair, bone or a single hair.

12. Malla Shastra

Malla wrote this science of gymnastics and sports. It analyses 82 kinds of gymnastics and sports and 24 kinds of infantry warfare.

13. Parkaya Pravesha

It analyses the method of entering one body from another body. **Valakhilyas** had written this. It analyses 32 kinds of yogas and 8 types of *siddhis* or superhuman capacities.

14. Science Of Horses

Agnivarma composed this. It analyses the different types of horses, their auspicious marks, their physiology, breeding and training.

15. Gaja Shastra

This is the science of elephants. This was composed by **Kumara Swami**. It analyses 16 methods of testing the various marks on the body of elephants.

16. Ratna Pareeksha

This deals with the testing of gems or precious stones. **Vatsyayana** who wrote this, has given 24 characteristics of gems, both natural and artificial. Their forms and weights are also discussed and classified. He has given 32 methods for testing the genuineness of precious stones.

17. Mahendrajala

This deals with magic. This was given by **Veerabahu**. It explains the method of creating illusions.

18. Shakti Tantra

This was authored by **Sage Agastya**. 64 kinds of external forces like, sun, moon, fire and air are explained and their applications are also explained in this. Nuclear Science also forms a part of it.

19. Saudamini Kala

This was given by **Sage Matanga**. It analyses the method of attracting bodies through shadows, ideas and also photographing of the interiors of earth and the mountains.

20. Science of Clouds

Sage Atri had composed it. It explains 12 kinds of clouds, their characteristics, 12 kinds of rains, 64 kinds of lightning and 32 varieties of thunderbolts.

21. Yantras

Sage Bharadwaja had composed it. 339 types of vehicles which are useful on land, 783 kinds of boats and ships, 101 varieties of air ships and means used by divine beings like *Gandharvas* are explained here.

Other Special Texts

Anukramika

These are indices, and provide the lists of Vedic deities, the meters of Vedic hymns, etc.

Vedic Koshas

These are in addition to *Nirukta*. These texts help in interpreting Vedic mantras.

Vrit

These are commentaries on *Upanishads* which explain the aphorisms or maxims in a more elaborate manner like *Bodhayana's Vrit* on *Brahma Sutra*.

Vartika

These provide a critical study of *Bhashyas* or commentaries for making them perfect, like *Katyayana's Vartikas* on Panini's *sutras*.

Vyakarana or Tika

They explain in simple language with some elucidation about what is contained in the original texts like the *Vyakarana* of *Darshanas.*

Tippani

A *tippani* explains the difficult phrases that are found in the original texts, like the work of **Kaiyata's** on the *Mahabhashya* of Patanjali.

In addition to these, there are also very many later works, like *Subhashitas* which contain wise sayings, instructions and stories in prose and poetry.

The *Kavyas*, which are dramas, and *Alankaras* which are prose and poetical rhetorical texts and scriptures, like *Prakarana Granthas*, the *Bhaja Govindam*, *Atma Bodha* and so on.

Then, there are also innumearable scriptures which contain *Strotas* and *Bhajans*.

There are also numerous scriptures in vernacular languages as well as translations from Sanskrit works.

Finally, in modern times, there are also innumerable works of the great saints and teachers about ancient scriptures and also about their own teachings.

This list, however, is not exhaustive. There are many other texts which are also important but not included here due to various limitations.

9

Itihasas and Puranas

Itihasas

Itihasas are epics. These are the books of legends. Itihasa means, "It happened thus." It is history as it truly happened. It tells the stories of past as well as present, about the remote areas of the Universe which are not perceived through the naked eye. These are meant for ordinary people, who cannot understand the Vedic philosophy as propounded in the Vedas.

In *Itihasas* and *Puranas*, the Vedic knowledge is explained in a very simple manner through several beautiful stories. The objective of Vedas and the *Itihasas* is, however, the same. Both try to convey the eternal truth. While Vedas make use of *karma*, *upasana* and *jnana* paths, *Itihasas* make use of the *bhakti marg* for attaining the same goal, which is *Mukti* or liberation.

With the two exceptions of *Yoga Vashishta* contained in the *Ramayana* and the *Bhagavad Gita*, the *Itihasas* and *Puranas*, in general, explain the material and transcendental teachings of the Vedas through interesting historical stories. The historical events pertaining to either a single hero or a few personalities in a particular lineage are described in them.

The two great *Itihasas* or epics are *Ramayana* and *Mahabharata*. Before the time of Valmiki, verses were only found in the Vedas. It is said that *Itihasas* kept Hinduism alive when it was at its low ebb, before the advent of Adi Shankara.

Ramayana

Ramayana is called *Adi Kavya* or the first epic. Sage Valmiki, who is considered as the *Adi Kavi*, wrote this great epic first in Sanskrit. Later, Goswami Tulsidas rewrote it in *Brijbhasha* which was the language of common man.

Before the time of Valmiki, there were only mantras of the Vedas. The epic Ramayana has 24,000 verses in seven *Kands*. The *Valmiki Ramayana* is dated around the 5th century BC.

Ramayana narrates the story of Sri Rama, the Lord Vishnu incarnate, a descendent of Ikshvaku clan belonging to the Solar Dynasty, and his three brothers who lived in *Treta Yuga*. (*Treta Yuga* is called the Silver Age that lasted for 3600 years. This *Yuga* came after *Satya Yuga*, also known as the Golden Age that is believed to have lasted for 4800 years. It is said that during *Satya Yuga,* humans had direct contact with the Divine, which diminished during *Treta Yuga*).

This epic tells how an ideal man and a king should act. The subject matter of this great epic is the story of Sri Rama, his brothers Bharata, Lakshmana and Shatrughna, their father King Dashratha, and their three mothers, Kaushalya, Kaikeyi and Sumitra. The story moves from their childhood, their marriage, the exile of Sri Rama, the abduction of the wife of Sri Rama, recovery of Sita by Sri Rama from Ravana, the demon king of Sri Lanka, to the war and destruction of Ravana by Sri Rama, and finally the reign of Sri Rama.

Ramayana is divided into seven *Kands*. They are —

1. Bal Kand

It deals with the birth and childhood of Sri Rama and his brothers in Ayodhya, his departure to the forest along with his brother Lakshmana accompanied by Sage Vishvamitra, the marriage of Sri Rama and his brothers, their return to Ayodhya and the preparation for the coronation of Sri Rama.

2. Ayodhya Kand

This *Kand* deals with Dashratha's grief over his promise to his wife Kaikeyi, and Rama's exile to the forest for fourteen years along with his brother Lakshmana and wife Sita.

3. Aranya Kand

This *Kand* tells about the life of Rama, Sita and Lakshmana in the forest and the abduction of Sita by Ravana, the demon king of Lanka.

4. Kishkindha Kand

This *Kand* is about the Monkey *(Vanara)* Kingdom in Kishkindha, Rama and Lakshmana meeting Hanuman who is Rama's staunch devotee, Rama making friendship with Sugreeva, the leader of the monkeys, and Rama, Lakshmana and the monkeys (*vanaras*) searching for Sita.

5. Sundar Kand

This *Kand* is dedicated to the moneky-god Hanuman. It includes details of Hanuman leaping over the ocean to reach Lanka in search of Sita, finding the imprisoned Sita there, burning the Lanka and returning back to Rama with the news of Sita.

6. Yuddha Kand

This *Kand* depicts the Rama-Ravana war, Rama and his army winning the war, Rama's return to Ayodhya with Sita, and becoming the king of Ayodhya.

7. Uttar Kand

It is an epilogue. It describes the life of Rama and Sita in Ayodhya, Sita being sent to forest by Rama, birth of Lava and Kusha, and the departure of Rama and Sita to their heavenly abode.

The Summary

Sri Rama, the hero of this epic, is portrayed in *Ramayana* as an *avatar* of Lord Vishnu. He was the eldest and the favourite among the four sons of King Dashratha. He was a very popular prince. When all the preparations for his coronation were in progress, Kaikeyi, one of the three wives of King Dashratha who was also the mother of Bharata, plotted against Sri Rama. Otherwise, she was very fond of him, but under the evil influence of her maid Manthara, she made the evil plan of sending Sri Rama to the forest for fourteen years.

She reminded Dashratha about his early promise of granting her any two boons as a reward for her skill and timely help in saving the life of her husband during his war with the demons.

Kaikeyi asked for her two wishes sending Rama to the forest as the first one and secondly to make her son Bharata, the younger brother of Rama, the king of Ayodhya.

Rama, the obedient son, in order to keep up his father's promise, left for the forest accompanied by his wife Sita and Lakshmana, one of his younger brothers born to Sumitra, the third queen of Dashratha.

In the forest, Sita was abducted by Ravana, the demon king of Lanka. Ravana as a result of his long and severe penance lasting about 10,000 years had got a boon from Lord Brahma according to which no God, demon or spirits could kill him. Ravana, the son of a Brahmin and a demon mother, was highly skilful and intelligent and had 10 heads and 20 arms. With this boon, he became invincible and created havoc harming all the good, pious and virtuous humans. Rama with the help of his staunch devotee Hanuman and the monkey (*vanara*) army of Sugreeva, the king of the monkeys, fought with Ravana, killed him and recovered Sita who was kept as a captive in Lanka.

Throughout *Ramayana*, we find powerful arguments about what is right and what is wrong. These arguments are as relevant even today as they were at the time of Sri Rama.

Through Sri Rama's life, Valmiki has explained the characteristics of an ideal human being. The epic clearly points out that one's life should be in accordance with *dharma,* whether it results in pain or pleasure. It also stresses the importance of keeping up promises whatever may be the outcome.

Sage Narada who originally narrated this story to Sage Valmiki, has listed sixteen qualities of an ideal man, which forms the first *Sarga* of *Valmiki Ramayana.*

Yoga Vashishta

The *Yoga Vashishtha* or the *Yoga Vashishtha Maha Ramayana*, or *Vashishtha Sudha*, or *Rama Gita* is a dialogue between Sri Rama and his Guru Vashishtha. Some people even consider it to be a separate epic. It is the most ancient work on Vedic principles.

In this work, Sage Vashishtha teaches Vedanta to Sri Rama. Advaita, the doctrine of non-duality, in its purest form is explained here through interesting stories. It says that *Jnana Yoga* is the only path to spiritual realisation. After Sri Rama returned from a pilgrimage to the *Gurukul*, on the conclusion of his education he became a changed person. He was always silent, quiet, thoughtful, detached and mentally disturbed. This worried King Dashratha and he informed his Guru Sage Vashishtha about change in Rama's behaviour. Sage Vashishtha then called Rama and enquired the reason for the same. Sri Rama told him about his disillusionment about the worldly life and its pleasures. He also asked Vashishtha some profound philosophical questions. Vashishtha realised that the right time had come to discuss the eternal truths with him. He wanted Rama himself to provide the answers as he noticed the divine glow on his face. Vashishtha taught Rama the ways to everlasting happiness through several stories and this formed the *Yoga Vashishtha*.

According to its philosophy, everything that we see around us is nothing but pure consciousness. The entire world is just an illusion. When that illusion disappears, all miseries vanish into nothing. The Self is the only one. Liberation or *Mukti* is the destruction of the feeling of 'I' or *Ahamkara*. When that knowledge or *Brahma Jnana* dawns, there are no more thoughts which is *Moksha*.

This scripture is considered to be the storehouse of wisdom. This book describes *jnana* or knowledge, but not rituals and worship for attaining *Mukti* or liberation. It stresses that knowledge alone is the means to enlightenment. Other means, no doubt, lead one to heaven, but after a pre-determined time, there is a fall back to the earth as per one's latent desires.

The marks of a liberated person, which are, dissolution of the mind, destruction of latent impressions, meditation on the Self, and exposition of Self are dealt with at great length in *Yoga Vashishtha*. It clearly explains how the individual soul gets unified with the supreme soul amidst all the trials and tribulations of life. It also explains about *Brahman* and the various methods of attaining self-realisation.

There are six sections or *Prakaranas* in this book. They are —

1. The *Vairagya Prakarana* (22), which deals with dispassion. It relates to the mental despondency of Sri Rama.

2. The *Mumukshu Prakarana* (28), that tells about the longing for liberation.
3. The *Utpathi Prakarana*, dealing with Creation. It is explained through the stories of —
    - Akashaja (The son of Akasha)
    - Lila (Sport)
    - Karkati
    - Aindreva, the son of Indra
    - The deceitful Indra
    - Manas (Mind)
    - Bala (Lad)
    - Siddha
4. The *Sthiti Prakarana* containing a description of existence or preservation. This contains the stories of —
    - Shukra (Venus)
    - Daman, Vyala and Kata
    - Bheema, Bhasa and Drudha
    - Dhasoora
    - Kacha
5. The *Upa Shanti Prakarana* is an explanation of dissolution of the Universe. It has the stories of —
    - King Janaka
    - Punya and Pavana
    - The Great King Bali
    - Prahalada, the great devotee of Lord Vishnu
    - Gadhi
    - Uddhalaka
    - Sureghu
    - Bhasha and Vilasa
    - Veetahavya

6. The *Nirvana Prakarana* contains the knowledge about liberation. It narrates the stories of —
   - Bhusunda
   - *Deva Puja* (Worship of God)
   - *Bilwa* fruit
   - Shila
   - Arjuna
   - Sata – The 100 Rudras
   - Vetala
   - Bhagiratha
   - Shikhidwaja
   - Kacha
   - Mithya Purusha
   - Bhringi
   - Ikshawaku

Mahabharata

The *Mahabharata* is said to have been written around 6th and 9th centuries BC. This epic describes about the life of the descendants of the Lunar race, particularly from the period of King Shantanu and his descendants Pandavas and Kauravas, who lived during *Dwapara Yuga.* This *yuga* is also known as the Bronze Age that was believed to have lasted for 2400 years. (It is believed that during this age, humans forgot their divine nature and materialism dominated, while spiritualism took a back seat.)

The childhood of Pandavas and Kauravas, their enmity, the exile of Pandavas, the great Mahabharata war at Kurukshetra, Sri Krishna's divine protection of Pandavas, the marvellous teachings of Sri Krishna in the battlefield in the form of *Bhagavad Gita*, the victory of the Pandavas, their reign, their departure to the Himalayas and finally the end of Krishna *avatar*, form the subject matter of this epic.

Linked with the main story, innumerable minor stories are found in this epic. All the stories are beautiful and contain excellent moral teachings. *Mahabharata* contains 100,000 verses. Sri Krishna

Dwaipayana Vyasa who is believed to be a contemporary of Sri Krishna wrote this great epic.

The most important part of this great epic is undoubtedly the *Bhagavad Gita*. It is in the form of dialogue between Lord Krishna and Arjuna, the third among the Pandava brothers on the battlefield just before the commencement of the great war at Kurukshetra. It is considered to be the essence of Vedic knowledge, particularly the *Upanishads*. It is considered as a universal gospel.

In the battlefield, Arjuna became depressed and refused to fight as soon as he saw his teachers and close relatives standing against him in the battlefield. At that moment, Lord Krishna who was Arjuna's charioteer imparted the knowledge of Self to him and made him realise his duty as a *Kshatriya* to fight against *Adharma,* unmindful of the results. After hearing Lord Krishna's words, Arjuna came out of his delusion. With all his doubts cleared, he fought against the Kauravas and finally the Pandavas won the war.

There are also stories of great sages, kings, demons, wise men and even Gods. It also contains philosophical parables.

Mahabharata clearly speaks about the four important goals of life namely, *Kama* or pleasure, *Artha* or wealth, *Dharma* or duty and *Moksha* or liberation.

The *Mahabharata* is eight times longer than Homer's *Iliad* and *Odyssey* put together. Nearly half of the *Mahabharata* is about the eighteen-day war in which innumerable people lost their lives. This epic covers almost all aspects of human life and knowledge both material as well as spiritual. There are countless arguments on *Dharma* and *Adharma*.

As Sri Jai Prakash Narayan has put it,

"*As long as human beings remain governed by passions and feelings, as long as the struggle between the good and evil continues to rage in human heart, as long as mankind is faced with the problems of war and peace, the Mahabharata will continue to remain a source of aesthetic enjoyment and moral and intellectual enjoyment.*"

It is said that there is nothing that we cannot find in *Mahabharata*. In the first *parva* it is said, that what is found in *Mahabharata* may be found everywhere but what is not found here may not be found elsewhere.

It is believed that originally this epic contained 20 *Parvas*, divided into 100 sub-*Parvas*. But now it has only 18 *Parvas*. The 18 *Parvas* are —

1. *Adi Parva* (*sub-parva* 1-19)

   Introduction, birth and upbringing of the Pandava and Kaurava brothers

2. *Sabha Parva* (*sub-parva* 20-28)

   Life at the palace, the game of dice, exile of the Pandavas

3. *Aranyaka Parva* or *Vana Parva* (*sub-parva* 29-44)

   Twelve years of exile of the Pandava brothers in the forest

4. *Virata Parva* (*sub-parva* 45-48)

   The year in exile of Pandavas in the palace of King Virata

5. *Udyoga Parva* (*sub-parva* 49-59)

   Preparation for the Mahabharata war

6. *Bhishma Parva* (*sub-parva* 60-64)

   The first part of the war with Bhishma as the commander or of the Kaurava army, and the famous *Bhagavad Gita*

7. *Drona Parva* (*sub-parva* 65-72)

   The war with Dronacharya as the commander of the Kaurava army

8. *Karna Parva* (*sub-parva* 73)

   The war with Karna as the commander of the Kaurava army

9. *Shalya Parva* (*sub-parva* 74-77)

   The last part of the war with Shalya as the commander of the Kaurava army

10. *Sauptaka Parva* (*sub-parva* 78-80)

    The manner in which Ashwathama, Drona's son and friend of Duryodhana, killed the sons of Pandavas while they were asleep, to avenge the defeat of Duryodhana in the war

11. *Stri Parva* (*sub-parva* 81-85)

    Gandhari, the mother of the Kauravas and other women lamenting over the death of Kauravas

12. *Shanti Parva* (*sub-parva* 86-88)

    Yudhishthira becoming the King, Bhishma's instructions and advice to Yudhishthira

13. *Anushasana Parva* (*sub-parva* 89-90)

    The final instructions from Bhishma to Yudhishthira

14. *Ashvamedhika Parva* (*sub-parva* 91-92)

    Ashvamedha yajna conducted by the Pandavas with Yudishthira as the king

15. *Ashrama Vasika Parva* (*sub-parva* 93-95)

    Departure of Dhritarashtra, Gandhari and Kunti to forest and their death in the forest

16. *Mausala Parva* (*sub-parva* 96)

    The fight among the Yadava clan with maces

17. *Maha Prastharika Parva* (*sub-parva* 97)

    The *mahaprasthana* or the final journey of the Pandavas

18. *Swargarohana Parva* (*sub-parva* 98)

    Pandvas ascend to heaven

    Appendix

    Khila-Hari Vamsa Parva (*sub-parva* 99-100)

    Life of Sri Krishna

The Summary

Devavrata who later came to be known as Bhishma was the son of Shantanu, the king of Hastinapur. His mother was the sacred river Ganga. He gave up his youth and his right for the kingdom for the sake of his father who wanted to marry a fisherwoman whose father had put a condition that if the king wanted to marry his daughter then he must agree to the condition that the son born to the king and his daughter alone would become the future king after Shantanu.

Bhishma made his father accept that condition and Shantanu married Satyavati. They had two sons namely, Chitrangada and Vichitraveerya. But unfortunately both of them died when they were young. Dhritarashtra and Pandu were the grandsons of Satyavati. Since Dhritarashtra, the elder one was blind, his younger brother Pandu ruled the kingdom.

When, once Pandu went to forest along with his wives Kunti and Madri, Dhritarashtra ruled the kingdom on behalf of his brother Pandu. But unfortunately, Pandu died in the forest and Madri, his wife, entered into the funeral pyre along with him. Kunti and the five children of Pandu returned to Hastinapur. Dhritarashtra had 100 sons. They were called Kauravas. Pandu's five children were known as the Pandavas. The Kauravas hated the Pandavas since their childhood. Even after they grew up, the Kauravas put Pandavas to a lot of hardship. Finally, a war became inevitable as the Kauravas refused to give even a bit of land to the Pandavas. This resulted in the famous Mahabharata war. Lord Krishna was an *avatar* of Lord Vishnu. He was also the cousin of the Pandavas and the Kauravas. They both asked him for his help. Sri Krishna helped the Kauravas by giving his entire army to fight for them and he helped the Pandavas by merely being with them without any weapons in the war. He became the charioteer of Arjuna, the third Pandava brother, who was his good friend.

With the divine grace of Lord Krishna, the Pandavas won the war after annihilating all the Kauravas. After the war, it was time for the Lord to go back from this earth and soon Lord Krishna departed from this earth. The loss and the sins committed by killing their kith and kin in the war made the Pandavas totally dejected and they along with their wife, Draupadi, left for the Himalayas for doing penance after making their grandson Parikshit the king. From the Himalayas, they departed to heaven.

Hari Vamsa

The *Hari Vamsa* is an appendix to Mahabharata. It deals with Krishna's life, particularly his childhood days, his *leelas* and his final exit. *Hari Vamsa* means the dynastic history of Lord Vishnu. It runs to 16,375 verses.

The great Sage Vaishampayana recited this first to King Janamejaya. In that assembly Ugrashrava, also called Suta, was also present.

Later, on the requests of the sages headed by Sage Shaunaka at Naimisaranya, Suta narrated *Hari Vamsa*.

Bhagavad Gita

Bhagavad Gita means **'song of the Lord'**. It forms the most important part of the epic *Mahabharata.* It is in the form of a dialogue between

Sri Krishna and Arjuna, the third among the Pandava brothers.

It is found in the *Bhishma Parva.* The central message of *Bhagavad Gita* is that one has to perform one's *dharma* or one's duty bravely and with dedication, even if it is unpleasant and hard, unmindful of the results or rewards.

Lord Krishna teaches this spiritual knowledge to Arjuna who faces mental conflict. In essence, it speaks about bringing about inner harmony whenever a man faces inner conflict. Through this, Lord Krishna taught Arjuna who represents the whole of mankind, about the eternal *Atman* which is neither born nor dies, about Self, about one's *dharma*, and about various types of *yoga* namely, the *Jnana, Karma* and *Bhakti Yoga.*

The Contents of Bhagavad Gita

Chapter	Subject
1	The despondency of Arjuna (46 verses)
2	*Sankhya Yoga*, the soul's immortality (72 verses)
3	*Karma Yoga*, duties of man (43 verses)
4	*Jnana Yoga* (42 verses)
5	Action and renunciation of action (29 verses)
6	Meditation and self-realisation (47 verses)
7	Wisdom and Realisation, the knowledge of ultimate truth (30 verses)
8	The imperishable *Brahman* (28 verses)
9	The royal science and the secret knowledge about ultimate truth (34 verses)
10	Divine glories (42 verses)
11	Vision of the cosmic form (55 verses)
12	Path of Devotion (20 verses)
13	The individual consciousness and the ultimate consciousness (35 verses)

14	The three *Gunas* or qualities of material nature (27 verses)
15	The Supreme spirit, realisation of the ultimate truth (20 verses)
16	Definition of Divine and demonical nature (24 verses)
17	The three-fold path (28 verses)
18	Liberation through renunciation, the final revelation of the ultimate truth (78 verses)

Puranas

After the great epics *Ramayana* and *Mahabharata*, came the *Puranas* which were written by Sage Vyasa. The *Puranas* contain the essence of the Vedas. These are similar to the *Itihasas*. These are also friendly treatises.

As Sri Aurobindo has very well put it,

"*The Puranas are only extension of Vedas. The change is in form only. They form a collection of mythology. They contain stories of Gods and Goddesses, kings, sages, demons and ordinary men, hymns, historical events, cosmology, code of conduct in life, rituals, future predictions and spiritual instructions. They were written to impress the teachings of the Vedas upon the common men who could not grasp the wisdom of the Vedas, and also to highlight devotion or Bhakti Marg, which is the easiest path for liberation or Mukti. Through the stories contained in them the Puranas try to influence the minds of masses and teach them the great wisdom of the Vedas. They explain the several incarnations of God, and how He rescues the devotees in times of need. They also give a detailed account of the process of Creation, the division of time into Kalpas, Manvantaras, Yugas, the Gods and sages in each Kalpa, the geography of the earth as well as the entire Universe, astronomy and the metaphysics of religious worships, and finally the struggle between good and evil forces of the Universe.*"

Puranas, like epics, were written from related historical facts. They are known as the fifth Veda. They glorify the *Saguna Brahman* aspects or *Brahman* in the form of Lord Vishnu, Shiva, Brahma,

Shakti and other deities. However, the objective of the Vedas and the *Puranas* is the same. While Vedas make use of *Karma*, *Upasana* and *Jnana* paths, the *Puranas,* like *Itihasas*, make use of *Bhakti* (devotion) for attaining *Mukti* or liberation.

In *Puranas*, the supreme truth is made known to one and all, including ordinary men, in a very simple manner. They also educate people in right and wrong and make them follow the path of religion for achieving lasting happiness. These are believed to have been written in different *Kalpas* by Vyasa.

There are many *Puranas*. It is believed that there were approximately 64 *Puranas* consisting of 18 *Maha Puranas*, 18 primary *Upa Puranas* and the rest secondary *Upa Puranas*.

Maha Puranas

The *Maha Puranas* contain 400,000 *slokas*. They are four times the size of *Mahabharata*. In these, six are *Satvic* or *Vaishnava Puranas* and glorify Lord Vishnu, six are *Rajasic* or *Brahma Puranas* and glorify Lord Brahma, and six are *Tamasic* or *Shaiva Puranas* and glorify Lord Shiva.

- The *Vaishnava Puranas* are *Vishnu Purana*, *Naradiya Purana*, *Vamana Purana*, *Matsya Purana*, *Garuda Purana*, and *Srimad Bhagavata Purana*.
- The *Brahma Puranas* that glorify Brahma are *Brahma Purana, Bhavishya Purana*, *Agni Purana*, *Brahma Vaivarta Purana, Brahmananda Purana* and *Padma Purana.*
- The *Shaiva Puranas* are *Shiva Purana*, *Linga Purana*, *Kurma Purana*, *Markandeya Purana*, *Skand Purana*, and *Varaha Purana.*

According to *Puranas*, there are five characteristic features or subjects dealt with in each *Maha Purana*. They are —

- *Sarga* – the process of creation of Universe
- *Pratisarga* – the periodical process of destruction and creation
- *Manvantara* – the various eras
- *Vamsa* – the histories of the solar and lunar dynasties
- *Vamsanucharita* – the royal lineage

It is also believed that Vyasa wrote the *Purana Samhita* and also taught them to his disciple Romaharshana. From him, the *Puranas* were passed on orally for a long time and in the process the sages added their own compositions as well, thus increasing the number of *Puranas*. Hence the date of the origin of *Puranas* cannot be ascertained with precision. In their final form, the *Puranas* were believed to have been written between 300 AD and 1000 AD.

Upa Puranas

The *Upa Puranas* are – *Sanat Kumara*, *Narasimha*, *Brihannaradiya*, *Shiva Dharma*, *Durvasa*, *Kapila*, *Vamana*, *Bhargava*, *Varuna*, *Kalika Purana*, *Samba*, *Nandikeshvara*, *Surya*, *Parasara*, *Vashishtha*, *Devi Bhagavati*, *Ganesha*, and *Hamsa*.

Vaishnava Puranas

1. Vishnu Purana

It has six major sections. It tells about the creation of the Universe as told by Sage Parashara to Sage Matreya. Its contents include —

- The creation of the Universe and beings like *rakshasas*, *yakshas*, *ghandharvas*, birds, sheep, horses, elephants, deer, camals and plants
- Birth of four classes of people namely *brahmins*, *kshatriyas*, *vaishyas* and *shudras*
- Rudra and the seven other names of Rudra
- Sati's self-immolation as a result of Daksha's arrogant behaviour insulting Lord Shiva
- Birth of Uma as a daughter of Himavan and Menaka
- Durvasa putting the garland on Iravata which is the white elephant of Indra
- The falling off of the garland to the ground from the head of Iravata
- Durvasa's anger and cursing Indra, Lakshmi leaving all the three worlds ruled by Indra
- Demons attacking the *devas*, *devas* approaching Brahma and Vishnu for help

- The advice of Vishnu
- Temporary truce between the *devas* and *asuras*
- The churning of the ocean of milk
- The empty promise of *devas* to the *asuras*
- The emergence of wonderful things from the ocean while churning
- Emergence of *amrit* and Lakshmi from the ocean
- Goddess Lakshmi going back to the God's abode
- Indra's prayers to Lakshmi to remain in the three worlds and to be with the one who prays to Lakshmi with the hymn uttered by Indra in praise of her
- *Amrita* taken away by the *asuras*
- Vishnu taking Mohini *avatar* and getting back the *amrita* and distributing it among the gods
- Gods becoming immortal
- Indra regaining his position and glory
- The story of Dhruva
- The kings Vena and Prachetas
- The story of Prahalada
- The geography of the earth, the underworlds
- The world of Sun, moon, stars, *navagrahas* and the *Saptarishis*
- The *Manvantaras* which is the cycle of creation and destruction
- The story of Sanjana and her husband Surya
- The four stages in life
- The cast divisions
- The rituals
- The creation of *Maya-moha* by Lord Vishnu to protect the *devas*, and to punish the *asuras*
- King Shatadhanu and his wife Shaivya
- The great dynasties in the line of Manu, Ikshavaku, Yuvanasha and Subhari, Sagara, Saudasa, Nimi, Chandra, Satyavathi and Richika , Raji, Nahusha and Yayati

- *Shyamantaka* jewel
- Shishupala, Shantanu,and Devapi, Kali, Vasudeva, and Devaki
- Childhood miracles of Sri Krishna
- The killing of Kansa by Sri Krishna
- Jarasandha
- Kalayavana
- Rukmi and Rukmini
- Balarama
- The *Parijata* flower
- Usha and Vanasura
- Pundraka, Shambha
- *Dvividha*
- The end of Yadavas
- End of Sri Krishna
- The Kali era
- *Pralaya*
- Keshidvaja
- Khandrikya and the manner in which *Puranas* came down through generations to form the subject matter of *Vishnu Purana*

2. Narada Purana

It is believed that Narada once revealed *Narada Purana* to Sanat Kumara on his request for knowing the mysteries of Vishnu and the methods by which meditation would become successful. The contents of this *Purana* are as follows —

- The geography of the earth
- Stories of Mrikandu and Markandeya, Ganga, Vahu, the son of King Vrika, Sagara, Saudasa, Aditi's *tapas*, Vali, the dwarf incarnation of Lord Vishnu, Bhagiratha and the descent of Ganga
- Rites and *Vratas* like *Ekadashi vrata, Poornamasi vrata, Dvajerohana vrata, Hari Panchaka*
- Bhadrashila son of Sage Galava

- *Varnashrama dharma*
- The various types of funeral ceremonies
- Yama's abode
- Attaing bliss
- Devamali, a devotee of Lord Viṣhnu
- Yajnamali and Sumali
- Sons of Devamali
- Karnika the hunter
- King Yadnadwaja, the *yugas* and so on

3. Vamana Purana

In this *Purana*, Sage Pulasya tells Narada about Vishnu's incarnation as Vamana. Its contents include —

- Righteousness and religiousness
- Nara Narayana
- Goddess Durga
- Prahalad
- Gajendra *moksha*
- Abode of Shiva and Sati
- Daksha's *yajna*
- Names of zodiacs according to their appearance
- Demon Andhak
- King Sukeshi's questions to the sages about the path towards benediction
- Respectability and contentment
- Sinful deeds
- Jambudweep
- Ten properties of *dharma*
- Rise and fall of Sukheshi's kingdom
- Manifestation of Nara-Narayana
- Meeting of Prahalada with Nara-Narayana and getting the blessings
- Manifestation of vegetation from the Gods

- The atrocities of Mahishasura
- The demons Chand and Mund and their end in the hands of Goddess Durga, Reincarnation of Goddess Durga
- Kuru and Kurukshetra
- Maha Bali, God's penance
- Appearance of Lord Vishnu
- Bali's questions to Prahalada
- Vamana *avatar* of Lord Vishnu
- His demands from Bali
- The river Saraswati
- The greatness of Sanihitya *sarovar* and Sitanu *teertha*
- The origin of four heads of Brahma
- Prithudal *teertha*
- Uma born to Mena
- Marriage of Uma with Shiva
- Palace constructed by Vishvakarma
- Killing of Nishumbh and Shumbh by Goddess Chandika
- Birth of Kartikeya
- Killing of Taraka and Mahishasura by Kartikeya
- Ritudhwaj injuring demon Patalaketu
- Penance of Lord Shiva
- Killing of Mura by Lord Vishnu
- Andhakasura
- Vishvakarma as a monkey
- The search for Chitrangatha and Vedavati
- *Danda* cursed by sage Shukracharya
- *Ganas* in Mandhara mountain and the battle
- Sanjeevani *vidya* used by Shukracharya
- Killing of Andhak by Lord Shiva
- Marutganas in different *manvantaras*
- Vishnu killing Kalaneni
- Bali, the king of heaven and his reign

- *Asvamedha yajna* performed by Dhundu
- Regaining his good looks by *Pururavanakshtra Purusha*
- Prahalad's pilgrimage
- Upamanyu and Shridhama
- Gajendra and the crocodile
- Greatness of *Saraswati strota*

4. Matsya Purana

Matsya Purana has 15,000 *slokas*. It is divided in to 291 chapters or *adhyayas*. Lord Vishnu is believed to have given this *Purana* during his incarnation as *Matsya* or fish. Sage Romaharshana narrated this *Purana* for the benefit of the sages at Naimisharanya. He acknowledged *Matsya Purana* as the holiest of all the *Puranas*.

The *Purana* starts with the time when Manu left to the forest to perform *tapas*, Brahma appeared before Manu and gave him a boon. Manu then became the protector of the world. Manu found a fish in the water, took in his hands and put it inside his *kamandal*. The fish grew in size enormously and occupied the entire ocean. Lord Vishnu who was in the form of the fish revealed his identity and asked Manu to save all beings of the world from the deluge, floods and draughts occurring on earth as a prelude to the great *pralaya.* The dark clouds soon appeared on the sky warning about the impending danger of deluge. Manu saved all beings in his boat as advised by Vishnu. The boat was dragged by Lord Vishnu with the snake as rope to which the boat was tied. Manu put several questions to the Lord while the boat tossed up and down on the water which forms the contents of the *Purana.*

The actual contents of this *Purana* include fthe following —

- The story of Creation starting with Brahma
- Brahma's creations
- His descendents
- Daksha's descendants
- The killing of demons
- Diti's penance for a son who would kill Indra

- Diti's observance of *Vrata*, her carelessness in observing the *Vrata*
- Indra cutting the baby in the womb of Diti into many parts by his *Vajrayudha*
- The parts of the child forming into *Marutas* who posed no threat to Indra
- *Marutas* becoming friend of Indra and getting elevated to the status of Gods
- Period in each *manvantara* the fourteen eras of the present *kalpa*
- Manu reigning in each *manvantara*
- Vena, the evil minded son of Anga
- Birth of Prithu from the dead body of Vena after the removal of all his sins
- Prithu, the good king who milked the earth for the sake of his subjects
- The solar lineage, the lunar lineage
- Daksha *yajna*
- Sati's anger
- Daksha's prayer to Sati
- The 108 names of Sati and the *teerthas*
- Self-immolation of Sati
- Sati reborn as Parvati
- The funeral ceremonies
- Brahmadatta and his lineage
- Kacha and Devayani
- Yayati
- Shukracharya and Brihaspati
- Details of various *Vratas* and other stories
- The science behind making idols
- The sixteen forms of donations
- The epilogue

5. Garuda Purana

This *Purana* tells about Lord Vishnu's incarnations. It consists of the tales of Lord Vishnu as told by Suta. It is called *Garuda Purana* because *Garuda* was the first one who narrated the tale to Sage Kashyap who in turn revealed it to Sage Vyasa.

According to this *Purana*, there are 22 incarnations of Lord Vishnu. They are —

- 1st incarnation – **Sanat Kumaras**, who were the extremely virtuous celibates
- 2nd incarnation – The Boar or **Varaha** for protecting the earth from demon Hiranyaksha
- 3rd incarnation – **Narada** for protecting the virtues of *Nishkama Karma*
- 4th incarnation – **Nara-Narayana**, who performed austerities for the protection and propagation of *dharma*
- 5th incarnation – **Kapila** for protecting the *Sankhya Shastra* from becoming extinct
- 6th incarnation – **Dattatreya** in the house of Sage Atri and Anasuya for propagating the secret of *Brahmavidya* to worthy people
- 7th incarnation – **Yagyadeva**, son of Ruchi Prajapati and Aakoothi
- 8th incarnation – **Rishabhadeva**, son of Sage Nabhi and Merudevi for establishing the norms of *Grihasthashrama*
- 9th incarnation – **Prithu** who milked (extracted) from the earth disguised as cow various nutrients like cereals and pulses
- 10th incarnation – **Matsya** or fish for protecting the life of Vaivaswat Manu
- 11th incarnation – Tortoise or **Kurma** who held the Mandarachala Mountain on his back when the ocean of milk was churned
- 12th incarnation – **Dhanvantari**, for revealing medicines for curing diseases

- 13th incarnation – The enchanting beauty **Mohini** for retrieving the pot containing *Amrita* or nectar from the hands of demons and distributing among the *devas*
- 14th incarnation – **Narasimha**, for protecting his devotee Prahlad and to annihilate the demon king Hiranyakashipu
- 15th incarnation – **Vamana**, to liberate the soul of the benovolent demon King Mahabali by asking for three steps of land
- 16th incarnation – **Parashurama**, wiping away by killing all the *Kshatriya* kings who had become immoral and wicked
- 17th incarnation – Born as **Vyasa** to Parashara and Satyavati for propagating Vedic knowledge
- 18th incarnation – **Sri Rama**
- 19th incarnation – **Sri Krishna**
- 20th incarnation – **Balarama**
- 21st incarnation – **Gautam Buddha**
- 22nd incarnation – **Kalki** in *Kaliyuga* as the son of a Brahmin named Vishnuyasha for liberating earth from sinners

Garuda Purana is considered to be the essence of all scriptures. Lord Vishnu himself revealed this to Lord Brahma and Lord Shiva. It is said that Sage Kashyapa had brought a withered tree back to life which was infected with snake's poison with the help of *Garuda Vidya*, a sacred mantra found in the Garuda Purana. It also tells about the following —

- Creation in various *Sargas* explaining the beginning of reproduction
- The various dynasties
- The powerful mantras like the *Navagraha mantras, Shiva mantra, Vishnu mantra, Saraswati mantra,* and *Lakshmi mantra*
- Astrology, yogas, *muhurtas* for various activities, *Griha Dasha*
- The predictions based on physical traits, predicting age on the basis of line on the forehead, predicting age by palmistry, predictions based on physical traits of women

- The various names of *Shaligram* on the basis of *chakras* present on it
- Origin of jewels
- Important places of pilgrimage, significance of *Gaya teertha* where the demon Gaya was killed by Lord Vishnu, the rituals for the dead
- Tales glorifying the significance of performing rites for the dead at Gaya through the story of King Vishal
- Tale of Prajapati Ruchi and his wife Manini
- Various consecrations to purify man
- *Upanayana* ritual
- *Keshant* ritual
- Ritual for *grihasthashram*
- Prohibited days for copulation
- Purification of different articles made of substances like gold, silver, conch, vegetables, leather and so on
- Description of rituals for the dead
- *Karma* and its consequences, atonement for sins
- Different kinds of austerities like *Yama* for restraining passions
- *Niyama* for daily routine
- *Mahasantapan vrata*, *Parnakrichchha vrata*, *Taptakrichchha vrata*, *Paad krichchha vrata*
- Virtues of observing fast on *Shiva Ratri*
- Power of chastity
- The story of *Ramayana*
- Sri Krishna
- The *Mahabharata*
- The eternal truth
- The supreme yoga
- Supremacy of devotion
- Various divine *strotas* like *Narasimha strota*, *Kalamirt strota*, *Mrityu Ashtaka strota*
- Salvation through yoga, self realisation

- *Brahma Gita*
- The existence of divinity in man
- Proper rituals for the dead for salvation as explained by Krishna to Garuda to clear his doubts
- Death and thereafter
- The significance of last rites – the *Pindadan*

6. Bhagavata Purana

It is said that even after compiling the Vedas and the great epic *Mahabharata*, Vyasa was not satisfied. He had some feeling of dissatisfaction that disturbed his mind constantly. It was Narada who told Vyasa that the reason for his discontentment was that while he had explained the *Karma* and *Jnana Marga* in detail in the Vedas and *Itihasas*, he did not pay adequate attention to *Bhakti Marga*, the path that could be easily followed even by ordinary humans and which will be most useful and easy path, especially in the *Kaliyuga*. As per the advice of Sage Narada, Vyasa wrote this *Purana* namely *Srimad Bhagavatam* which became the most popular among all *Puranas*.

This *Purana* describes the various incarnations of Lord Vishnu and gives a detailed picture of Lord Krishna's birth and life and contains the famous *Bhagavad Gita* too. It has 12 chapters and is divided into 18 cantos (*Skandha*) and has 18000 verses. Vyasa after writing this *Purana* imparted the knowledge to his son Sukha Brahma Rishi. He subsequently recited the entire *Purana* to King Parikshit who was cursed to die within seven days as a punishment for insulting Sage Sameeka. Sage Suta who was present in the assembly there at that time heard the entire *Purana* and later he narrated the *Bhagavata Purana* in the assembly of sages of Saunagati in the forest of Naimisaranya. The sages, thereafter, spread the entire wisdom to others.

Brahma Puranas

1. Brahma Purana

This *Purana* was imparted by Romaharshana, Vyasa's disciple to the sages at Naimisharanya while they were arranging for a *yajna*. Vyasa had given this knowledge to Romaharshana.

This knowledge was originally imparted by Brahma to Daksha and the other sages. Romaharshana started the discourse as follows—

- The process of creation, starting from Brahma's creation of a man and a woman namely, *Svayambhu* Manu and Shatarupa
- Their descendants starting from their three sons, namely Vira, Priyavrata and Uttanapada, father of the great Dhruva
- Pracinavarhi, and his ten sons called Prachetas and Marisha, who was known as Prajapathi
- The 5000 sons of Daksha and Asikdi known as Haryashvas and Dakshas, loss of these sons and another of his 1000 sons known as Shavalashvas
- How Brahma was the cause for this loss and made to marry one of the 60 daughters of Daksha by name Priya
- The birth of Narada as the son of Brahma
- The story of other daughters
- About Vishvakarma, the chief architect of the world who was one of their sons
- About Vishvadevas who are the children of Vishwa
- The daughter of Daksha Prajapati
- Kashyapa and Aditi and Diti, gods who are the children of Aditi and demons who are the children of Diti
- The solar and lunar dynasties
- The geography of the world
- How the earth looks like, its limits, the underworld, the hell, *Prithvi*, importance of *Konaditya* in Konarka in Orissa, the 12 Adityas, the 108 names of Surya
- The story of Indradyumna, and Purushotamakshetra, Markandeya, King Shveta, Vali, Gautama, Garuda, the Doves, Garuda and Maninaga, Vishvamitra and Indra, Shveta, Kubera, Harishchandra, Vriddha Gautama, Pippalada, Nageshvara, Shiva cutting the 5th head of Brahma
- The owl and the dove
- The hunter
- Gautama and Manikundala

- Kandu, the *chandala*
- The *Brahmarakshsas*
- Yoga

2. Bhavishya Purana

This *Purana* is in five parts.

The **first** part deals with a description of genesis, greatness of deities, worship of Shiva, Vishnu and Surya.

The **second**, **third**, and **fourth** parts relate to the description of the greatness of Shiva, Vishnu and Surya, prediction of Adam and Eve, Noah's arc, decline of Sanskrit language, the birth of other languages, birth of Buddha, *Aharyas*, kings like Chandragupta, Ashoka and Saints like Jayadeva, Chaitanya and the muslim rulers of India.

The **fifth** part describes heaven, description of kings of Solar race, description of a game similar to chess, supremacy of Brahma, prediction of future events including biblical and modern history, Islam, Buddhism, future kings, Nimbarka Acharya, Madhavacharya, Sridharacharya and Jayadevacharya.

3. Agni Purana

There are 15,000 to 16,000 *slokas* in this *Purana*. It is a *Rajasic* Purana. *Agni*, the fire God narrated this Purana to Sage Vashishtha, who in turn passed it on to Vyasa and he, in turn to his disciple Suta. Finally, Suta narrated this *Purana* for the benefit of Sages headed by Shaunaka in Naimisharanya forest.

There are 383 brief chapters in this *Purana*. The last chapter gives a description of *Brahma jnana*. This *Purana* contains a summary of Vedas and *Upanishads*. It also describes rituals. It was written much later, and is like a supplement to other *Puranas*.

Its contents include —

- The essence of cosmic soul or *Brahman*, various *avatars* of Lord Vishnu
- *Hari Vamsa* and *Mahabharata*
- The process of Creation
- How to pray

- How to build temples
- How to make the idols of deities
- The places of pilgrimage
- The geography of earth
- Astrology
- *Manvantras*
- *Varnashrama dharma*
- Sins and their atonement
- Various *Vratas*
- Hells
- Importance of giving alms
- The power of *Gayatri mantra*
- Duties of a king
- Different kinds of dreams and their remedies
- Omens and signs
- Preparation for battle
- Rama's precepts about the duties of a king
- *Dhanur Veda* – the science of weapons and warfare
- Property
- Debt
- Will
- Detection of lie
- Good effects of alms
- The *Puranas* and the number of *slokas* in each *Purana* together with the mantra
- Benefits of hearing *Purana*
- The various dynasties
- *Ayurveda* – the treatment of humans, animals and plants
- Literature and grammar
- Use of *alankaras*
- Three types of poetry and their subdivisions
- How an epic is written and its theme

- The nine sentiments to be used in literature along with the *rasas* or feelings
- The 64 *kalas* or skills
- The grammatical rules of *Sandhi* and *Samasa*
- Declensions of words
- Periodic destruction or *Pralaya* of the world at the end of every 4000 *yugas*
- *Yama* and hell
- Rebirth
- Yoga to counteract the miseries of life and their pre requisites
- Meditation and posture
- Control of breathing or *prana*
- *Pranayama, Dhyana*, and different ways of gaining concentration, and *Samadhi*
- The knowledge of *Brahman*
- The *Atma* that is in the heart
- The five possible ends of life
- The story of Bharata
- *Bhagavad Gita*
- *Yama Gita*, taught by Yama to Nachiketa

This *Purana* ends with the description of the virtues of *Agni Purana.*

4. Brahma Vaivarta Purana

This *Purana* has four parts and contains 32 chapters. *Suta* explained this *Purana* to the sages at Naimisharanya. The four parts are —

1. *Brahma Khand* explaining the creation of the Universe, origin of Narayana, Radha, Gopis, Gopas and cows and all animate and inanimate beings
2. *Prakriti Khand* describing the greatness of Goddess Durga, Radha, Lakshmi, Saraswati, and Savitri in creation, story of Savitri and Satyavan, Surabhi Swaha, Swadha the clan of Surat, Ganga, tales from *Ramayana*, Indra cursed by Durvasa, and Lakshmi worship

3. *Ganesh Khand* narrating the greatness of Lord Ganesh, Jamadagni, Kartevirya, Parashurama
4. *Sri Krishna Khand* elaborating the life and *leelas* of Sri Krishna

5. Brahmanda Purana

Lord Vayu narrated this *Purana* to Veda Vyasa and he in turn taught it to Suta. Suta later narrated this Purana in Yakshakshetra. It has four parts. They are —

- *Prakriya*
- *Anushanga*
- *Upotaghat*
- *Upasamhar*

Its contents include —

- The creation of the Universe
- *Kalpas*, *Yugas*, *Manvantaras*, Jambudweep and Bharatvarsh, Anudweep, Ketumal Varsh, *Bharat Vamsa, Prithu Vamsa, Dev Vamsa, Rishi Vamsa, Agni Vamsa*
- Preceptor's form
- Sages, rulers, legends
- Conflict between Kartikeya and Parashurama
- King Sagar, his sons and the recovery of the sacrificial horse
- Dissolution and annihilation of the Universe
- The seven parts of *Adhyatma Ramayana*
- Penance of Agastya, preaching of Brihaspathi
- Birth and reign of Bhandasura, manifestation of Lalita devi and her triumphant *yatra*
- War preparation of Bhanda
- *Shakti sena*
- *Vighna Yantranasam*
- Destruction of Vishukra and Vishanga
- Rebirth of Kama
- Description of Sripura

- *Matanga Karya*
- Components of precious stones
- Palace of Chintamani
- *Moksha Ekadashi* wherein Yudhishthira prays to Krishna and the reply of Sri Krishna

6. Padma Purana

Padma Purana describes tales glorifying Lord Vishnu. It contains 50,000 *slokas*. There are five parts in *Padma Purana*. They are —

- *Srishti Khand*
- *Bhumi Khand*
- *Swarga Khand*
- *Patala Khand*
- *Uttara Khand*

These tales were originally told by Lord Vishnu to Brahma. Later, Romaharshana revealed the contents of all *Puranas* to his son Ugrashrava also known as Suta and instructed him to narrate the *Purana* to the sages doing penance at Naimisharanya. Accordingly, Suta narrated the contents of *Padma Purana* to the sages.

Srishti Khand contains a dialogue between Bhishma and Sage Pulastya. It deals with metaphysical knowledge. It also explains the following —

- The process of Creation as narrated by Pulastya to Bhishma after blessing him on his penance at Gangadwar
- Lord Brahma's life span
- The chronological order
- The four prominent castes
- The manifestation of Goddess Lakshmi
- Self-immolation of Sati
- Origin of deities
- Demons and serpents
- Origin of *Marutganas*
- King Prithu, and the Surya Dynasty

- The demon King Bashkali
- Killing of Shambuk by Sri Rama
- Manifestation of Ganesha and Kartikeya
- Significance of *Gayatri mantra*
- The ideal Brahmin
- Significance of *Rudraksha*, *Amla* and *Tulsi*
- Importance of worship of Surya

Bhumi Khand describes the following —

- Earth
- Tales of kings like Prithu, Nauhsh, Yayati and Ashru Bindumati, Prabhriti
- Stories related sages like Shiva Varma Suvrata, Chyavan
- The different types of sins and virtues, propagation of *Vaishnavism*
- The enlightened parrot Kunjal

Swarga Khand explains —

- The sequence of Creation
- The sanctity of the holy places like Bharatvarsh, Jambumarg, river Narmada and Amarkantak
- *Dharma teertha* and sacred bath in Yamuna, Kashipuri, Kapardishwar, Gaya, and Puras
- Lord Vishnu
- Sri Rama's return from Lanka
- The geographical expansion of Bharat

Patala Khand relates to the following —

- Tales of Sri Rama and Sri Krishna
- The demon king Ravana
- Lakshmana sent to bring back Sita from Ashok Vatika and Sita's return to Ayodhya with Rama
- *Ashvamedha Yajna* performed by Sri Rama on the advice of Sage Agastya
- Fastening of the *yajna* horse by Lava and Kusha and then defeating of the army of Sri Rama

Uttara Khand contains the aspects given below —

- Dialogue in the form of discussion between Lord Shiva and Goddess Parvati about the metaphysical knowledge of religion
- The 1000 names of Lord Vishnu and 100 names of Sri Rama
- Descent of Bhagirathi
- Encountering Shani by Dharashad
- Qualities of a Vaishnav
- Indra Prastha
- Vaikunta — the abode of Lord Vishnu
- The incarnations of Vishnu
- The story of Sri Rama
- The story of Sri Krishna
- Jarasandha
- Rukmini *Svayamvara*, queens of Sri Krishna
- Aniruddha and Usha
- Decline of Yadava dynasty
- Rituals of Vishnu worship
- Lord Vishnu — the supreme God
- Parashuram

Shaiva Puranas

1. Shiva Purana

This *Purana* is subdivided into six *samhitas* or sections. They are —

- *Jnana Samhita* with 78 chapters
- *Vidyeshwara Samhita* with 16 chapters
- *Kailasha Samhita* with 12 chapters
- *Sanat Kumara Samhita* with 59 chapters
- *Vayaviya Samhita* with 30 chapters
- *Dharma Samhita* with 65 chapters

This *Purana* was narrated by Romaharshana also known as Lomaharshana to the sages at Naimisharanya. Brahma originally imparted this to his son Narada. This *Purana* starts with the beginning of Creation when there was the presence of *Brahman* only but not any Creation. It goes on with the following aspect —

- Story of Creation with the birth of Brahma from the lotus sprouted from the *nabhi* of Lord Vishnu
- The emergence of *Linga*
- The process of Creation
- The appearance of Rudra
- Tarakasura the son of demon Tara, burning of Manmatha the Lord of Love by Lord Shiva
- Parvati's meditation to get Shiva as her husband and the marriage of Lord Shiva with Goddess Parvati
- Tripura the fort made of gold, silver and iron
- Sita and the Ketaki flower
- Birth of Ganesha and Kartikeya
- *Linga* manifestation of Lord Shiva
- Nandikeshwara *teertha*
- Rishivara *teertha*
- The twelve Jyotirlingas
- Arjuna and Lord Shiva
- Arjuna obtaining *Pashupatastra*
- Lord Shiva's grace
- *Sudarshana Chakra*
- Lord Shiva's one thousand names
- Importance of *Shiva Ratri vrata*
- *Veda nidhi*
- Chandra Shekhara and Neelakantha
- Smearing ashes by Shiva
- Nandi the son of Sage Shilada
- The units of time
- Daksha *yajna*
- Parvati becoming Gowri
- Upamanyu, son of Sage Vyaghrapada and Shiva's blessings
- Andhakasura

- The demon brothers Hiranyanetra and Hiranyakashipu, slaying of Ruru by Parvati
- A false Parvati
- Yama's story
- King Shatanika and his son Shasranika
- Parashurama
- Geography of earth
- Astronomy
- The fourteen *manvantaras* of each *Kalpa* and the sages and Gods on each and the birth of Vaivasvata Manu.

2. Linga Purana

Sage Romaharshana narrates this *Purana* for the benefit of the sages. The *Purana* starts with a description of the creative process of Brahma and the measure of time. Its contents are given below —

- Yoga, particularly *Pashupata Yoga* taught by Lord Shiva
- Various *avatars* of Lord Shiva in each of the 28 *Kaliyugas* to teach *Pashupata Yoga*
- The names of four disciples of each of these *avatars*
- Components of *Pashupata Yoga*
- Why Shiva is worshipped in the form of *Linga*
- The sacred *Gayatri mantra* taught by Lord Shiva to Lord Vishnu and Brahma
- The Devadaru forest
- Sudarshana and his wife
- Dadhichi and king Kashyapa
- The *yugas*
- The geography of Universe
- Astronomy
- Dhruva
- Daksha's descendents
- Parashara
- Tripura

- Omens of impending death
- The city of Varanasi
- Andhaka son of Hiranyaksha
- Hiranyaksha and the boar
- Hiranyakashipu and Narasimha
- The demon Jalandhara
- One thousand names of Lord Shiva
- Daksha's *yajna*
- Parvati and her *tapasya*
- Tarakasura
- Upamanyu

3. Kurma Purana

Lord Vishnu himself is believed to have preached this *Purana* during his *Kurmavatara* to Sage Narada. Narada, in turn, narrated the *Purana* to Suta who in turn described it to the sages. It is said that this originally was in four parts —

1. *Brahmi Samhita*
2. *Bhagavati Samhita*
3. *Gauri Samhita*
4. *Vaishnavi Samhita*

But now only *Brahmi Samhita* is available in two parts, the *Purva* and *Uttara* parts.

In the *Purva* part is found the story of Indradyumna, description of *Kurma Purana*, *varnashrama*, origin of geosphere, description of the various *avatars*, preaching of Gods, description of Manu, Daksha *yajna*, Hiranyakashipu, *Vamanavatar*, Ikshvaku, Pururava clans, Rama and Krishna *avatars*, *Satya, Treta, Dwapara,* and *Kali yugas*, greatness of Varanasi, *Lingas*, Prayag and Yamuna.

The *Uttara* part contains yoga, Rudra during his *tandava*, metaphysical knowledge of *Ashtanga yoga*, duties of a celibate, edible and non-edible things, rituals and its regular performance, duties of *vanaprasthas* and *sanyasis*, expiation, expiation for drinkining wine, greatness of the places of pilgrimage.

This *Purana* also contains subjects relating to the following —

- Churning of the ocean of milk
- Appearance of Goddess Lakshmi
- History of Creation
- The descendents
- Killing of demons Madhu and Kaitabha by Vishnu, the 1000 names of Goddess Parvati
- Descendents of Uttanapada
- Daksha, Hiranyaksha
- Andhaka
- Solar dynasty
- Lunar dynasty
- Lord Krishna, geography and astronomy
- Manus in the six *manvantaras* which are over
- The present seventh *manvantara*
- Seven more *manvantaras* in this *yuga* before *pralaya*
- Veda Vyasa
- The 28 names of Veda Vyasa
- Lord Shiva's 28 incarnations and their names
- The *Ishwara Gita*
- Vyasa's discourse about the path of true knowledge
- Yoga as a technique of meditation
- Rituals
- Chanting of *Gayatri Mantra*
- Major *vratas*
- Penance for sins committed
- *Maya* Sita whom Ravana abducted
- Lord Shiva and Brahma
- Kala Bhairava
- Nandi
- Epilogue

4. Markandeya Purana

In this *Purana*, Markandeya clears the doubts of Jaimini. This is the shortest of all *Maha Puranas*.

Its contents include – Jaimini, the disciple of Veda Vyasa requesting Markandeya for the answers to his questions —

- Why did the Lord take human incarnation even though He was the Supreme and the cause of the origin, perpetuation and destruction?
- How did Draupadi become the wife of the Pandavas?
- How did Balarama expiate for the sin of killing a Brahmin?
- How did Draupadi's sons die?

The further contents of this Purana are —

- Markandeya asking Jaimini to approach the birds which were proficient in the contents of the epic *Mahabharata* to clear his doubts
- Markandeya telling the story of the birds to Jaimini
- The birth of the birds
- The birds migrating to Vindhyachala
- The birds clearing the doubts of Jaimini
- The two sons of Vipulasvan
- Sukrish and Tumburu
- Vipulasvan cursing his sons for disobeying him
- The divine *leela* of God Vishnu
- The four forms of Narayana, the first as Vasudev
- The second as Narayana
- The third as Pradyumna, and the fourth as Aniruddh
- The birth of Pandavas, the incarnation of deities to relieve *Prithvi* of her overburden
- Shuchi, the wife of Indra taking birth as Draupadi
- Balarama killing Suta
- Expiation of Balarama for the sin
- Harishchandra losing his kingdom on account of Vishvamitra's orders

- Vishvamitra's anger and cursing of Harishchandra
- The five guardian deities of directions condemning Vishvamitra's actions
- Vishvamitra cursing them
- Their birth as the sons of Draupadi
- Vishvamitra asking for *dakshina* (fee paid to a teacher) from King Harishchandra
- Haishchandra selling his wife Shaivya for giving the *dakshina*
- Brahmin buying the queen
- Vishvamitra's anger at the small amount of *dakshina*
- Harishchandra selling himself to a *chandaal* who was *Dharma* himself
- Death of Rohit, the son of Harischandra
- The queen bringing the son for cremation without recognising Harishchandra and knowing the truth later and lamenting over their fate
- Lord *Dharma* appearing before them and praising Harishchandra
- Harishchandra and his family attaining heaven
- Vashishtha's appearance
- Vashishtha cursing Vishvamitra to become a stork
- Vishvamitra cursing Vashishtha to become a partridge
- Brahma helping them to regain their form
- Birth of living creatures
- Peaceful death for those endowed with good qualities, hell for sinners who take birth again and again as imperfect human beings until their actions improve for attaining the position equal to that of Indra

5. Skand Purana

It is the largest of all the *Puranas*. It has seven parts – *Maheshwar*, *Vaishnava*, *Brahma*, *Kashi*, *Avantikshetra*, *Nagar* and *Prabhasha*.

The main theme of this *Purana* is the reason and outcome of the birth of Skand or Kartikeya or Subramanyam which is the slaying of Tarakasura by Skand who headed the army of Gods. This *Purana* was supposed to have been told by Lord Shiva to Goddess Parvati, then to Skand to Nandi and Nandi to Sages like Sanaka, Sanaka to Vyasa, Vyasa to Suta who finally narrated the story to the sages at Naimisharanya.

Maheshwar Khand

It contains —

- Daksha's animosity towards Lord Shiva
- Sati's self-immolation
- Worship of Lord Shiva
- Churning of the ocean of milk, emergence of *Amrit*
- Brahma's boon to Tarakasura
- Shiva testing Parvati's devotion
- Arrival of *Saptarishis*
- Birth of Kartikeya
- Katikeya slaying Tarakasura
- Virtues of *Shiva Ratri* fasting
- Sorrow of Kartikeya, destruction of the demon Pralamb
- The austere penance of Kaal Bhiti or Mahakaal
- King Karandama's questions
- How to worship Lord Shiva
- Glory of Arunachal Shiva Linga
- Shiva, the creator of the Universe
- Destruction of demons Shumbh, Nishumbh and Mahishasura
- Arunachaleshwar's grace to Parvati

Vaishnav Khand

The contents include —

- Lord Varaha satisfying Prithvi's curiosity
- *Varaha mantra*
- The manifestation of Padmavati
- The reincarnation of Vedavati of *treta yug* to Prithvi

- Marriage of Lord Vishnu with Padmavati
- Story of King Parikshit
- Importance of Krishna *teertha*
- Places of importance on Venkatachala Hills
- The 180 *teerthas* there
- The 6 *teerthas* namely, *Swami Pushkarini, Akasha Ganga, Papa Vinasham, Panduteertha, Kumara Dhara teertha,* and *Thuburu teertha* said to be capable of bestowing salvation
- Anjana's penance at *Akash Ganga teertha*
- Lord Vishnu asking Brahma to go to *Purushottam kshetra* Sage Markandeya worshipping Lord Vishnu
- Markandeya Kund
- Holy places near *Purushottam teertha*
- Vidyapati worshipping Lord Neel Mahadev
- Indradyumna leaving for *Purushottham kshetra* and worshipping Lord Neel Mahadev, installation of idol Narasimha by Narada near Neelkanth temple
- Indradyumna performing *Ashvamedha yajnas*
- Carving and consecration of Jagannath idols and *Rath Yatra*
- A few important places of pilgrimage
- The importance of Bhadrikashram
- Importance of the month of Kartika
- Holy dip in Margashirish
- Charities made in the month of Vishakha and Ayodhyapuri

Brahma Khand

Its contents include —

- Supremacy of *Rameshwar kshetra*
- Setu bandhanam
- Rameshwar Linga
- Importance of *Dharmaranga kshetra*
- Decline of moral values in *Kaliyuga*
- Significance of *Chaturmasa* the four months

- *Vratas*, importance of abstinance in *Chaturmasa*
- Methods of performing *Shodashaupachar* rituals

Kashi Khand

It includes the following —

- Vindhyachala Mountain obstructing the path of Surya
- Agastya ordering the Vindya Mountain to diminish in size
- Kashi – the supreme pilgrimage centre
- The majesty of Kashi as described by Kartikeya and the origin of Kashi

Avanti Kshetra Khand

It provides the account of the following —

- Glory of Mahakaal *teertha* as told by Sanat Kumara
- *Kapaal mochan*, different names of Ujjain
- The grandeur of Avantipuri
- The descent of Narmada river
- Narmada marrying Purukutsu
- A boon from Narada to King Manu
- Sage Jamadagni receiving Kamadhenu
- Description of hell

Nagar Khand

It includes —

- Vashishtha's son cursing Trishanku
- The creation of Trishanku *swarga* by Sage Vishvamitra

Prabhas Khand

Its contents are as follows —

- Description of *Puranas* and *Upa Puranas*
- *Prabhasa teertha*
- Somnath Linga and his varied names
- Siddeshwara Linga and Siddha Linga
- Chandra worshipping Lord Shiva at *Prabhas kshetra*

- Significance of tonsure
- Emergence of Saraswati in *Prabhas kshetra*
- The abode of trinity Godsdesses
- Dwaraka *mahatmya*
- Questions put by sages to Prahlad
- Sanctity of the city of Dwaraka

6. Varaha Purana

This *Purana* tells how Varaha, the boar rescued the earth. It contains prayer to Lord Vishnu by *Prithvi*, the earth, the process of Creation, origin of Rudra, Sanat Kumara and Marich.

It mentions the following —

- The origin of Agni
- Stories relating to the great men of those days
- Gauri and destruction of Daksha *yajna*
- Wedding of Lord Shiva and Goddess Parvati
- Ganesha
- Naga
- Kartikeya
- Aditya
- The killing of Andhakasura
- Matrigana
- Katyayani
- Kumara
- Dharma
- Rudra
- Aruni
- *Agastya Gita*
- *Shubhvrata*
- *Dhanyavrat*
- Dialogue between Lord Vishnu and Sage Narada
- Agastya

- Geographical description of Jambudweep, Kushadweep, Kraunchdweep
- The origin of Vaishnava
- Destruction of Mahishasura
- *Kapalikvrata*
- Dialogue between Prithvi and Sanat Kumara
- Dialogue between Narayana and Prithvi
- Sorrow and happiness
- Twelve kinds of crime
- Expiation from sins for *mukti*
- Vishnu worship methods, *Sanatan dharma*
- Illusion
- *Karma* for salvation
- History of Gridhra and Shringati
- Dialogue between *chandaal* and *brahmarakshasas*
- Greatness of Kokamukh
- Badrikarshrama
- Importance of *Madura kshetra*
- *Shaligram*
- Shalanhayanak
- Greatness of *Stutswami teertha*
- Lohargalam
- *Panchar kshetra*
- *Vishram teertha* and *Devana*
- Worship of Narayana at the confluence of Yamuna and Saraswati rivers
- Greatness of Krishna Ganga, Sambh, *Dwadashi Vrata* in *Ram teertha*
- Installation of various idols
- Origin of *shraddha*
- Methods of wiping out impurities
- *Medhatipati pitrasambad*

- Kinds of *pinda sankalpa*
- *Madhupaih* ritual and donation
- Yama and his court
- Sinner's fate
- Hell
- *Yamadoot*
- Chitragupta, his instructions for expiation
- Fruits of good and bad *karmas*
- *Pativrat*
- Dialogue between Yama and Narad
- Greatness of Prabhodini Gokarneshwar
- Shringeshwar
- Ashvarisha's unification with Vishnu
- Unification of Sage Raimya and King Vasu with Vishnu
- Agni
- Ashwinikumaras
- Goddess Parvati
- Ganapati
- Naga devata
- Kartikeya
- Aditya
- Ashta Matrikas
- Goddess Durga
- Kubera
- Lord Vishnu
- *Dharma*
- Lord Rudra
- *Tanmantras*
- Chandra
- Various *vratas*
- Various types of charities
- Holiness of *Kokamukh teertha*

- Mayapuri
- *Kubjamarak teertha*
- Badrikashram
- *Mandur teertha*
- Someshwar Linga
- *Shaligram kshetra*
- *Ruru kshetra*
- *Gonishhaman teertha*
- *Stootswami teertha*
- Dwaraka
- Sanandoor thurli
- *Lahargal teertha*
- Mathura
- *Chakra teertha*
- *Kapila teertha*
- *Govardhan teertha*
- *Gokarn teertha*
- Wood idols
- Stone idols
- Earthen and copper idols
- Bronze idols
- Silver and gold idols
- Rituals concerning the last rites for the dead
- *Madhupark*
- Nachiketa's experience
- Virtues of chastity
- Liberation from sins
- Gokarneshwar
- Means of realisation of Lord Vishnu
- Sage Gautama
- *Prakriti* and *Purusha*
- Geography of earth

- Jambudweep
- Shakdweep
- Kushadweep
- Kraunchadweep
- Shalimalidweep
- *Trishakti*

Limitations of this Study

The first limitation relates to the comprehensiveness of this study. If the ancient Indian wisdom contained in the *Shruti* and *Smriti* literature can be compared to all the oceans in the world, this study forms only a small part of a single wave of all the oceans put together. The ancient Indian literature is so vast that it becomes almost impossible to cover and comprehend them completely and correctly.

Secondly, the study and knowledge of the ancient Indian literature is limited to the translated versions of the scriptures and is not based upon a thorough study of the original works written or composed in Vedic Sanskrit. A study of the translation can never come anywhere near a complete study of the works in its original form and language.

Moreover, there are differences of opinions regarding the number of *Shakhas*, *Brahmanas*, *Aranyakas*, *Upanishads*, and the number of *Upanishads* in each group and under each Veda.

In general, views differ regarding what are to be considered as *Smritis*. While some view that all the scriptures other than the four Vedas are born out of the Vedas and are therefore to be considered as *Smritis*, the others believe that *Agamas* and *Dharma Shastras* are not derived from the Vedas and therefore they are to be treated as *Shruti* and not as *Smriti*.

Last but not the least, in this book, the *Samhitas* and *Upanishads* are comparatively dealt with more elaborately than the *Brahmanas* and *Aranyakas* sections of the Vedas. This is because the *Samhitas* form the first and foremost portion of the Vedas and sometimes the Vedas refer to *Samhitas* only, and *Upanishads* that form the fourth and final section of the Vedas are considered to contain only the essence of the Vedas. Further the *Brahmanas* and *Aranyakas* explain the mantras and rituals contained in the *Samhita* portion of the Vedas and also the *Brahmanas*. The *Aranyakas* and *Upanishads* merge into one another and cannot be separated clearly.

Thus, this book provides only a macro outline of many, if not all the scriptures. It is meant for everyone who wishes to have a bird's eye view of them.

References

1. Adyatma Upanishad - Eng. Trans. Dr. A. G. Krishna Warrier
2. Advaya Taraka Upanishad - Eng. Trans. P. R. Ramachander
3. Aitareya Upanishad - Eng.Trans. Swami Gambhirananda
4. Aksha Malika Upanishad - Eng. Trans. K. Srinivasan
5. Akshi Upanishad - Eng. Trans. Dr. A. G. Krishna Warrier
6. All about Hinduism - Swami Sivananda
7. Amrutha Bindu Upanishad - Eng. Trans. Swami Madhavananda
8. Amrutha Nada Upanishad - Eng. Trans. K. Narayana Swamy Iyer
9. Annapurna Upanishad - Eng. Trans. Dr. A. G. Krishna Warrier
10. An Essay on the Vedas - Sri Aurobindo
11. An Essay on the Upanishads - Sri Aurobindo
12. Aruneyi Upanishad - Eng. Trans. Swami Madhavananda
13. Atharva Sikha Upanishad - Eng. Trans. P. R. Ramachander
14. Atharva Siras Upanishad - Eng. Tran. P. R. Ramachander
15. Atharva Veda - Eng. Trans. Maurice Bloomfield
16. Atma Upanishad - Eng. Trans. Dr. A. G. Krishna Warrier
17. Atma Bodha Upanishad - Eng. Trans. Dr. A.G. Krishna Warrier
18. Avadhutha Upanishad - Eng. Trans. Prof. A. A. Ramanathan
19. Bahvricha Upanishad - Eng. Trans. Dr. A. G. Krishna Warrier
20. Bhavana Upanishad - Eng. Trans. Dr. A. G. Krishna Warrier
21. Bhikshuka Upanishad - Eng. Trans. Prof. A. A. Ramanathan

22. Bihad Aranyaka Upanishad - Eng. Trans. Swami Madhavananda
23. Brahma Upanishad - Eng. Trans. Swami Madhavananda
24. Brihad Jabala Upanishad - Eng. Trans. P. R. Ramachander
25. Britannica - Concise Encyclopedia
26. Chandogya Upanishad - Eng. Trans. Swami Swahananda
27. Commentaries on the Vedas, the Upanishads, and the Bhagavad Gita - The Three Branches of India's Life Tree by Sri Chinmoy
28. Dakshinamurthy Upanishad - Eng. Trans. P. R. Ramachander
29. Dhyana Bindu Upanishad - Eng. Trans. K. Narayanaswami Aiyar
30. Ekakshara Upanishad - Eng. Trans. Dr. A. G. Krishna Warrier
31. Encyclopedia - Cambridge University Press
32. Garbha Upanishad - Eng. Trans. Dr. A. G. Krishna Warrier
33. Greatness of the Vedas - Jeffrey Armstrong
34. Hamsa Upanishad - Eng. Trans. K. Narayanaswami Aiyar
35. Hayagreeva Upanishad - Eng. Trans. P. R. Ramachander
36. Hinduism - Swami Vivekananda
37. Hindu Scriptures - V.A.K. Ayer
38. Hindu View of Life - Dr. S. Radhakrishnan
39. How I became a Hindu - David Frawley
40. Hymns of the Mystic Fire - Sri Aurobindo
41. India: What can India teach us - Max Muller
42. Indian Mythology - Apam Napat
43. India's Priceless Heritage - Nani Palkivala
44. Integral Yoga Literature - Sri Aurobindo
45. Isavasya Upanishad - Eng. Trans. Vidyavachaspathi V. Panoli
46. Jabala Upanishad – Eng. Trans. Prof. A. A. Ramanathan
47. Jabala Darshana Upanishad - Eng. Trans. P. R. Ramanathan
48. Jabali Upanishad - Eng. Trans. P. R. Ramachander
49. Kaivalya Upanishad - Eng. Trans. SwamiMadhavananda

50. Kali Santarana Upanishad - Eng. Trans. K. Narayana Swami Aiyar
51. Katha Upanishad - Eng. Trans. Vidyavachaspathi V. Panoli
52. Katha Rudra Upanishad – Eng. Trans. Prof. A. A. Ramanathan
53. Kaushitaki Upanishad - Eng. Trans Dr. A. G. Krishna Warrier
54. Kena Upanishad - Eng. Trans. Vidya Vachaspathi V. Panoli
55. Krishna Upanishad - Eng. Trans. P. R. Ramachander
56. Kshurika Upanishad - Eng. Trans. P. R. Ramachander
57. Kundika Upanishad - Eng. Trans, Prof A. A. Ramanathan
58. Lecture on Vedic Knowledge and Modern Science - B.G. Siddarth
59. Maha Narayana Upanishad - Eng. Trans. Swami Vimalananda
60. Maha Upanishad - Eng. Trans. Dr. A. G. Krishna Warrier
61. Maha Vakya Upanishad - Eng. Trans. P. R. Ramachander
62. Maitrayani Upanishad - Eng. Trans. Dr. A. G. Krishna Warrier
63. Maitreya Upanishad – Eng. Trans. Prof. A. A. Ramanathan
64. Mandala Brahmana Upanishad - Eng. Trans. K. Narayanaswami Aiyar
65. Mandukya Upanishad - Vidya Vachaspathi V. Panoli
66. Mantrika Upanishad - Eng. Trans. Dr. A. G. Krishna Warrier
67. Mudgala Upanishad - Eng. Trans. Dr. A. G. Krishna Warrier
68. Muktika Upanishad - Eng. Trans. Dr. A .G. Krishna Warrier
69. Mundaka Upanishad - Eng. Trans. Swami Gambheerananda
70. Nada Bindu Upanishad - Eng. Trans. K.Narayana Swami Aiyar
71. Narada Parivarjaka Upanishad - Eng. Tran. Prof A. A. Ramanathan
72. Niralamba Upanishad- Eng. Trans. Dr. A. G. Krishna Warrier
73. Nirvana Upanishad - Eng. Trans. Prof. A. A. Ramanathan
74. Nrsimha Poorva Tapaniya Upanishad - Eng. Tran. P. R. Ramachander

75. Paingali Upanishad - Eng. Trans. Dr. A. G. Krishna Warrier
76. Pancha Brahma Upanishad - Eng. Trans. P. R. Ramachander
77. Para Brahma Upanishad - Eng. Trans. Prog A. A. Ramachander
78. Parama Hamsa Parivarjaka Upanishad - Eng. Trans. Prof. A. A. Ramanathan
79. Parama Hamsa Upanishad - Eng. Trans. Swami Madhavananda
80. Pasupatha Brahmana Upanishad - Eng Trans. P. R. Ramachander
81. Pranagni Hotra Upanishad - Eng. Trans. Dr. A. G. Krishna Warrier
82. Prasna Upanishad - Eng. Trans. Swami Gambheerananda
83. Rama Tpaniya Upanishad - Eng. Trans. P. R. Ramachander
84. Rig Veda - Eng. Trans.T. H. Griffith
85. Sama Veda - Shri Veda Bharathi
86. Sama Veda - Eng. Trans. T. H. Griffith
87. Sandilya Upanishad - Eng Trans. K. Narayana Swami Aiyer
88. Sanyasa Upanishad - Eng. Trans. Prof. A. A. Ramanathan
89. Sarabha Upanishad - Eng. Trans. P. R. Ramachander
90. Saraswati Rahasya Upanishad - Eng. Trans. Dr. A. G. Krishna Warrier
91. Sareerika Upanishad - Eng. Trans. Dr. A.G. Krishna Warrier
92. Sarva Sara Upanishad - Eng. Trans. Swami Madhavananda
93. Satyayaniya Upanishad - Eng. Trans. Prof. A. A. Ramanathan
94. Savitri Upanishad - Eng. Trans. Dr. A. G. Krishna Warrier
95. Sita Upanishad - Eng Trans. Dr. A. G. Krishna Warrier
96. Skand Upanishad - Eng. Trans. Dr. A. G. Krishna Warrier
97. Sowbhagyalakshmi Upanishad - Eng.Trans. Dr. A. G. Krishna Warrier
98. Subala Upanishad - Eng. Trans. Dr. A. G. Krishna Warrier

99. Sukha Rahasya Upanishad - Eng. Trans. Dr. A. G. Krishna Warrier
100. Surya Upanishad - Dr. A. G. Krishna Warrier
101. Svetasvatara Upanishad - Eng Trans. Swami Tyagi Sananada
102. Taittariya Upanishad - Eng. Trans. Swami Gambheerananda
103. Tara Sara Upanishad - Eng. Trans. K. Narayana Swami Iyer
104. Tejo Bindu Upanishad - Eng Trans. K. Narayana Swami Aiyar
105. The Book of the Vedas - Timeless Wisdom from India's Tradition - Virendra Kumar Arya
106. The Early Hindu Civilization - Romesh Chunder Dutt
107. The Principal Upanishads - Dr. S. Radhakrishnan
108. The secret of the Veda - Sri Aurobindo
109. The Upanishads - Sri Aurobindo
110. The Upanishads - Eng. Trans. F. Max Muller
111. The Upanishads - Shayam N. Shukla
112. The Vedas - V.A.K. Ayer
113. The Vedas - Swami Sivananda
114. The Vedas and Upanishads - Sanderson Beak
115. Tripura Rahasya Upanishad - Eng. Trans. Dr. A. G. Krishna Warrier
116. Tripura Upanishad - Eng. Trans. Dr. A. G. Krishna Warrier
117. Trisikhi Brahmana Upanishad - Eng. Trans. P.R. Ramachander
118. Turiyatitha Avadhutha Upanishad - Prof. A. A. Ramanathan
119. Upanishads - Gateways of Knowledge - M.P. Pandit
120. Vajra Suchika Upanishad - Eng. Trans. Dr. A. G. Krishna Warrier
121. Varaha Upanishad - Eng Trans. K. Narayana Swami Aiyer
122. Vasudeva Upanishad - Eng. Trans. P. R. Ramachander
123. Vedas - An essence - Ashok Dilwali
124. Vedas, Soul of India – Dina Nath Misra

125. Wisdom of the Vedas - J.C. Chatterjee
126. Wisdom of the Veda - M.P. Pandit
127. Wisdom of the Vedas - S. Vidyalankar
128. Wisdom of the Ancient Seers - David Frawley
129. Wisdom of the Vedas - J. C. Chatterjee
130. Wisdom of the Veda - M. P. Pandit.
131. Yajna, the Vedic Sacrifice (Offering) - Octavian Sarbatoare
132. Yajnavalkya Upanishad - Prof. A. A. Ramanathan
133. Yajur Veda - Eng. Trans. - Arthur Berriedale Keith
134. Yoga Choodamani Upanishad - Eng. Trans. P. R. Ramachander
135. Yoga Kundalini Upanishad - Eng. Trans. K. Narayana Swami Aiyer
136. Yoga Sikha Upanishad- Eng. Trans. P. R. Ramachander
137. Yoga Tattva Upanishad - Eng. Trans. K. Narayana Swami Aiyer